# TEXT-BOOK OF TEMPERANCE.

BY

DR. F. R. LEES, F. S. A.

AUTHOR OF "TEMPERANCE BIBLE COMMENTARY," "DOCTORS, DRUGS AND DRINKS," "CONDENSED ARGUMENT FOR PROHIBITION," ETC., ETC., ETC.

PUBLISHED BY

Z. POPE VOSE & CO., ROCKLAND, ME.

J. N. STEARNS, 172 WILLIAM ST., NEW YORK.

1869.

# PREFACE.

This Text-Book was originally designed for the use of young people between the ages of fourteen and twenty, as a means of teaching them the great *facts* and *principles* which lay beneath the Temperance Reformation. It was desirable, therefore, that very simple language should be used. A glance at the Table of Contents will show how comprehensive is the argument, and that it is adapted to meet the actual wants of our age, and the special hindrances of our time, rather than to give a dry cyclopædic summary of all the facts and details of the subject. Within the limits of a small volume, this, indeed, was found to be impossible; and we therefore accepted the alternative of a thorough and original exposition. As we proceeded, however, we found that, without the sacrifice of scientific accuracy and the rejection of the very words of high medical authorities in the sections bearing upon Chemistry and Physiology, we must occasionally use learned terms. The *Questions* prepared for each part, carefully read and pondered by the pupil himself, — or, what is better, put by a teacher, who will examine his pupil upon them, — will enable every youth of ordinary capacity and education to understand the matter quite well.

# CONTENTS.

# TEXT-BOOK OF TEMPERANCE.

## I.

### Temperance as a Virtue.

1. "It is an ancient artifice of fraud," says Dean South, "to prepossess the mind by representing bad things under a good name." Hence the need of revising our definitions and verifying them by comparison with facts.—TEMPERANCE is a word in everybody's mouth; yet what particular actions it commands, or forbids, and why, are points generally unsettled. This is rather owing to the fact that people are not taught to think in a precise method, than to anything hard or obscure in the nature of the subject itself. A very simple process of reasoning will bring every honest and candid mind to the true use of words upon this matter. All persons are agreed that Temperance is at least a moral virtue, and consequently concerns a course of life dictated by the intellectual and moral powers. It is the governing of passion and appetite; therefore, it can never be the mere gratification of them. What virtue is there in doing what one merely *likes* to do, and what is pleasant or natural to do? Animal instincts and fleshly appetites cannot rise to the dignity of virtues;

---

**1. What does Dean South remark in regard to falsehood putting on the livery of virtue? Why are people's notions so unsettled on the subject of Temperance? What is Temperance,—an appetite or a virtue? What is**

for virtue is only and always moral strength shown in restraining the lower nature and its blind impulses. A boy, for example, who sucks his barley sugar, is no more virtuous or temperate than a dog that gnaws his bone; but a child that, at the request of its parent or superior, cheerfully gives up some sweets that have been given him, because he is told and believes that they are injurious, really displays a virtuous and temperate disposition. In other words, the mind rules, and not the appetite. Hence, Temperance, the virtue, always *begins* with self-denial, and is not possible without it. But the *temperate* action or state may exist where there is no self-denial. A person may be so well-instructed, and so obedient and faithful to the best instincts of nature, as to have no unruly desire seeking to transgress the higher law; and the state or practice of such individual will be "temperate" because it expresses *obedience* to Divine law; that is, manifests a just relation between animal desire and the moral will. The one is servile, the other magisterial. Thus, while the motive will be a criterion as to the true character of a man, it is "the fitness of things" which must be the sole test of the rightness of the action.

2. How is this "fitness" to be ascertained? Just as all other truth is to be known, — by seeking for it, — through the use of our perceptive and rational powers. He who seeks will find, provided he searches in the love of

---

**the meaning of virtue? Is it virtuous to do what one *likes*? Where does Temperance begin? What is implied in the *state* of Temperance? How are the Desires and the Will related? What is the sole *test* of the rightness of actions?**

**2. How is the fitness of things to be known? What are such relations called?**

truth as the manifestation of the Divine will, and observes the known conditions of sound reasoning. Just as a man may, by carelessness and inattention, add up a column of figures wrongly, so by carelessness he may violate the laws of sound thinking, and form an "opinion," instead of reaching a conclusion; but the fault rests with the man and not with the relations fixed by God, that show forth his wisdom and power. The relations of fitness are the *laws* which man has to obey,— the rules of his life, knowable by reason through experience.

3. The practical conclusion from this examination is, that while Temperance, the virtue, is always a state of mind *opposed* to sensual gratification, and therefore founded upon the recognition of the higher law,— Temperance, the right action, is *obedience* to the intellectual perception of those relations of fitness among things, which we call the adaptation of right means to good ends. He, consequently, who drinks or smokes merely because he "likes" it, or because it is pleasant or fashionable, acts upon a motive beneath morality, and therefore below Temperance; and he who drinks or smokes, without any perception or proof of the usefulness of drinking or smoking, acts upon an impulse that contains no element of intellectual law or truth. What is neither good in *motive*, sound in *sense*, nor useful in *result*, can have no title to the sacred name of Temperance. We add the definitions of Temperance given by several great and philosophical writers, some of them separated by centuries of time from each other.

---

3. State the conclusions deducible from this line of remark. What are the three essential elements which must be united in Temperance?

4. Socrates [B. C. 450] says, —

"He who knows what is good and chooses it, who knows what is bad and avoids it, is learned and temperate."

Aristotle, the most scientific mind of antiquity, says,—

"Temperance is a mean state on the subject of pleasures, — bodily pleasures, — and not all even of these. . . . . . In the *natural* desires few err, and only on one side, — that of *excess, the object of our natural desire being the satisfaction of our wants.* But in the case of peculiar [or artificial] pleasures, MANY people err, and frequently; for people who are called 'lovers' of such pleasures are so called, either from being pleased with *improper objects*, or in an improper degree or manner, or at an improper time. A man is called intemperate for feeling more pain than he ought, at not obtaining pleasant things [as wine]; but the temperate man is called so from *not feeling* pain at the absence of, or the *abstaining* from, *pleasure.* Now the intemperate man desires all things pleasant, and *is led by his mere desire to choose these things.* But the temperate man is *in the mean* on these matters, for he is not pleased, but rather annoyed, at the principal pleasures of the intemperate man; nor is he pleased with any *improper objects*, or pained at their absence; nor does he feel desire when he ought not, or in any case improperly. But he feels moderate and *proper desire for all those pleasant things* WHICH CONDUCE TO HEALTH."

5. The philosopher Hobbes [A. D. 1640] defines —

"Temperance, the habit by which we *abstain* from all things that tend to our destruction; Intemperance, the contrary vice; as for the common opinion, that virtue consisteth in mediocrity, and vice in extremes, I see no ground for it. Courage may be

---

4. What is the moralist Socrates' definition? How does Aristotle, in his *ethics*, respectively define the temperate and the intemperate man?

5. Give the definition of Hobbes, the philosopher of Malmesbury.

virtue when the daring is *extreme, if the cause be good,* and *extreme* fear no vice when the danger is extreme. To give a man *more than his due* is no injustice, though it be to give him less. In gifts, it is not the *sum* that maketh liberality, but the *reason;* and so in all other virtues and vices."

6. "Most people," says David Hume, "will naturally assent to the definition of the elegant and judicious poet,—

> "'Virtue (for mere good-nature is a fool)
> Is *sense* and *spirit,* with humanity.'
>
> ARMSTRONG.

"The prudence explained in Cicero's *Offices* is that sagacity which leads to the discovery of Truth, and preserves us from error and mistake.

"To *sustain* and to *abstain,* that is, to be patient and continent, appeared to some of the ancients a summary comprehension of all morals.

"With the Stoics, as with Solomon and the Eastern moralists, folly and wisdom are equivalent to vice and virtue."

"Men will praise thee," says David, "when thou doest *well unto thyself.*" (Ps. xlix.) "I hate a wise man," says a Greek proverb, "who is not *wise unto himself.*"

7. Thomas De Quincey, the acute critic, gives an admirable definition from the physiological stand-point, namely, "Temperance is *adaptation* to the organism;" while the late Dr. Samuel Brown, of Edinburgh, has a

---

**6. Give the historian and philosopher Hume's definition. What does he quote from Cicero? Did the Ancients exclude abstinence from their conception of virtue? What rule did David and the Greeks lay down?**

**7. What was the objective definition of Mr. De Quincey? What the subjective one of Dr. S. Brown, the chemist and reviewer?**

no less luminous and comprehensive definition from the moral point of view, —

"True and universal Temperance is the spirit of obedience to all the laws of man's manifold and miraculous nature."

8. It is a plain inference from all this that dietetic Temperance is the proper use of food, which includes as truly abstinence from bad, as the use of good things: and hence, if *alcoholic liquors are bad*, true Temperance teaches, and demands, entire abstinence from them.

---

## II.

## The Chemical History of Alcohol.

9. The intoxicating constituent in strong drinks that is specially objectionable on the ground of Temperance morals, is technically called ALCOHOL, or Spirit of Wine. It is common to ale and beer, to cider, perry, and other fermented drinks, and of course to every form of fermented wine, and of ardent spirit distilled from fermented liquors. It is a *product* of fermentation, an *educt* of distillation; in other words, it must be generated by the one process, before it can be drawn out, or extracted, by the other. To understand this fact in all its fulness, and to meet a large number of difficulties urged by the ignorant, it will be needful to explain the general principles of chemistry, and to show *how* alcohol comes into being.

---

8. State the general conclusion; and the proposition *assumed*, which, being established, will render abstinence a moral duty.

9. What is the intoxicating constituent of strong drinks technically called? Is it a product, or an educt, of distillation? By *what* process is it generated?

One fallacy, however, may be anticipated, namely, "Fermentation is a natural law or power." This is quite true, but it by no means either destroys the distinction between "nature" and "art," or throws the responsibility from man who uses natural power for his own ends, upon the Divine Author of it. All works, whether bad or good, — whether the manufacture of powder, bullet and pistol, and the discharge of them at the head of a noble patriot by a foul assassin, — whether the moulding of iron into ploughshares, or the production of gun-cotton for the blasting of rocks, — are *equally* done by borrowed power, expressed by natural law; but the character of the work must nevertheless determine the moral position of the worker, according to the old and everlasting test, "a tree is known by its fruit."

10. A celebrated English bishop and botanist, Dr. Stanley, once said in Exeter Hall, by way of objection to the "teetotalers" (i. e., thorough abstainers from *all* alcoholics), that "their chemistry was at fault, since they took sugar, which contained alcohol." A lady wittily retorted with the *argumentum ad episcopum*, —

> "If in sugar, *rum* there be,
> The bishop drinks it in his tea!"

Clearly, *Saccharum* is one thing, and '*Rum* another; and before it can be truly alleged that the "thing" *rum* is in the "thing" saccha*rum* (as the one word is in the other),

---

Is fermentation a Natural law? Is not *all* power derived, through nature, from God? For what is man "responsible"? — is it for the *fact* of power, or the *use* of it? Give examples of the difference of use, as good or bad. What is the distinction between nature and art? What is the final test of good or evil?

10. What celebrated man asserted that alcohol was in sugar? Does not

it must be extracted from the sugar while it remains sugar, and this cannot be done. Certainly if it is *in*, it will come *out;* but if it will NOT come *out*, there is no proof that it is *in*. In fact, however, while by the action of sulphuric acid, imitating the natural process of the growth of vegetable juices into sugar, an old linen shirt can be *changed into sugar*, not the most purblind of theorists would ever argue that, therefore, there is sugar in linen! Stated in the plainest terms, the truth is, that while the "matter" of all organic life is very much the same, the forms of it are forever varying. Now we have the air, the water, and the mineral, as the food of plants; then we have the infinite variety of vegetable organism, food and poison, built up out of these; here the precious wheat, and there the poisonous poppy, flourishing side by side in the same field; and then again we have, fed by grass, roots, grain, and fruit, one flesh of birds and beasts, and another flesh of man at the head and crown of creation. As Paul says, in reference to plant, seed, and animal, though all springing originally out of the common elements of the globe, "God giveth to each a body as it pleaseth Him." — Though things, in infinite variety and endless procession and circulation, having a tri-unity at bottom, may assume *every form in turn*, they can never be *two* forms at the same time. The thought, when analyzed, is seen to be an absurdity: for *change is a fact of succession;* and to affirm that one change is *within* another, or *is* another, is simply to talk nonsense.

---

*rum* come from the fermentation of sugar? If the bishop be right, what is the correct inference? How do you explain the fallacy? *Does* alcohol come out of sugary matter? Explain the *changes* involved in the chemistry of nature, and show how variety springs from combination. What is change? Can one change be *in* another?

11. Professor Frankland, of the Royal Institution, defines CHEMISTRY as "the science which treats of the *atomic composition* of bodies, and of those *changes which result* from an alteration in the relative position of their atoms." Substances are either (1.) *simple* bodies, incapable of being resolved into more than one kind of matter, or (2.) *compound*, separable into two or more distinct substances. The simple substances, up to the present condition of our knowledge, are sixty-two, and are technically called *elements*. They manifest a more or less intense affinity (or *attracting force*) amongst themselves, when in contact, which induces aggregation of some, and consequent separation of others. It is through the "combination" of these elements, that all the infinitely varied forms of earthly matter are successively brought about. This force of chemical affinity has five modes of action at present known: (1.) *Direct combination* of substances with each other. (2.) *Displacement* of one element or group of elements, by another. (3.) Mutual *exchange* of elements. (4.) A *rearrangement* of the constituents of a body. (5.) The *resolution* of a compound into a more simple compound, or into its elements.

12. Each atom has its atomic weight or specific gravity (see table of elements), which represents, as nearly as possible, 1. The smallest proportion by weight, in which it is found to unite with, or be thrust from, a

---

**11. Give Professor Frankland's definition of the science of Chemistry. What are the two great classes of substances? How many *simple* substances are known? What relation do they hold to each other? In other words, how do they behave? Are they *attached* to each other, and, so to speak, "given in marriage"? How many forms of union and dissolution, or of marriage and divorce, do they exhibit? Name the five kinds.**

compound; the smallest weight of *Hydrogen* so entering or leaving a substance being taken as unity, or the standard to start from. 2d. The weight of the element in the solid state which contains the same amount of heat as seven-fold by weight of solid Lithium at the same temperature. 3d. The weight of the element which, as gas or vapor, under like conditions of heat and pressure, occupies the same volume as one part by weight of Hydrogen.—Of course the weight of a compound substance is the sum of the atomic weights of its elements.

13. When atoms exist not combined with *other* kinds of matter, they nevertheless sometimes group themselves together in pairs, trios, quartettes, etc., and are then termed elementary molecules.

Hence the "molecular-*volume*" of an element in a state of gas or vapor, must be the same as the molecular-volume of Hydrogen, under the same conditions, while the molecular *weight* of an element will be generally found to be double or treble that of its own atomic weight. Oxygen, for example, is both a diatomic, and (as ozone) a triatomic-molecule. Sulphur is also diatomic and hexatomic.

As a rule, however, the molecular weight of a *compound* is identical with its atomic weight. The molecular volume, or the space filled by the combining proportions of a compound, is equal to that filled by two combining proportions (one molecule) of Hydrogen.

---

**12. What does an atomic weight represent? Of what is *Hydrogen* the unit? What else measures specific gravity?**

**13. What are "elementary molecules"? What is "molecular *volume*," and how is it related to "molecular *weight*"?**

Hence the law, "Equal volumes of all gases and vapors contain, at the same temperature and pressure, an equal number of molecules." Under this law, therefore, the molecules of nearly all compounds, however great the aggregate volume of their constituents, have one uniform volume, which is precisely the same as that of one molecule of Hydrogen: Thus, in regard to volume, —

2 of Hydrogen + 1 Oxygen, form 2 of Steam.
3 of Hydrogen + 1 Nitrogen, form 2 of Ammonia.
6 of Hydrogen + 1 Oxygen +2$x$Carbon Vapor, form 2 of Alcohol-Vapor.

14. Elements that combine with each other readily, develop much heat, which in fact measures intestine chemical affinity or motion. Such elements are possessed of widely different properties, and when their compounds are decomposed by an electric current (which is but another form of motion), the constituents are separated at opposite poles. Those that appear at the positive pole are called "Negative" elements; those that appear at the negative pole, "Positive" elements. (For another purpose and reason, the Negative are also called *chlorous;* the Positive, *basylous.*) The difference, nevertheless, is one of degree only, since they merge insensibly into each other, and both series exhibit a graduated intensity of the two qualities.

15. The Book of Nature has in truth its natural Al-

---

**14.** What is the effect of rapid combination of elements? What results from their separation by an electric current?

**15.** To *what* may the 62 primitive elements be compared? What is the *result* of their varied combination? Name the 21 elements most essential to life, man, and civilization.

phabet, out of which its simple syllables, and its varied and distinct words, its atmospheres and fluids, its earths and minerals, and its living and illuminated chapters of the vegetal and animal kingdoms, are all elaborated by a process of progressive combination, — a process whereby its 62 primitive elements are put together in different quantities and different ways, resulting in an ever increasing number and complexity of compounds. The following is the Primer of this Natural language. The 21 most necessary and important of these elements are put in *large* type, the next in importance in italics, and those rarely found in Roman type : —

| NAME. | Symbol. | Atomic Weight. | NAME. | Symbol. | Atomic Weight. |
|---|---|---|---|---|---|
| ALUMINIUM | Al. | 27.5 | Molybdenum | Mo. | 92 |
| *Antimony* | Sb. | 122 | *Nickel* | Ni. | 58.8 |
| *Arsenic* | As. | 75 | Niobium | Nb. | 97.6 |
| *Barium* | Ba. | 137 | NITROGEN | N. | 14 |
| *Bismuth* | Bi. | 208 | Osmium | Os. | 199 |
| *Boron* | B. | 11 | OXYGEN | O. | 16 |
| BROMINE | Br. | 80 | *Palladium* | Pd. | 106.5 |
| Cadmium | Cd. | 112 | PHOSPHORUS | P. | 31 |
| Cæcium | Cs. | 133 | *Platinum* | Pt. | 197.4 |
| CALCIUM | Ca. | 40 | POTASSIUM | K. | 34 |
| CARBON | C. | 12 | *Rhodium* | Rh. | 109 |
| Cerium | Ce. | 92 | Rubidium | Rb. | 85.5 |
| CHLORINE | Cl. | 35.5 | Ruthenium | Ru. | 104 |
| *Chromium* | Cr. | 52.5 | *Selenium* | Se. | 79 |
| *Cobalt* | Co. | 58.8 | SILICON | Si. | 28.5 |
| COPPER | Cu. | 63.5 | SILVER | Ag. | 108 |
| Didymium | D. | 96 | SODIUM | Na. | 23 |
| FLUORINE | F. | 19 | *Strontium* | Sr. | 87.5 |
| Glucinum | G. | 14 | SULPHUR | S. | 32 |
| *Gold* | Au. | 196.7 | Tantalum | Ta. | 137.5 |
| HYDROGEN | H. | 1 | Tellurium | Te. | 128 |
| Indium | In. | 74 | Thallium | Tl. | 204 |
| IODINE | I. | 127 | Thorium | Th. | 231.5 |
| Iridium | Ir. | 198 | *Tin* | Sn. | 118 |
| IRON | Fe. | 56 | Titanium | Ti. | 50 |
| Lanthanium | La. | 92 | *Tungsten* | W. | 184 |
| LEAD | Pb. | 207 | *Uranium* | U. | 120 |
| Lithium | L. | 7 | Vanadium | V. | 137 |
| *Magnesium* | Mg. | 24 | Yttrium | Y. | 68 |
| MANGANESE | Mn. | 55 | ZINC | Zn. | 65 |
| MERCURY | Hg. | 200 | Zirconium | Zr. | 90 |

16. These elements are arranged in two great classes, — *Metals* and *Non-Metals* (or metalloids). The latter are 13 in number, — Boron, Bromine, Carbon, Chlorine, Fluorine, Hydrogen, Iodine, Nitrogen, Oxygen, Phosphorus, Selenium, Silicon, and Sulphur. Eight of these elements are Negative or *Chlorous* toward the other 54 Positive or *Basylous* ones, — namely, Fluorine, Chlorine, Bromine, Iodine, Oxygen, Sulphur, Selenium, Tellurium.

17. The meaning of *Chemical Notation* — a scientific or precise system of naming which tells the history of the combination — should now be understood by every educated young man; for without this it is impossible truly to explain the most important problems in biology or life. Let the following points, then, be carefully borne in mind, —

(*a.*) A chemical compound of the first order is called "*binary*," because it represents the union of two elements; and the special name is taken from that of the constituents; that of the "positive," ending in *ic*, being placed before that of the "negative" ending in "*ide*," as, —

Potassium united with Sulphur becomes Potassic Sulphide.

Sodium united with Oxygen becomes Sodic Oxide.

Silver united with Chlorine becomes Argentic Chloride.

---

**16. What are the two great classes into which the primitive elements are divided? What are the names of the *non*-metals? How many, and which of them, are "Negative" towards the more "Positive" elements? What else are the Negative ones called? What the Positive?**

**17. What is Chemical Notation? Give examples of a "binary" compound. (*a.*) How are the Positive and Negative distinguished by the ending**

(*b.*) When the same elements form two compounds, in the one containing the least of the Negative element the name of its Positive ends in "*ous*," the *ic* being reserved for the compound containing the larger proportion of the Negative element.

(*c.*) So an acid which contains Oxygen, its name has generally the terminal *ic* added to the name of the element to which the Oxygen is united (or to an abbreviation), as, —

Sulphur united with Oxygen forms Sulphur*ic* Acid.
Nitrogen united with Oxygen forms Nitr*ic* Acid.
Phosphorus united with Oxygen forms Phosphor*ic* Acid.

(*d.*) But when the same element with Oxygen forms two acids, the *ic* is added to the name of the acid containing the larger amount of Oxygen, and the ending *ous* is adopted for the other.

(*e.*) The symbols attached in the table to the primary substances, when conjoined in use, always *denote a certain definite proportion by weight of each element.* HCl, for instance, not merely signifies a compound of Hydrogen and Chlorine, *but a molecule of that compound containing exactly one atom* (i. e., one part by weight) *of Hydrogen, and one atom* (35.5 parts by weight) *of Chlorine.* Hence, if the molecule of a compound contains more than one combining ratio of any element, the formula expresses the fact by a figure *after* and *below* it, as —

---

of their names? (*b.*) In a double compound how do you mark which contains the *least* of the Negative element? (*c.*) What is the terminal form of an oxygen acid? (*d.*) What mark is adopted when the same elements form two acids? (*e.*) What do the symbols in the table (par. 15) denote? How

Zincic Chloride . . . . . . . . . **Zn** $Cl_2$
Ferric Chloride . . . . . . . . . **Fe**$_2$ $Cl_6$

(*f.*) When a *large* figure is placed before the formula of a compound, it is designed to apply to every symbol in that formula: thus — $3SO_4H_2$ denotes 3 molecules of the compound $SO_4H_2$ (Sulphuric Acid).

18. In the case of the Acids containing no Oxygen, the prefixes *sulpho* and *hydro*, for Sulphur and Hydrogen, are respectively used.

If a binary compound contains Oxygen, and forms an acid when united with water, or a salt when added to a base, it is termed an *anhydride*, or anhydrous acid. Thus:

1 atom of C and 2 atoms of O form Carbon*ic* Anhydride.
2 atoms of N and 3 atoms of O form Nitr*ous* Anhydride.
1 atom of S and 2 atoms of O form Sulphur*ous* Anhydride.
1 atom of S and 3 atoms of O form Sulphur*ic* Anhydride.

19. The systematic names have not yet entirely displaced the trivial names in the following examples, —

---

is a combining proportion of *more* than one atom expressed? (*f.*) What does a *large* figure before the symbols denote? Give an example.

18. What device is adopted to express the acids of Sulphur and Hydrogen? What is an *anhydride*? Give examples.

19. What are the scientific names for Water? for Sulphuretted Hydrogen? for Hydrochloric acid? for Light Carburetted Hydrogen? for *Ammonia*?

Hydric Oxide for Water.
Hydric Sulphide for Sulphuretted Hydrogen.
Hydric Chloride for Hydrochloric Acid.
Hydric Carbide for Light Carburetted Hydrogen.
Hydric Nitride for Ammonia.

Nor in several of three classes of compounds called *Bases*, convertible into Salts by the action of acids. As, for example, in compounds of metals with Oxygen, where

Baric Oxide is commonly known as Baryta.
Calcic Oxide is commonly known as Lime.
Magnesic Oxide is commonly known as Magnesia.
Aluminic Oxide is commonly known as Alumina.

20. A second class of compounds of Metals with *hydroxyl* have their names formed by changing the terminal syllable of the metal into *ic* or *ous*, and "hydroxyl" into *hydrate*. Thus Cæsium and hydroxyl become cæsic hydrate; iron and hydroxyl, ferric-hydrate, ($Fe_2$ $HO_6$). Potash properly should be Potassic-hydrate, and Soda, Sodic-hydrate. This *hydroxyl*, Ho, is the root, or radical, of Water, and the explanation is important. It belongs to a class of inorganic radicals, which are compounds of one or more atoms of a polyad element, *of which some of its bonds are unsatisfied;* and is named

---

What compounds are called *bases?* What is the scientific name for Baryta? Lime? Magnesia? and Alumina? What sort of compounds are these called?

20. Name a second class of *bases.* What is *Hydroxyl?* What is a "Radical"? What is an *hydrate?* Name the third class of *bases.* In what do their names terminate? What is the single exception?

*monad* (one), *dyad* (two), *triad* (three), *polyad* (many), just according to the number of monad-atoms wanted to fulfil its atomic attachment. (See par. 24.)

A third class of bases, compounds of nitrogen, phosphorus, arsenic, etc., have their names ending in *ine*, except *ammonia*, which keeps its vulgar title.

21. If a Salt be free from Oxygen and Sulphur, like table-salt (NaCl), it is termed a *haloid;* if it hold Oxygen, it is termed an *oxysalt;* and if that element be replaced by Sulphur, a *Sulpho-salt*. They are named according to the rule for binary compounds; namely, Sodic Chloride, etc.

22. The OXYSALTS are either normal, acid, or basic. In a *normal* salt (erroneously called "neutral"), the displaceable hydrogen of the acid is all exchanged for an equivalent amount of a metal, or of a positive compound radical. In the following, the displaced and sub stituted elements are put in italics,—

Nitric Acid . . . $\mathbf{N}O_3\,\mathit{H}$ $\begin{cases} \text{Sodic Nitrate, } \mathbf{N}O_3\,\mathit{Na}, \\ \text{Calcic Nitrate, } (\mathbf{N}O_3)_2\,\mathit{Ca''}. \end{cases}$

Sulphuric Acid, $\mathbf{S}O_4\,\mathit{H}_2$ $\begin{cases} \text{Potassic Sulphate, } \mathbf{S}O_4\,\mathit{K}_2, \\ \text{Calcic Sulphate, } \mathbf{S}O_4\,\mathit{Ca''}. \end{cases}$

23. In an *Acid*-salt the displaceable hydrogen of the

---

21. What is a Salt called when free from oxygen and sulphur? Give an example. What is it called when it holds oxygen? What when oxygen is replaced by sulphur?

22. Name the three kinds of *Oxysalts*. What is a *normal* salt? What was it formerly but falsely called? Give examples, on the black-board, of Nitric and Sulphuric acid. Mark with a *line* underneath the *displaceable* hydrogen and the *substituted* metals.

23. What is an *acid*-salt? Give an example on the board.

acid is but partially exchanged for a metal or positive compound radical, as,—

Carbonic Acid $CO_3\,H_2$ . . Hydric Potassic-Carbonate, $CO_3\,HK$

24. When the number of BONDS—that is, of affinity for other elements—of a metal, or compound positive radical, in a Salt, is greater than the number of atoms of displaceable hydrogen, the compound is termed a *basic* Salt, as,—

Carbonic Acid $CO_3\,H_2$ { Malachite $CO_5\,H_2\,Cu''_2$
Blue Cupric Carbonate $C_2\,O_8\,H_2\,Cu''_3$

These bonds are expressed by the *marks* ''' up to four, by Roman numerals (v., etc.) beyond; but still better *symbolically*,

H' or Hydrogen
Zn'' " Zinc
B'' " Boron
C'''' " Carbon
N$^{v}$ " Nitrogen
S$^{vi}$ " Sulphur

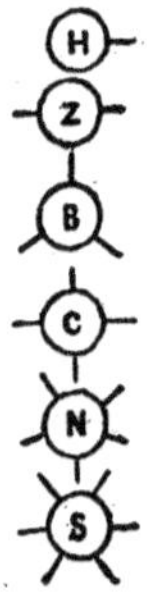

24. What is a *basic* salt? Give an example from two compounds of Copper (*Cuprum.*) Show on the board the *signs* of the number of "bonds," from one to three, and from three upwards. Draw a *diagram* of these "bonds," symbolically expressed in six substances. What is the inference as to chemical reaction?

It follows, from this variation of *attachment* (or atomic power), that the atoms, and their relative weights, *display very different values in chemical reactions.* An atom of Zinc is equal, in that respect, to two atoms of Hydrogen; so that, when Zinc is brought into contact with Steam at a great heat, one of Zn expels from the Steam two of H, taking their place, thus,* —

$$\underset{\text{Water.}}{\mathbf{O}H_2} + Zn = \underset{\text{Zincic-oxide.}}{\mathbf{O}Zn} + H_2$$

So, when Zincic-oxide is in contact with Hydrochloric-acid, and the Zinc is exchanged for Hydrogen, two atoms of this are found to be necessary to replace the one atom of the zinc, as, —

$$\underset{\text{Zincic oxide.}}{\mathbf{O}Zn} + \underset{\text{Hydrochloric-acid.}}{2HCl} = \underset{\text{Zincic oxide.}}{\mathbf{Zn}\ Cl_2} + \underset{\text{Water.}}{\mathbf{O}H_2}$$

25. The scholar, having mastered the notation, will begin to see into the secret and meaning of *combination.* A series of fundamental examples shall now be given, expressed in various ways, commencing with WATER (*Hydric oxide*).

Symbolically (H)—(O)—(H) Formula $\mathbf{O}H_2$

*Molecular weight* = 18. *Molecular volume* ☐☐ 1 *litre*

---

25. What is Water called, chemically? Give its symbol and explain its formation. What are its chief characteristics? What its actions and reactions? What is the meaning of Water of Crystallization?

* *The thick* type is used to show that the element represented by the first symbol of a formula is *directly united* with all the active-bonds of the other elements following upon the same lines. Thus $\mathbf{S}O_2\ Ho_2$ shows that the hexad atom of S is in union with the *four* bonds of the two atoms of O and H, and with the two bonds of the two atoms of *Hydroxyl* (Ho).

of *Water-vapor* weighs 9 criths. *Fuses* at 0°. Boils at 100° Centigrade.

Water is formed by the *direct union* of Hydrogen and Oxygen. It occurs abundantly in nature; and is, in fact, the very blood of all vegetal life, the vehicle of movement and transformation! It is a secondary product in an incalculable number of chemical reactions. It acts on many metallic-oxides, and converts them into hydrates. For example, Potassic oxide *plus* Water, becomes Potassic hydrate. It transforms anhydrides into acids. For example, —

| $P_2O_5$ | $+ 3OH_2$ | $= 2POHo_3$ |
|---|---|---|
| Phosphoric anhydride. | Water. | Phosphoric acid. |

It unites also molecularly with many compounds as *Water of Crystallization*, as in sodic-sulphate and alum. This is a peculiar combination, called *Molecular union*, as distinguished from the atomic, attended by the splitting up of the atoms, and a change in the active atomicity of the molecules.

26. *Water-vapor*, it is probable, is not an assemblage of single molecules of the compound $OH_2$, but of very complex *groups* of them, united without lessening their size. It is this which adapts Water for the great purpose of retaining radiant heat, having a greater power of absorption than any other known substance; and

---

26. What is the probable state of Water-vapor? What are its *uses* in respect to the temperature of our globe? In what condition does Oxygen exist in the air? State its atomic and molecular weights. How do plants supply a store of this element? What is the allotropic form of Oxygen called? State its property, and draw the symbols of both states.

thus acting as a blanket for the world, keeping its temperature up to the living-point. Without this property, the earth would become in a few hours too cold to live upon.

As examples of the alteration or intensifying of properties by union *in different positions*, besides Water, we may take the dyad element of OXYGEN ($O_2$). Its atomic weight $=16$; its molecular, therefore, being dual, $=32$. It occurs in a free state in the atmosphere; and in most minerals, and nearly all vegetable and animal compounds. It is given out in nature abundantly by the decomposition of Carbonic anhydride, $CO_2$, by the foliage of plants, the pores taking up the Carbon for structure, leaving the Oxygen to escape; so that the growth of plants is a perpetual source of this vivifying gas. But it exists in *another form* (allotropic), as OZONE, $O_3$, and in that state is strongly oxidizing, rusting silver and mercury, and decomposing organic matters, at common temperatures. If $O_2$ is represented as $O{=}O$, Ozone may be symbolized as

27. *Hydric peroxide* (or Hydroxyl) is transformed into Water by the action of nascent Hydrogen. It is a powerful oxidizing agent. Heat converts it into Water and Oxygen, thus,—

$$\underset{\text{Hydroxyl.}}{2\left\{\begin{matrix}OH\\OH\end{matrix}\right.} = \underset{\text{Water.}}{2\,OH_2} + \underset{\text{Oxygen.}}{O_2}$$

27. **Give the formula of *Hydric peroxide*, and of its decomposition by heat. What is its potent property?**

28. It can now be understood how *Alcohol* can come into existence as the result of *artificial combinations*, under the power of latent affinities. *Vinous Alcohol*, in fact, is one of a tribe of ALCOHOLS. They have been called "hydrated oxides" of the basylous radicals, but erringly, since they contain no Water. They are really *compounds of hydroxyl with the basylous organic radicals*; so that each series of radicals forms a corresponding one of Alcohols. They act upon and saturate acids (according to the number of atoms of hydroxyl), forming *ethereal salts*. The monad radicals give monacid alcohols; the dyad radicals, diacid alcohols, etc.

29. The simplest or first-born of this family of Alcohols is *Methylic alcohol* (wood-spirit) derived from Marsh-gas by the substitution of one atom of hydroxyl (Ho) for one of hydrogen, thus,—

| $CH_4$ | $CH_3$ Ho |
|---|---|
| Marsh-gas. | Methylic alcohol. |

or, symbolically expressed, as follows,—

It is also produced by the *destructive* distillation of wood.

---

28. To what tribe of Organic Compounds does *Vinous Alcohol* belong? What sort of compounds are they? What do they form by saturating acids?

29. Name the first-born of the family of Alcohols. Explain its derivation from Marsh-gas. Why is it also called Wood-spirit?

30. ETHYLIC ALCOHOL, or "*Spirit of Wine*," has the following formula and properties, —

$$\left\{\begin{matrix} CH_3 \\ CH_2 \end{matrix}\right. Ho \text{ or EtHo (i. e., Ethylene and Hydroxyl).}$$

*Molecular weight* = 46. 1 *litre* of *the vapor weighs* 23 *criths*. Specific *gravity*, 0.792 at 20° Centigrade. Boils at 78°. 4 C.

(*a*) It is prepared from Ethylene treated with HCl and KHo, as follows, —

$$\underset{\text{Ethylene.}}{\left\{\begin{matrix} CH_2 \\ CH_2 \end{matrix}\right.} + \underset{\text{Hydrochl. acid.}}{HCl} = \underset{\text{Ethylic chloride.}}{\left\{\begin{matrix} CH_3 \\ CH_2 \end{matrix}\right. Cl}$$

(Hydrobromic or hydriodic acids would do as well.) Next treat the chloride with Potassic hydrate, and the following changes occur, —

$$\underset{\text{Ethylic chloride.}}{\left\{\begin{matrix} CH_3 \\ CH_2 \end{matrix}\right. Cl} + \underset{\text{Potassic hydrate.}}{KHo} = \underset{\text{Ethylic alcohol.}}{\left\{\begin{matrix} CH_3 \\ CH_2 \end{matrix}\right. Ho} + \underset{\text{Potassic chloride.}}{KCl}$$

(*b*.) Ethylic Alcohol results from the *fermentation* of grape sugar with yeast, at about 22° Centigrade.

$$\underset{\text{Grape Sugar.}}{C_6H_{12}O_6} = \underset{\text{Ethylic alcohol.}}{2C_2H_5Ho} + \underset{\text{Carbonic anhydride.}}{2CO_2}$$

(*c*.) Distilled with Chloride of Lime, ethylic alcohol

---

**30. Give the formula of ETHYLIC ALCOHOL, or "Spirit of Wine." State its boiling point and specific gravity. (*a*.) Show how it is *prepared* for Ethylene. (*b*.) Give the formula of its formation by *fermenting* grape sugar with yeast. (*c*.) What does it form when distilled with Chloride of Lime?**

produces *Chloroform*, which is an anæsthetic of the same class, paralyzing nervous functions.

31. By *oxidation*, ethylic alcohol is converted into (1) ALDEHYDE, and then (2) into ACETIC ACID. Hence, whoever alleges that, under any circumstances, whether *in* the body or *out* of the body, this alcohol is decomposed, there is no scientific proof of the fact until the *derivatives* (as they are called) are demonstrated to be present as the result. The change will be as follows, —

$$\underbrace{\left\{\begin{matrix} CH_3 \\ CH_2\,Ho \end{matrix}\right.}_{\text{Ethylic alcohol.}} + O = \underbrace{\left\{\begin{matrix} CH_3 \\ COH \end{matrix}\right.}_{\text{Aldehyde.}} + \underbrace{OH_2}_{\text{Water.}}$$

$$\underbrace{\left\{\begin{matrix} CH_3 \\ COH \end{matrix}\right.}_{\text{Aldehyde.}} + O = \underbrace{\begin{matrix} CH_3 \\ COHo \end{matrix}}_{\text{Acetic acid.}}$$

32. It must, by this time, be plain to the meanest capacity, that no blunder can be greater than to rank *Alcohol* amongst the productions of Nature. It is, to all intents, like the golden images of the Ephesian Shrine, "the work of *Art* and man's device," using and abusing the *powers* and *possibilities* latent in Nature. This truth, of course, has been always known to chemists of repute, and it will be as well to put the fact upon record, showing how the simple truth *can* be perceived where no blinding prejudice, or perverting appetite, darkens the understanding.

---

31. What are the *resulting* products of the Oxidation of Ethylic Alcohol? Explain (1) the conversion of the Alcohol into *aldehyde* and water, and (2) the change of aldehyde into *acetic acid*.

32. Is Alcohol a *natural* product? Why not? What is the argument of

"The formation of Alcohol," said the great French chemist, A. F. Fourcroy, "takes place at the expense of the *destruction of a vegetable principle:* thus spirituous fermentation is a commencement of the destruction of principles *formed* by vegetation. The *acid*, or acetous, fermentation is *the second natural movement* which contributes to reduce vegetable compounds to more simple states of composition. Wine, in turning sour, absorbs air; so that a certain portion of the oxygen of the atmosphere appears to be necessary to the formation of the acetous acid. Finally, after vegetable liquors, or their solid parts moistened, have passed to the *acid state*, their decomposition continuing, under favorable circumstances (namely, a warm temperature, exposure to air, and the contact of water), leads them into putrefaction, which terminates in volatilizing most of the principles under the form of gas. Water, carbonic acid, carbonated and even sulphurated hydrogen gas, volatile oil in vapor, and sometimes even azotic gas and ammonia are evolved; and after this there remains nothing but a brown or black residuum, known by the name of mould. Though all the circumstances of putrefaction are not yet described, or even known, we have discovered that they are confined to the conversion of *complex substances* into substances *less compound;* that nature restores to new combinations the materials which she had but lent, as it were, to vegetables and animals; and that she thus accomplishes the perpetual circle of compositions and decompositions, which attests her power, and demon-

---

**Fourcroy regarding the process of fermentation? Give the testimonies of Count Chaptal and Prof. Turner.**

strates her fecundity, while it announces equal grandeur and simplicity in the course of her operations." ("Philosophy of Chemistry," ch. xii. 1785.)

"NATURE," said Count Chaptal, "NEVER FORMS SPIRITUOUS LIQUORS; *she rots the grape upon the branch, but it is* ART *which converts the juice into* [alcoholic] *wine.*" ("L'Art de Faire le Vin.," p. 2. Paris, 1819.)

"ALCOHOL," said Dr. E. Turner, "is the intoxicating ingredient of all spirituous and vinous liquors. IT DOES NOT EXIST READY FORMED IN PLANTS, but is a *product* of the vinous fermentation." ("Elements of Chemistry," 2d. ed. p. 664.)

33. The significant fact may here be noted which shows the chemical *contrast* between Food and Alcohol, as regards the way in which their elements are combined. "The substances," says Liebig, "which constitute THE PRINCIPAL MASS of every vegetable, are compounds of carbon, with oxygen and hydrogen *in the proper relative proportions for forming water.* Woody fibre, *starch*, *sugar*, and *gum*, for example, are such *compounds of carbon with the elements of water.* In another class, the proportion of oxygen is greater than would be required for producing water by union with the hydrogen. The numerous organic acids met with in plants belong, with few exceptions, to this class. A third class may be regarded as compounds of carbon, with the elements of water and an *excess of hydrogen.* Such are the *volatile and fixed oils*, wax, and the resins." ("Organic Chemistry," 1843.) To this class Alcohol belongs, in

---

33. In what respect do Food and Poisons stand contrasted? Explain the contrast by examples of grape sugar and alcohol.

which we have carbon 2, hydrogen 6, oxygen 1. Eight-tenths of all vegetal food is constructed of carbon and *the elements of water*, whence the blandest properties result, like water itself, —

"Honest water, too weak to be a sinner."

On the other hand, *poisons* are generally virulent in the ratio of the *disproportion* between the H and O.

34. Alcoholic liquors are known as the result only of *one process*, operating upon *one substance*, — the process is FERMENTATION, the substance GRAPE SUGAR (*glucose*). By no other process, upon any other substance, have they ever been produced.* Hence, it follows that no

* Though alcoholic drinks are exclusively made by inducing the fermentation of saccharine substances, it should be known that Flennel long ago, and Berthelot more recently, discovered a method of making alcohol by *synthesis*, — that is, instead of the method of undoing nature's work of growth in fruit and grain, by the conjoint processes of *malting* and *fermenting*, they put together certain compounds containing the elements of alcohol, when affinity does all the rest. The method, however, will probably always remain too costly even for the manufacture of pure alcohol for chemical purposes. It consists in subjecting to mutual action, in a closed retort, at common temperatures, sulphuric acid and olefiant gas ($C_2 H_2$), adding five or six volumes of water. Sulpho-vinic acid results, and from this, after repeated distillations, using a little carbonate of potash to absorb the water, alcohol distils over. Practically, then, the objection that alcoholic drinks are obtained only by the decomposition of food cannot be evaded.

It is Man that transforms by art's chemical spell
"The sweet milk of the earth to an essence of hell."
He *fermenteth* the fruit, and *corrupteth* the grain,
To engender a spirit that maddens the brain.

Cowper, the Christian Poet, who saw clearly the evils of drinking, and of "the styes that law hath licensed," asks and answers the pertinent question, —

"Will Providence o'erlook *the wasted good?*
Temperance were no virtue if He could."

---

34. From what *substance*, and by what *process*, are alcoholic liquors ob-

compound-substance in the universe, not excepting sugar itself, can possibly contain alcohol *prior* to, or independent of, that process on which its genesis depends. Neither, as we have seen, can this process take place in any living organism, plant or animal, nor even in lifeless substances, unless certain conditions exist which conspire to produce it.

*Glucose* consists of the following elements: $C_6\ H_{12}\ O_6$, according to the new system, with Hydrogen for unity; but the older chemists, now to be cited, have the formula of $C_{12}\ H_{12}\ O_{12}$.

35. What is the *nature* of the *vinous fermentation* which generates Ethylic Alcohol? The following from Turner's *Chemistry* will answer fully, —

"This name is given *to the peculiar decomposition* which the different species of sugar undergo *in certain circumstances;* and by which their elements combine to form *new compounds*, which, under similar conditions, are always the same. When a saccharine solution is placed in contact with substances in a state of decomposition or putrefaction, it is observed after about twenty-four hours, if the temperature be kept between 38° and 86° F., that *the taste of the sugar has disappeared;* pure *carbonic acid* is disengaged, and the liquid has *acquired* intoxicating properties. It *now* contains alcohol, which may be *separated* by distillation. If we compare the composition and quantity of these products with that of

---

**tained? Give the new and old formula of *glucose*. Is alcohol producible by synthesis? (Note.)**

**35. What is the *nature* of the process operated on grape sugar which gives rise to Alcohol? How does Liebig define Fermentation, etc.?**

the sugar employed, we shall find them to contain the same weight of carbon."

Baron Liebig, in a later work, thus defines the processes, —

"FERMENTATION, PUTREFACTION, and DECAY. — These are processes of *decomposition*, and their ultimate results are to *reconvert* the elements of organic bodies into that state in which they exist *before they participate in the processes of Life*, [whereby] complex ORGANIC ATOMS of the *highest order* are REDUCED into combinations of *a lower order*, into that state of combination of *Elements* from which they sprang." ("Letters on Chemistry," 2d series, pp. 127–9.)

36. Turner's *Chemistry*, edited by Liebig, goes into particulars, —

"*Fermentation is nothing else but the putrefaction of a substance containing no nitrogen.* It is excited by the contact of all bodies, the elements of which are in a state of active decomposition. In nitrogenized substances of a very complex constitution, *putrefaction* (*or fermentation*) is spontaneously established when water is present, and when the temperature is sufficiently high, and *it continues till the original compounds are wholly destroyed.** Substances containing no nitrogen, on the contrary, *require*, in order to their undergoing this metamorphosis, *the presence of a nitrogenized substance* already in a state of putrefaction (fermentation). The

* Hence the error talked some years ago, about "*inceptive* fermentation."

---

**36. What is the difference between Fermentation and Putrefaction? How long will Fermentation go on if not artificially arrested?**

substances which best promote the change are gliadine, gluten, vegetable albumen, in short, all substances in a state of *spontaneous decomposition*, to which the general name of *ferment* is given. Putrefying animal substances are equally capable of exciting the same action [as in the Lamb wine of the Chinese].

37. "Ferment, or yeast, *is a substance in a state of putrefaction*, the atoms of which are in a continual motion.* This motion, or conflict of the elements, communicating itself to the sugar, *destroys* the equilibrium of its atoms. These no longer retain the same arrangement, and group themselves according to their special attractions. The carbon of the sugar is divided between the hydrogen and the oxygen; there is *formed*, on the one hand, a carbonized compound, containing almost all the oxygen (carbonic acid); and, on the other, a second carbonized compound, containing all the hydrogen (alcohol).

"It is highly probable that cane sugar, before it undergoes the vinous fermentation, is converted into grape sugar by contact with the ferment; and that, consequently, it is *grape sugar alone which yields alcohol and carbonic acid*.†

*This explains why ferment and fermented substances were prohibited in the typical and symbolical institutions of the Jews, and were applied to *bread*, as well as *wine* and *honey*.

† "Whatever denomination of sugar you start with, it becomes *grape sugar*; this is the preliminary step. *This grape sugar then suffers dismemberment*, and is resolved into *carbonic acid* and into *alcohol*."—Professor Brande (Lectures, "Medical Times," vii. p. 179).

---

37. What is *Yeast*? What does it do on the atoms of sugar? Is there such a thing as "*inceptive* fermentation," or does the process, once begun, go on *continuously*? What is the observation of Prof. Brande concerning grape juice?

"In the fermentation of vegetable juices containing sugar, it appears that the elements of certain other principles therein dissolved take an essential part in the formation of the new products *occasioned by the action of the air on the juice of the grape*, of fruits, and of other plants.

"The nitrogenized matters in solution, such as gluten, gliadine, vegetable albumen, etc., are spontaneously decomposed; and it is then that the decomposition of the sugar is commenced, and continues alone till the sugar has entirely disappeared. *When* the juice *has once begun to ferment*, it may be preserved from the contact of the atmosphere *without the action being thereby arrested.** *The nitrogenized* [nourishing] *matters of the juice are constantly precipitated in the shape of ferment, or yeast;* and in the fermented liquors, besides alcohol, there are found other substances, such as *œnanthic ether*, oil of potato, oil of grain, etc., the presence of which could not be detected *previous* to fermentation."

38. In the light of these explanations, the notion that Alcohol is *in* Sugar or *in* Grapes, or that nature has adapted her arrangements to the production of Alcohol, must appear simply absurd. Against the first of these

* "The ferment may exist and lie dormant till *the presence of oxygen* renders it active, and capable of communicating its activity to other bodies. If, for instance, I express the juice of grapes, cautiously avoiding the contact of air or oxygen, *the grape juice remains unchanged*, though the azotized ferment is contained in it; but throw up a little oxygen into the juice — a bubble is sufficient — and now the ferment begins to change, and has become capable of inducing a *new arrangement of the elements* of sugar." — Prof. Brande.

---

38. Is Alcohol in Sugar? Give the reasons of Prof. Liebig.

objections, however, we may place the following passage from the "Organic Chemistry" of Baron Liebig (1843) —

"FERMENTATION OF SUGAR. — The peculiar decomposition which sugar suffers may be viewed as a type of *all* the transformations designated fermentation. The analysis of sugar from the cane proves that it contains the ELEMENTS of carbonic acid and alcohol, *minus* 1 atom of water. *The alcohol and carbonic acid produced* by the fermentation of a certain quantity of sugar *contain* together 1 equivalent of oxygen, and 1 equivalent of hydrogen *more than the sugar contained.* It is known that 1 atom of sugar contains 12 equivalents of carbon, both from the proportions in which it unites with bases, and from the composition of saccharic acid, the product of its oxidation. Now, *none of these atoms of carbon are contained in the sugar as carbonic acid*, because the *whole quantity* is obtained as oxalic acid, when sugar is treated with hyper-manganate of potash; and as oxalic acid is a lower degree of the oxidation of carbon than carbonic acid, it is impossible to conceive that the lower degree should be produced from the higher, by means of one of the most powerful agents of oxidation which we possess.

"It can be also proved, that the hydrogen of the sugar *does not exist in it in the form of alcohol*, for it is converted into water and a kind of carbonaceous matter when treated with acids, particularly with such as contain no oxygen; and this manner of decomposition is never suffered by a compound of alcohol. SUGAR, therefore, CONTAINS NEITHER ALCOHOL NOR CARBONIC ACID, so that these bodies must be produced by *a different arrangement of its atoms*, and by their union with the elements of water."

39. An American serial having, in 1847, given currency to some erroneous views regarding the *sudden* production of alcohol in newly expressed grape juice,* we induced an esteemed friend and careful analyst, to institute a number of experiments, and now republish his "Report," with an advertisement prefixed, that appeared for several years in the papers, —

EXPERIMENTS OF AN ENGLISH CHEMIST.

"The Committee of the *British Temperance Association* having received, from Dr. Lees, the detail of the following experiments conducted by a practical chemist, in the presence of competent witnesses, are prepared to offer a premium of £50 to any person who will *extract* any appreciable quantity of *Alcohol* from grapes, ripe or otherwise, *provided the fruit has not in any way been meddled with by art;* they believing that the intervention of man is necessary to the placing of fruit in a condition such as will permit of the *vinous* fermentation." After twenty years' lapse of time, these experiments remain unrefuted.

"Dr. Pereira ("Elements of Materia Medica") of the Manufacture of Wine, says, —

* As Liebig says, "*Vegetable juices in general become turbid when in contact with the air*, BEFORE FERMENTATION COMMENCES." — (*Chemistry of Agriculture*, 3d Ed.)

---

39. Do sound or even rotting Grapes *contain* Alcohol? Give the experiments of a British Chemist in the negative.

"'Grape juice does not ferment in the grape itself. This is owing, not [solely] as Fabroni ("de l'Art faire le Vin;" Paris, 1801) supposed, to the gluten being contained in distinct cells to those in which the saccharine juice is lodged, but to the exclusion of atmospheric oxygen, the contact of which, as Gay Lussac ("Ann. de Chim." lxxvi. 245) has shown, is necessary to effect some change in the gluten; whereby it is enabled to set up the process of fermentation. The expressed juice of the grape, called *must* (mustum), readily undergoes the vinous fermentation when subjected to the temperature of between 60° and 80° F.'

"Here we find two celebrated philosophers, natives of wine countries, quoted as *knowing* that grape juice does not ferment in the grape itself; and how each attempted to *account* for the fact. Yet now, after a lapse of forty years, we hear the assertion (from the other side of the Atlantic, indeed) that alcohol is contained in ripe grapes, whole or bruised! It may be asked, reasonably we think, *what* new evidence these new-world luminaries have to adduce; for, after it has been ascertained that a certain sort of decomposition in a certain substance *cannot* take place, we are entitled to remain incredulous till doomsday, or until proof shall be produced that nature's laws no longer continue the same as formerly. Nevertheless, we have been willing to make a few experiments, in order to see, with our own eyes, whether the old truths, or the new assertions, best agree with the laws of nature.

"(I.) One pound of fully ripe grapes (Black Hamburg) were put into a glass retort, with half a pint of water, and distilled very slowly until three fluid ounces had passed into the receiver. This product had no alcoholic smell. It was put into a small glass retort, with an ounce of fused chloride of calcium, and distilled very slowly till a quarter fluid ounce was drawn; this second educt had no smell of alcohol, nor was it in the slightest degree inflammable.

"(II.) A flask was filled with grapes, none of which had been deprived of the stalks, and it was then inverted in mercury.

"(III.) Another flask was filled with grapes from which the stalks had been pulled, and many of which were otherwise bruised: this flask was also inverted in mercury.

The flasks were placed, for five days, in a room of the average temperature of about 70° Fah. In the perfect grapes no change was perceivable. In the bruised grapes *putrefaction* had proceeded to an extent, in each grape, proportionate to the degree of injury it had sustained; the *sound parts* of each continuing unchanged.

"(IV.) The grapes were now removed from the flasks, and the juice expressed from each.

"The juice from the bruised grapes had, not an alcoholic, but a *putrescent* flavor. Dr. A. T. Thompson ("Dispensatory," p. 644) says "that in wine countries, before the grapes are subjected to the press, *the sound are separated from the unsound with great care,*" — evidently to prevent this putrid flavor in the wine. The juice from the sound grapes was perfectly sweet.

"Both these juices were placed in lightly corked phials, half-filled, and subjected to a proper fermenting temperature. It was THREE DAYS before the *commencement* of fermentation, in each, was indicated by the evolution of carbonic acid gas, as also by the odor of the alcohol, and of the aromatic oils always generated in such cases.

"I therefore still believe it to be A FACT, that grapes do not produce alcohol; that it can result only where the juice has been *expressed* from them, and then not *suddenly;* and that, where the hand of man interferes not, alcohol is never formed.

"JOSEPH SPENCE,
"*Chemist to the Yorkshire Agricultural Society.*
"9th Mo., 1847."

40. The physical and social effects of drinking alcohol *in* wine, and alcohol distilled *from* wine, are everywhere the same, differing only in degree. Both engender, according to their strength, the terrible and debasing appetite for themselves which it is the object of Temperance Societies to suppress. Yet, such is the force of prejudice, that an old theory is revived by Prof. Kranichfeld, of Berlin, that alcohol in wine is not alcohol, but *the vinous principle!* — a theory which had been exploded by Gay Lussac above thirty years before, as well as by Prof. Brande. (See "Philosophical Transactions" for 1811–13.) After the celebrated Berzelius had pronounced the Berlin experiments to be inadequate, they were held, it seems, rather with hope than confidence; for, at a general assembly of Deputies of the German

---

**40. Is there any material difference in the physical and social effects of drinking *wine* and *spirits* respectively? Do they not both produce criminals, drunkards, and madmen? Is Alcohol *in* wine different from Alcohol distilled *out*?**

Temperance Societies, held in Hamburgh, August, 1843, Dr. Kranichfeld proposed, "A prize of two or three hundred louis d'or, to award to the solution of this question, —

"Is the *animating principle* in spirituous liquids before the distilling (or any other chemical operation) of the very same kind and quality as after; or is it after such process different from before; and what are — if the latter is the case — the medical, physical, and chemical qualities and effects of the one as well as of the other?"

41. There is nothing whatever in the experiments contrary to the accredited doctrine of chemists. On testing wine, "*the first portions which distil contain water*, and are followed by absolute alcohol;" and this impure compound, consisting of alcohol, united with the *œnanthic acid* and the volatile oils which pass over before the end of the process, is what Dr. Kranichfeld calls the "*vinous principle*"*!* Considering it as *a collection* of principles, is it any wonder that it should not burn, taste, and smell *exactly like* absolute alcohol? But when it was exposed to a second distillation, and to a higher degree of heat, which separated the water and heterogeneous principles, it then appeared as undisguised alcohol. All this accords with the established theory; it does not in the least contradict it.

Professor Brande, in a lecture at the Royal Institution, thus satisfactorily disposes of the doctrine under discussion, —

---

**41. State the error of Dr. Kranichfeld, and give Prof. Brande's answer to it.**

"Some chemists have suggested the probability of the *non-existence* of ready formed alcohol in wine, and have supposed that the alcohol is *generated by the action of heat*, and is altogether a *product* of distillation. But, inasmuch as I can obtain the same quantity of alcohol by distilling wines *at very low* as at very high temperatures, and as I can get the full complement of alcohol from the stronger wines *by the action of carbonate of potash*, which abstracts water and separates alcohol without any distillation or any other interference of heat, we must not allow those who indulge in wine to

"'Lay this flattering unction to their souls,'

or to use any such argument in opposition to the teetotalists." ("Medical Times," viii. p. 180, 1843.)

42. Wines, Ales, Beers, Porters, and other *fermented liquors*, such as Cider and Perry, differ from *distilled spirits* only in this, that the latter have more thoroughly got rid of the *small remains* of the original substances from which they were made, whether grain, fruit, or fruit juices. Under the "Physiology of Diet," we shall supply TABLES indicating the true facts in relation to various drinks; but for all essential purposes of the present argument it is sufficient to say that intoxicating liquors are, in the main, *but Alcohol and Water, more or less strong*, and injurious in proportion to the *quantity* of the alcohol contained in them. Adulteration, no doubt, is very extensively practised; but, so far as

---

**42. What is the common character of intoxicating liquors in relation to Temperance? What is the purpose of the brewer? What says Dr. Druitt? (Note.)**

Temperance is concerned, it may be stated as a rule that no other drug is worse than alcohol. The purpose of the brewer (whether of wine, ale, or cider) is *not* to make a "nourishing" beverage; and every pretence of the kind is, therefore, an impudent imposition upon public ignorance and credulity. The object of the brewer is to *clear the liquor* of the natural gluten or albumen dissolved in malt *wort*, apple *juice*, or wine *must*, changing that precious element of nutrition into *yeast* (or barm as it sometimes is called), and to convert the valuable *sugar* into alcohol and carbonic acid. The *chief*, if not the sole, end of all the elaborate processes of artificial fermentation is *the production of an intoxicant*, and the destruction of the nitrogenous or blood-forming elements of food.* Whatever salts or acids of alleged value, medically or dietetically, may remain after the process of "clearing" is over, were contained in *far greater measure* in the original cereal or fruit from which the drink was made.

43. In order to exhibit the complete contrast between the "fruit of the vine" and the various products of its fermentative or putrefactive destruction, tables of their

*Dr. Druitt in his "Report on Wines," got up in the interest of the wine importers, says, indeed, that "alcohol is a *mere drug*, and is *not* the valuable element in wine." He praises and puffs as the very element of life, certain volatile *aromas* and *scents!* But it must be plain that wines that fetch high prices *exclusively*, or *chiefly*, on account of their flavor and aroma, are of a very limited range, accessible only to the wealthy connoisseur, and quite beyond the reach or appreciation of the general public; so that such refined evasions or apologies, are altogether beyond the real practical question.

---

43. For what *diseases* are grapes and grape juice prescribed in "Syria" and in Switzerland? *Why* are they good in consumption?

different compositions are subjoined. But first of their "MEDICAL PROPERTIES AND USES. The ripe FRUIT OF THE VINE is cooling and antiseptic; and when eaten in large quantities, diuretic and laxative. Grapes are very useful in febrile diseases, particularly in bilious and putrid fevers, dysentery, and *all inflammatory affections.* In Syria, the juice of ripe grapes, *inspissated*, is used in great quantities in these diseases. (Russell's "Nat. His. of Aleppo," i. 83.) Grapes have been strongly recommended as *an article of common diet in phthisis* (Moore's "View of Society in Italy," ii. Lett. 62); and they certainly contain *much bland nutritious matter*, well fitted for phthisical habits." (Dr. A. T. Thompson, "London Dispensatory.")

"In the inflammatory form of *dyspepsia*, and in pulmonary affections, ripe grapes are eaten in considerable quantities, in Switzerland and other parts of the continent, occasionally with considerable benefit, and forming what is called the *cure de raisins.*" (Dr. Pereira, "Treatise on Food," p. 355.)

44. CONSTITUENTS OF "WINE IN THE CLUSTER."

1. Gluten, a blood-former, plentiful.
2. Sugar, in varying, but always large amount.
3. Gum, which, however, is chiefly a mechanical lubricant.
4. Various *odorous* matters, or aromas.

5–6. Malic acid and citric acids in small quantities.

7–8. Phosphorus and sulphur in combination.

9. Bitartrate of Potash (Cream of Tartar).

---

**44. What are the constituents of "Wine in the Cluster"? Name the main results of *fermenting* it, and the substances lost for dietetic ends.**

10. Tartrate of Lime.

11. Water, etc.

When these mingled elements are "worked," the old products are in great part destroyed. The *nourishing* gluten putrefies by exposure to air and moisture; "*carbonic acid* and pure *hydrogen gas* are evolved; *phosphate, acetate, caseate*, and *lactate of ammonia* being at the same time produced in such quantity that the further decomposition of the gluten ceases. But when the supply of water is renewed, the decomposition begins again, and in addition to the salts just mentioned, *carbonate of ammonia* and a white crystalline matter resembling mica (*caseous oxide*) are formed, together with the *hydrosulphate of ammonia*, and a *mucilaginous substance* coagulable by chlorine. *Lactic acid* is almost always produced by the putrefaction of organic bodies." (Liebig, "Org. Chem.," p. 259.) As the gluten decays, and the yeast fungus is developed, the *Bitartrate of Potash*, in great part, settles, in bottle or cask, as "crust of wine," being insoluble in alcohol, and is thus lost as a salt of the blood. When the first working is over, and the wine is bottled, we find, on opening it after a few months, the following constituents, —

45. "Wine, the Mocker" — or, "*Old Red Port.*"

*Alcohol*, a powerful narcotic.

*Œnanthic acid* (an oily, inodorous liquid).

*Œnanthic ether* (of a vinous, unpleasant smell).

*Essential or volatile oils.**

* *Nicotine*, a frightful poison (one-fourth of a drop will kill a rabbit; one drop, a dog), is one of these essential oils; formula, $C_{10}H_8N$. It is the in-

45. Enumerate the *new* constituents in "Wine the Mocker"? What follows the "Keeping of Wine"?

Bouquet or aroma.
*Acetic acid.*
*Sulphate of potash.*
Chlorides of potassium and sodium.
Tannin, and coloring matter from the grape husk.
Undecomposed sugar, gum, and extractive matter, in *small* quantities.

The substances in *italics* are new compounds.

After a time, the alcohol suffers a slow decomposition, and the wine becomes milder. This, probably, is owing to the gradual conversion of part of the alcohol into *ethers*, by union with the different acids. But, on exposure to air, in a proper temperature, wine will at once enter into the *acetous fermentation*, during which the alcohol *quickly disappears*, and is replaced by acetic acid, or vinegar.

A more complete contrast between the natural and the artificial wine can hardly be conceived than these analyses present.

46. The following (determined by Dr. Bence Jones) is the percentage of alcohol contained in samples of the liquors named, as given by the Alcoholometer.

| | | | |
|---|---|---|---|
| Port Wine, | 20 to 23. | Rum, | 72 to 77. |
| Sherry, | 15 to 24. | Whiskey, | 59. |

toxicating principle of *prepared* tobacco, but was not present in the *natural leaf*. It results, like alcohol, from *fermentation*; several other volatile oils are generated at the same time.

---

46. Give the percentage of alcohol in eight of the most celebrated Wines? Also of Spirits and fermented liquors?

| | | | |
|---|---|---|---|
| Madeira, | 19. | Brandy, | 50 to 53. |
| Champagne, | 14. | Geneva (Gin), | 49. |
| Burgundy, | 10 to 13. | Bitter Ale (new), | 6 to 12. |
| Rhine Wine, | 9 to 13. | Porter, | 6 to 7. |
| Claret, | 9 to 11. | Stout, | 5 to 7. |
| Moselle, | 8 to 9. | Cider, | 5 to 7. |

47. Alcohol can in no sense be regarded as "a good creature of God," in respect to diet. For, in the first place, it is not constructed *like* food, being neither solid nor innocent; and, in the second, whether good for any proper end, it is still an artificial, and not a natural, product. In a strict and scientific sense, man can make nothing, — he can only *modify;* the ultimate power which effects every change belongs exclusively to that all-pervading Spirit in whom we "live and move and have our being." There is nothing done or developed by the creature, which is not also done *by the agency of God* empowering or sustaining it. In this last case, however, the result is called Art, not Nature. When we speak of the "creations" of the poet or the painter, we employ the word figuratively. "Creature," therefore, in a strict sense, is the minor relative, of which "Creator" is the major. Hence "creature" must signify, in this discussion, either some substance which formed a part of the *original creation*, or which is still produced in *nature*, independent of human aid or agency; for vital and vegetative nature may be viewed as a "perpetual creation," in which the types of all original products are constantly renewed,

---

**47. Is alcohol, in any sense, "a good creature"? Was it placed or provided in Paradise? Can such words as creation, or growth, be fairly applied to it? Why not?**

bearing fruit after their several kinds. When the original creative act was accomplished; when the spirit of God brooded over the face of the waters, and chaos retired before the reign of order; when the sun was fixed, and the planets were appointed their courses in the heavens; when the fiat went forth, "Let Light *be*," and "Light *was;*" when radiant heat cheered and quickened the fresh creation, and animated every living thing; when silence gave place to praise, and the songs of birds made vocal the bowers of Paradise; when from the rocks fountains of living water gushed forth, and eastward the silvery stream rolled on; when "the Morning Stars sang together, and all the Sons of God shouted for joy" at this fresh outbirth of creative power, — is it recorded that *Alcohol* was there?

48. If we pass from the records of Revelation to the open and illuminated volume of Nature, — if we search throughout the wide range of vegetative and animated forms for the presence of alcohol, — there is not one plant or flower, not one creature or compound, resulting from the formative processes of life and growth, in which it can possibly be detected or developed. Creation, growth, maturity, — these are terms which refer to *life;* but alcohol has nothing to do with life, except to destroy it; it is a poison alike to plants and animals; it is the outcome of vegetable *death and decay*, not of life, growth, or creation. It is not a *creature*, but the result of the death and decomposition of a creature. The clusters of the grape are but so many natural air-tight bottles, each

---

**48. Is alcohol found in nature? Does any living cell secrete it? What is the character of a "grape" berry?**

containing within it an exquisite apparatus for nourishment and preservation, — the only "fruit of the vine" which nature "creates" and "matures." But neither in this nor in any other "fruit" have chemists ever detected the presence of alcohol; at least, in the records of their multitudinous experiments and analyses, we find no memorial of the discovery.*

49. But the indications of Nature's design do not terminate here. Even when fermentation is established by the interference of Art, it still requires the continued exertion of human ingenuity to secure the object sought. The art of the brewer and the maltster is, in fact, a battle with Nature. The sweet juice of the young grain is the natural precursor of the flour in the ripe one. Nature aims to *mature* her fruits, so as to adapt them to the wants and laws of her animated creatures; or, when they cease to be thus used, to reduce them again to their simple "elements." It needs little reasoning to establish the position, that neither *immature* nor *decaying* fruits were ever designed to be the food of man. Nature exerts her energies and processes in perfecting the gluten of the barley; this the maltster destroys and reconverts into less compound elements; Nature, again, seeks rap-

* Some years ago, indeed, a medical man professed to have discovered a small quantity in a jar of gooseberries! Possibly, but then these were neither in their *natural* place, nor natural state: they were decaying *in artificial circumstances*, for Nature does not put her "fruits" into jars and cupboards. She keeps them for weeks and months upon the living tree, and so long as the skin bottle is unbroken which contains their pulp, both are preserved. Even when her "wine" is left ungathered (Jer. xl. 10, 12), and decomposition at last begins, nature still avoids the brewing process.

---

49. What are the further indications of natural design? Give a summary of Dr. Shaw's statement. Is alcohol "the *fruit* of the vine"?

idly to reduce her waste and decaying products to their original elements, fitting them (as manure) for the food of vegetables, when they have ceased to be adapted to the wants of animals; here, too, the brewer steps in and thwarts her obvious intentions. "WINES," says Dr. Shaw, "having once finished their fermentation as wines, *do not naturally stop there;* but, unless prevented by the care of the operator, proceed directly on to vinegar; where again they make no stop, but, *unless prevented here also, spontaneously go on* to vapidity, ropiness, mouldiness, and putrefaction. To speak philosophically, the *intention* or tendency of nature is to *proceed* from the very beginning of vinous fermentation, directly, *in one continued series, to putrefaction;* and thence again to a new generation; which appears to be the grand circle wherein all natural things are moved, and all the physical or rather chemical phenomena are produced."—("Chemical Lectures;" London, 1731, pp. 126, 127.) Alcoholic wine, then, is no more entitled to be called "*the fruit of the vine*" than any of the other contemporaneous or subsequent products of its decay, such as carbonic acid, vinegar, yeast, volatile oils, œnanthic acid, or ammonia. To apply the phrase "fruit of the vine" to any of the substances resulting from its *decay*, is just the same absurdity as to call *death* the fruit of *life;* and the prevalence of this mode of speech amongst divines and others is a disgrace to our age and country. It exhibits a humiliating extent of ignorance and confusion of thought. In the hope of assisting to remove this opprobrium, the author has entered into more detail on the Principles of Chemistry than he would, otherwise, have deemed needful in treating of the genesis of alcohol.

50. "It is a very general error," says Liebig, "to suppose that organic substances have the power of undergoing change spontaneously, *without the aid of an external cause.* The *juices of the fruit*, or other parts of a plant which very readily undergo decomposition, retain their properties *unchanged* as long as they are protected from immediate contact with the air; that is, *as long as the cells or organs in which they are contained resist the influence of the air.* The beautiful experiments of Gay Lussac upon the fermentation of the juice of grapes are the best proofs of the atmosphere having an influence upon the changes of organic substances. The juice of grapes which were expressed under a receiver filled with mercury, so that air was completely excluded, *did not ferment.*"* ("Org. Chem." p. 271.)

In fact the grape is plainly constructed with a view to prevent the fermentative process taking place upon its contents.

The tannin, coloring, and resinous principles are determined to the coat or husk, for the purpose of forming a skin-bottle impervious to the action of the air, and excluding the operation of those external agents which promote decay. Next to the skin is placed the acid, beyond that the saccharine pulp, then comes the glutinous *central pulp*, protected by a treble barrier from the influ-

*On this principle, Mr. F. Wright, of Kensington, has prepared, for sacramental use, *the pure juice of grapes*, free from alcohol, and supplies above three hundred of the churches.

---

50. Do *organic changes*, such as fermentation, take place spontaneously? Is not a distinct agent always necessary? State the general structure of the grape, after Fabroni, and show how provisions are made to *prevent* the alcoholic fermentation. Give, finally, the solemn testimony of Holy Writ.

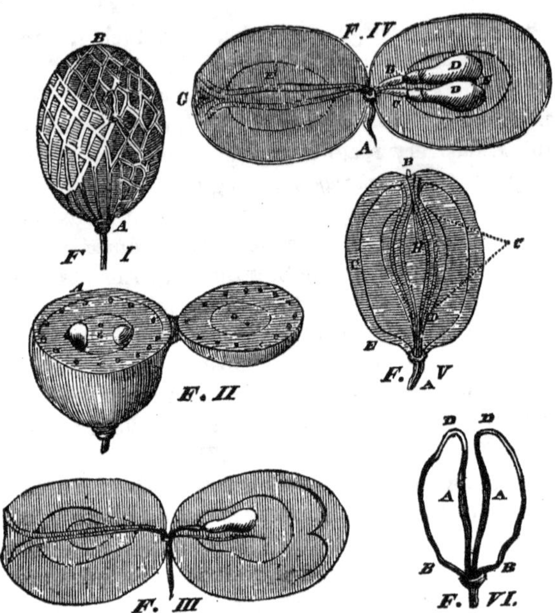


THE ANATOMY OF THE GRAPE.

See Adam Fabroni "On the Art of Making Wine," ch. 1.

EXPLANATION.

Figure I. exhibits the grape stripped of its skin ; beneath the transparent superficial pulp may be traced the texture of the conduits or *veins* coming from the crown, B, and, after ramifying into a species of fine network, descending into the stem, A.

Fig. II. represents a horizontal section, made a little above the seeds. The superficies, A, is clearly divided into three parts; through the central part run two arteries (AA, Fig. VI.); the outward region borders on the skin and extends to the conduits or veins (marked C, Fig. V); while a third substance is placed between the *central* and the external (or *cortical*) pulp, which may be called the *intermediate* pulp.

Fig. III. presents a vertical section, with a seed in one half.

Fig. IV. presents another section, containing both seeds, DD, enclosed in the *central pulp*, E; the seeds are united by means of a gelatinous ligature, to the two funicles, BC, running from A. The other half, G, represents more distinctly the two arteries which run through the central pulp, E.

Fig. V. displays the two arteries, CD, which rise from the centre of the stem, A, and ascend through the middle of the fruit, to the crown, B, from whence they fold back and ramify into the beautiful network described in Fig. I. (Their course backward is marked C in the cut.)

Fig. VI. represents the *arteries* and *veins* separated from the pulp.

ence of oxygen. It is in this central part, and in the organic structure of cells and vesicles, that the gluten resides, and it is this nitrogenized substance which is most susceptible of decay, and from the putrefaction of which the *yeast* is formed; hence, so long as the pulp remains excluded from air, and the cells unbroken, it is impossible that the alcoholic fermentation can take place. This, however, is done by the violent crushing or treading of the fruit; but it is not done *by nature*. Indeed, nature adopts the most wonderful precautions to prevent the alcoholic fermentation, and to preserve the "fruit of the vine" unchanged, as wholesome and nourishing *food* for that being who exerts his utmost ingenuity to convert it into a poisonous *drink!*

Thus beautifully do the designs of Nature and the discoveries of Science, harmonize with the declarations of God's most Holy Word,—

"THUS SAITH THE LORD, AS THE GRAPE IS FOUND IN THE CLUSTER, AND *one saith*, DESTROY IT NOT,* FOR A BLESSING IS IN IT: SO WILL I DO FOR MY SERVANTS' SAKE, THAT I MAY NOT DESTROY THEM ALL." (Isaiah lxv. 8, "Septuagint" Translation.)

*The word translated "*destroy*" signifies "*corrupt*" (as in Mal. i. 14).

# III.

## The Dietetics of Temperance.

51. THE important, practical question concerning Alcohol, is not, How is it generated, but what does it *do* in the healthy human body when introduced there? No one holds that it is indifferent or neutral, — mere "chip in pottage," — for in that case, as no one would *like* it, so no one would take it, much less buy it. Does it then act as diet, or as drug? as food, or as poison? In other words, will it help to sustain health and strength, which are the ends of food? — or will it, on the contrary, impair health and lessen strength? If it really has any "adaptation to the organism," then its timely use is no violation of Temperance; but if it is, in its properties and operation, unsuitable to the normal wants of man, Temperance imperiously dictates that we should totally abstain from it. These questions can now be answered satisfactorily. The researches and discussions of the last thirty years, forced upon the world of so-called "Science" by the Temperance reformers, have, amidst many changing hypotheses and conflicting theories, left amongst the settled truths of the question, a large number of clear principles and demonstrated facts and laws. To these we will now call attention.

---

**51. What is the real question of importance concerning Alcohol? How is it to be determined?**

52. The EXPERIENCE of many hundreds of thousands of abstainers, often under the most crucial conditions,—an experience embracing all regions, and the most varied circumstances of life,—has shown that people are not only as well able to perform the duties and enjoy the natural pleasures of existence, without strong drink as with it, but that their strength is increased, their health improved, and their enjoyments augmented. In England, where Government and Life Assurance statistics are accessible, it has been established, that the health of teetotalers is, on the average, one-half better than that of moderate and free drinkers together; and that the *value of life* amongst abstainers is increased by *one-third* as compared with the moderate drinkers.* And this fact holds true, equally of abstaining soldiers,—in India, China, Afghanistan, the Crimea,—of peasants in agricultural counties, and of artisans in large, manufacturing cities. In India, the percentage mortality amongst the British troops, in one presidency, after an experiment extending over several years, stood thus:—Abstainers, 1; Moderate drinkers, 2; Free-drinkers, 4.† In the Crimean

*Notwithstanding the disadvantage, that in the ranks of Temperance Men are included an *extra* proportion of men (now reclaimed) who *once* were drunkards.

†The "South India Temperance Journal" for 1844 records the following facts in relation to the 25th (British) Regiment, stationed at Cannamore:—

| | | |
|---|---|---|
| 241 Teetotalers, in a year sent to the Hospital | 198 = 80 | per cent. |
| 767 Non-teetotalers sent . . . . . | 2,202 = 286 | " |
| The Teetotalers had of deaths . . . . | 5 = 2 | " |
| The Drinkers had . . . . . . . . | 23 = 3 | " |

---

52. What has *Experience* shown in regard to abstainers? What is the verdict of Life Assurance Societies? What was the result of the trial of abstinence by the English soldiers in India? In the Crimea? What does Dr. Lyons report? What is the meaning of the Indian statistics?

war, the Turkish troops, though badly camped and fed, never had a death-rate higher than 5 per cent., even when scurvy prevailed, and the British troops never sank lower than 10. Dr. Lyons' Report on the Army of the Crimea admits that the porter rations were injurious; while the rum rations were simply deadly. The army returns from India illustrate the same truth. In the Bengal presidency, where rum rations were given (of course in "moderation"), the army had 73 deaths per 1000 over an average of 20 years. In the Bombay presidency, when porter was tried, after a short trial, the deaths were reduced to 1 in 50. In the Madras presidency, after a *long* trial the deaths diminished to 38 per 1000. But amongst the Temperance soldiers, the death-rate sank to the normal rate of 11 per 1000. The plain teaching of this is, that spirits *killed* 62 soldiers per 1000; porter *only* 27 per 1000; pale-ale, owing to its greater approximation to water, will simply kill about 12 per 1000; or, in other words, double the natural mortality.

53. It is a remarkable fact, which may be stated in this connection, that Sales' Brigade, when exposed to great hardship and privation in Afghanistan, but happily beyond the reach of "drinks," enjoyed an unexampled exemption from sickness, crime, and death.* Generals Napier and Havelock † bore the same testimony to

* The words of Gleig, the historian, are, "*No* sickness, *no* crime."

† "Having been attacked with fever, Havelock says, 'There was nothing in surrounding localities to cause such an affliction, and therefore I attributed

---

**53.** What was the experience of Sales' Brigade in Afghanistan? What famous Indian Generals ascribed their health to the practice of abstinence? What was Havelock's experience? What was the testimony of Sir R. Sladen, physician general?

the advantages of abstinence in India, and Sir Ramsden Sladen, Physician General of Madras, states the result of his tropical experience as follows: "I have enjoyed an uncommon share of health; but I find I can go through bodily and mental exercise *much better* when I abstain altogether from alcoholic or fermented liquors." The celebrated Cavalry Generals, STUART and STONEWALL JACKSON, who fought so well in a bad cause, were both abstainers, and ascribed their power of endurance to their abstinence, and no system could be more severely tested than was abstinence from strong drink during the burning heat and the freezing cold of their summer and winter campaigns.

54. Extreme exertion under high artificial tempera-

it partly to a rather prolonged exposure on one occasion to the rays of the sun, and partly to having, at the suggestions of friends, modified the habits which they deemed too austere for the fatigues of active service, *and consented to drink a few glasses of wine daily*, instead of restricting myself, as I had done for many months, to pure water. The fever was speedily checked; and on the disappearance of its symptoms under skilful treatment, I resolved henceforth to legislate for myself in dietetics; and, resuming my former system, abjured entirely the use of wine. A single example does not prove a rule; but my own experience, as well as that of a few others in the Bengal Contingent, certainly goes to establish the fact, that water-drinking is the best regimen for a soldier.'

"Although after this he was exposed to rain and sun, and made long and painful marches in a heated atmosphere, and endured cold and fatigue, his health remained firm and unshaken. He was willing to drink wine as well as water if it could be *proved* beneficial. A man of fact in this, as well as in everything else, he abjured the use of all stimulants because they were injurious to his health, and strove to drive them from the army because he knew they made soldiers worse in every respect, instead of better."—*Headley's Life of Havelock.*

---

54. What was the result of two remarkable trials of abstinence in the Government Yards at Portsmouth and Woolwich? What is the experience of the Sheffield Armor-Plate-rollers?

ture is also borne far better by abstainers than by drinkers. Above seventy years ago, the celebrated Dr. Beddoes, of Bristol, tried the experiment amongst the Anchorsmiths of Portsmouth, and, in his "Hygeia," records that the abstainers worked far better and with less subsequent fatigue. In the attempt to make the "Lancaster shells," at Woolwich, three sets of men broke down in the process, so excessive were the labor and heat; and only when a band of abstainers undertook the work was this "monster shell" actually made. The London "Times" of Sept. 11, 1867, in describing the rolling of the 15-inch armor-plate at the Atlas works, Sheffield, gives the following splendid testimony to the physical excellence of abstinence. The slab of iron to be rolled weighed 21 tons. "Sometimes one came on groups of men who were saturating in water the rough bands of sacking in which they were enveloped before going to wrestle with some white-heat forging; sometimes on men nearly naked, with the perspiration pouring from them, who had come to rest for a moment from the puddling furnaces, and to take a long drink of the thick *oatmeal and water*, which is all that they venture on drinking during their labor, and which long experience has proved to be *the most sustaining of all drinks* under the tremendous heats to which they are subjected."

55. A difference of climate, of heat or cold, does not appear to make any material difference in the result, as to the advantages of abstinence. In the Army of the

---

55. Does climate make any material difference in a trial of abstinence? What was the result of the experiment in the Army of the German Confederation? What is the verdict of British Life Assurance, as regards Alcohol? What of the Preston Sick Clubs?

German Confederation, when the experiment was made above twenty years ago, amongst 27,000 troops, it was found that the strong country levies from Holstein, Mecklenburgh, and Hanover, chiefly laborers and woodcutters, to whom the usual grog rations were given, had 90 cases of sickness per 1000; while the city-bred troops, less inured to toil, from the Hanse-towns and Brunswick, from whom they were withheld, had only 42 cases. So, in the British Temperance Provident Life Assurance Society, taking the most favorable adult period, it is found that the rate of mortality is 11 per 1000, while in other offices, very careful in the selection of their lives, it ranges from 16 to 23 at the same age. In the Provident, during the last twelve years, separate books have been opened for the insurance of good lives of non-abstainers; but when the quinquennial profits were divided, it was discovered that *one-third* more profit accrued to the teetotaler than to the respectable, limited drinker. The first report of the Health of Towns Commission, in England, shows another striking fact, arising from a comparison of the statistics of the Temperance Sick Club with that of a large number of others, including a Manager's Sick Club, composed of members living under sanitary conditions superior to those which the majority of working-men can now enjoy. 1000 drinkers had 23 sick per year, for an average of 7 weeks and 4 days, at a cost per head of 56s.; while 1000 abstainers had only 13 sick, for a period of 3 weeks and 2 days, at a cost of 29s. per head; so that the teetotalers extend to each other more pecuniary help, and save themselves much protracted pain. Compared with them, there is, in the average community of "moderate drinkers," twice as many persons sick, for twice as long a time, and at twice as much expense. This, again, amounts to the significant fact, that abstainers save themselves from three-fourths of the common miseries of mankind. The pains and depressions of the sick-bed are diminished, the cost of sickness abridged, the prolonged and painful nursing of wife and daughter rendered needless, and a vast train of inconveniences that attend disease, especially amongst the poor, are saved to the sufferer and his friends. Over the household of the truly temperate, the cloud of affliction rests neither so densely nor so frequently, and while it casts a shadow less sombre, passes quickly away, dispelled by the bursting sunlight of health and hope.

56. The great navigators to the polar regions, both English and American,—Ross, Parry, Franklin, Richardson, Kennedy, and Kane,—have demonstrated the actual perniciousness of alcoholics in high latitudes, where all the powers of life are needed to resist the destructive energies of physical nature. Whatever tends to lower the vital activity, or to depress the heat-generating powers of the living frame, must be specially avoided under the rigorous climate which prevails within the Arctic and Antarctic circles. Hence the rule of abstinence was enforced by authority, but with undoubted benefit to the health and strength of the men.* If alcoholics cannot

* To the numerous testimonies of *Experience* referred to, we add that of Sir John Richardson, M. D., one of the most distinguished members of the Arctic Expeditions:

"I am quite satisfied that spiritous liquors, *diminish the power of resisting*

---

56. How did the Arctic Navigators deal with Alcoholics? What is the inference from their experience? What is the testimony of Sir John Richardson and Dr. McRae? What is the verdict of experience, as stated by Brinton, Smith, Lallemand, etc.?

*give power* in circumstances of such extremity and need, it is simple folly to use them with such a view, in the ordinary circumstances of daily life. The late Dr. W. Brinton, of London, a man of large experience, thus admits this truth in his great work on "Dietetics," —

"Careful observation leaves little doubt that a moderate dose of beer or wine would in most cases at *once diminish the maximum weight* which a healthy person could lift. *Mental acuteness, accuracy of perception*, and *delicacy of the senses, are all so far opposed by alcohol*, as that the *maximum* efforts of each are *incompatible* with the ingestion of any moderate quantity of fermented liquid. A single glass will often suffice to *take the edge off* both mind and body, and to reduce their capacity to something below their perfection of work." (p. 389, 1861.)

Dr. E. Smith, in his experiments recorded in the "Philosophical Transactions" for 1859, had proved the same thing of alcohol, —

*cold*. Plenty of food and sound digestion are the best sources of heat. We found on our northern journey that *tea was far more refreshing than wine or spirits, which we soon ceased to care for*, while the *craving* for the tea increased. Liebig, I believe, considers that spirits are necessary to northern nations, to diminish the waste of the solids of the body, *but my experience leads me to a contrary conclusion*. The Hudson's Bay Company have for many years entirely excluded spirits from the fur-countries in the north, over which they have exclusive control, to the great improvement of the health and morals of their Canadian servants, and of the Indian tribes."

[Dr. McRae's testimony at the meeting of the American Association for the Advancement of Science, at Montreal, in 1856, was as decisive, and is as reliable, as either of the others. "The moment that a man had swallowed a drink of spirits, it was certain that his day's work was nearly at an end. It was absolutely necessary that the rule of total abstinence be rigidly enforced, if we would accomplish our day's task. Whatever it could do for a sick man, its use as a beverage when we had work on hand, in that terrific cold, was out of the question." I. F. H.]

" It greatly *lessens muscular tone and power.* There is *no* evidence that it increases nervous influence, whilst there is much evidence that it *lessens nervous power.*"

Professors LALLEMAND and PERRIN, of Paris, a year later, state the same truth amongst their experimental conclusions, —

" *Muscular power is weakened*, and (in extreme cases) extinguished."

Volumes of concrete experiences might be given, bringing us to the conclusion that alcohol depresses power rather than increases it; and science will explain the reason.

57. If experience has settled the fact, *as a fact*, that men are really more healthy and more vigorous, in body and mind, by abstaining than by using intoxicants, science, by technical and special experiments, has no less certainly determined several elements of the theory, which account for the fact. It is now universally admitted that alcohol is not an element that *makes* blood, out of which is restored or built up the various parts and tissues of the living framework. It has not the proximate elements of nutrition, for cell or membrane, for bone, muscle, nerve, or brain. It cannot, therefore, *nourish.*

Baron LIEBIG says: " Beer, wine, spirits, etc., furnish no element capable of entering into the composition of blood, muscular fibre, or any part which is the seat of the vital principle."

Prof. MOLESCHOTT, in his work on the " Chemistry of

---

**57. What is the final conclusion in regard to Alcohol as *nutriment*? State the opinions of Professors Moleschott, Liebig, and Carpenter?**

Diet," says: "Alcohol does not deserve the name of an alimentary principle." ("Erlangen," 1853.)

Dr. W. B. CARPENTER, in the fourth edition of his "Manual of Physiology" (1865), says: "Alcohol cannot supply anything which is essential to the due nutrition of the tissues." (p. 327.)

In short, it has no lime and phosphorus for the bones; no iron or salts for the blood; no nitrogen, in any form, for vital tissue of any kind; and it is not even a solid, as all real food is and must be.

58. But a hypothesis was broached by Liebig, in 1843, that since alcohol is not found in the secretions and excretions, when taken in limited quantities (which, however, it *is*), it must be *decomposed* (i. e., combusted or burnt) in the blood, through the action of oxygen, and by this oxidation supply *heat* to the body, and therefore energy or force. To this the author of this volume replied, at the time: (1) that several experimenters have detected alcohol in the renal secretion, and that it is patent to all, by mere smell, that some of the associated alcohols (and therefore alcohol itself) with the characteristic *odors* of whiskey, wine, rum, beer, etc., rapidly escape from the breath of the drinker; (2) that if, possibly, some of the alcohol is burnt up, it must necessarily be by *robbing the blood of oxygen* (a fixed quantity) intended, first, to burn up the effete tissues of the frame, and, second, to oxidize the innocent and normal oils and fatty matters in the blood; (3) that if it does that, then it

---

**58. What was the hypothesis of Liebig, in regard to Alcohol as an element of respiration? What were Dr. Lees' five reasons for rejecting that hypothesis, and ignoring the conclusion?**

leaves a more valuable fuel than itself *undecomposed*, and consequently the body becomes cooler; while (4) at the same time, waste matter being unduly kept in the system, the vital tone is lowered, and diseases of congestion are set up; and (5) that the experiments of Fyfe and Prout, published in the "Annals of Philosophy," in 1813, clearly show that *less carbonic acid is eliminated* in the breath after the use of wine, and therefore less heat is produced, — which result corresponds to actual experience.

59. Two years later this fact became admitted by continental experimenters, including Liebig himself, who confessed that alcohol, *if oxidized*, would yield *less heat*, at greater cost, than the normal fuel of the body. He says, —

"If 1 part by weight of Sugar of Milk can keep up the temperature of the body at the normal height for 33 hours, then an equal weight of *Alcohol* will keep it up for 65 hours, and an equal weight of Fat for 87 hours." ("Animal Chemistry," 3d ed., p. 117. Lond. 1846.)

Thus he admits that, taking both cost and consequence into account, the poison, Alcohol, is *four* times dearer than the natural fuel, Oil. Moreover, whatever amount of alcohol is *oxidized*, leaves a proportionate amount of carbonaceous food unconsumed; and, in some cases, compels nature to *protest*, by setting up a disinclination for fermented liquors, —

---

**59. Does Alcohol hinder the elimination of Carbonic Acid from the body? What great authorities admit the fact? What is the evidence wanted, but not obtained, to prove that Alcohol is *oxidized*, or burnt up within the body? What is the concession of Dr. Anstie?**

"When Cod-liver oil is administered to persons accustomed to drink daily a certain quantity of wine," says Liebig, "it often happens that the *inclination for wine is diminished*, so that at last they can take no wine at all; obviously *because alcohol and fat-oil* in this case *mutually impede the excretion of each other* through the skin and lungs." (Ibid., p. 97.)

Dr. VIERORDT, of Carlsruhe, says, as the result of experiment: "The mean number of expirations in a minute is fourteen; that number increases after meals. *The amount of carbonic acid expired diminishes considerably after the ingestion of fermented liquors, and does not return to its natural quantity for the space of two hours.* During moderate exercise at least *one third* more carbonic acid is exhaled with each expiration than during repose." ("Physiology of Respiration," 1845.)

In other words, the benefits of *fresh air* and *exercise* are counteracted by the use of alcoholic fluids, and the body is not healthily ventilated.

Professor LEHMANN says: "We should forbid the use of spirituous drinks, and not prescribe tinctures, which might *hinder* the necessary excretion of carbonic acid." ("Physiological Chemistry.")

No doubt, alcohol *does* hinder the excretion of foul air from the body, and retains effete, bad matter of various kinds — thus promoting, on the one hand, the production of diseases like rheumatism and gout, and, on the other, of bilious and typhoid fevers; but there is no evidence *yet* furnished which proves that alcohol *is* decomposed in the blood. If it be, where are the oxides? When steel is oxidized, we can find the *rust* in evidence. So far as chemistry can tell us, by experiment and analogy, oxidizing alcohol would produce *aldehyde*, *acetic acid*, and finally carbonic acid and water. But while the latter two have not been shown to be produced in greater quantities, the former have not been found *at all* after the use of pure alcohol, though their presence is easily detected in the blood when directly introduced through the stomach. If the wood and coal have been here, we say, show us the *ashes*. If the eggs have been consumed, produce the *shells*. So, if alcohol is decomposed in the body, produce in evidence its derivatives. This is a fair challenge; yet one physician, who clings to his theory with singular pertinacity, confesses that, after *twelve years' research and experiment*, he has not been able to produce this proof. But even he,—Dr. F. E. Anstie, the author of "Stimulants and Narcotics,"—in a lecture to the Royal College of Physicians, in August, 1867, is compelled to abandon the notion that alcohol *warms*. He says: "Alcohol, as has been abundantly proved by the admirable researches of Dr. Sidney Ringer, *does not elevate but reduces bodily temperature*, when given in even the largest *non*-intoxicating doses, except in the case where the temperature is already below the normal standard. There can be no doubt of the correctness of this observation, which I have repeatedly verified." General experience, special experiment, the quantitative measurement of the lessened oxidized products of combustion in the blood, and the test of the thermometer, all unite in a demonstration of the *fallacy* that alcohol is a warming agent, or fuel to the body; and whatever the science of the future may settle as to the destiny of alcohol, cannot disturb in the least the certainty of this fact.

60. *The end of food is the generation of force, with which man performs the work of life.* But the possible methods by which food can generate power are only three: (1) by the organization of tissue; (2) by the supply of the chemical ingredients of the blood; and (3) by furnishing fuel for oxidation and the consequent production of heat. It is now seen that alcohol can do none of these things: it cannot make tissue, or supply salts, and phosphates, or feed the furnace. Prof. LEHMANN, in his "Physiological Chemistry," says: "We cannot believe that alcohol, theine, etc., belong to the class of substances capable of contributing towards the maintenance of the vital functions." Dr. E. SMITH, F. R. S., says: "Alcohol is *not* a true food. It interferes with alimentation." (1859.)

If it be not food, however, is it not possibly drink?

61. DRINK *is needed as the* VEHICLE *of all vital movement.* Adapted to this end, Providence has given us, in wonderful abundance,

"*Honest* water, too weak to be a sinner."

As Dr. W. B. CARPENTER, in his "Manual of Physiology," impressively observes, —

"Water serves as the medium by which all alimentary material is introduced into the system; for until dis-

---

60. What is the end of Food, and the *threefold* means by which it can accomplish that end? What eminent Physiologists deny that Alcohol is capable of being food? Give their words.

61. Can Alcohol be *drink*? What are the varied uses, and adapted properties, of water? How does Alcohol antagonize the work of water? Why does Alcohol precipitate salts and organic compounds? How do Turner Liebig, and Hooper describe its relations to water?

solved in the juices of the stomach, food cannot be truly received into the economy. It is water which holds the organizable materials of the blood either in solution or suspension, and thus serves to convey them through the minutest capillary pores into the substance of the solid tissues. It is water which, mingled in various proportions with the solid components of the various textures, gives to them the consistence they require. And it is water which takes up the products of their decay and conveys them, by a most complicated system of sewage, altogether out of the system. . . . *No other liquid can supply its place;* and the deprivation of water is felt even more severely than the deprivation of food. . . . Alcohol *cannot* answer any one of those important purposes for which the use of water is required in the system; whilst, on the other hand, it *tends to antagonize many of those purposes* by its power of *precipitating* most of the organic compounds whose solution in water is essential to their appropriation by the living body." (1865.)

Alcohol is thus described in the sixth edition of Dr. Turner's "Elements of Chemistry," edited by Professor Liebig: "Pure alcohol is a clear, colorless, mobile liquid; specific gravity 0.792—0.791 at 68°, or 0.7947 at 60°. It boils at 172°, and has not been frozen by any cold hitherto produced. Is a non-conductor of electricity. The *odor* of alcohol is agreeable and penetrating, and intoxicates powerfully. It is highly inflammable, and its combustion, with a sufficient supply of oxygen, yields only carbonic acid and water. Alcohol greedily absorbs water from the atmosphere; and *deprives animal substances of the water they contain, causing them to shrivel up. Hence its use in preserving anatomical preparations.*"

"Alcohol," says Dr. Hooper, in his "Lexicon Medicum," "has a very strong affinity for water, combining with it in every proportion; it even *separates* the water from several salts when they are dissolved in it, and *precipitates* the solid matter."

This, as we shall afterwards see, renders alcohol an agent hostile to digestion. Two agents more utterly antagonistic in their function than alcohol and water cannot be found, for what the one does, the other directly undoes.

These *facts*, if not self-evident, are undeniable. Everywhere "water" is hailed as a friend by the voices of vital Nature, — at least in all ordinary measures. The flower in the garden, the grain in the field, the tree in the forest, unite with "the cattle upon a thousand hills," in illustrating the *necessity* and the *benefaction* of this simple and beautiful liquid, — the blood of Nature, the "Water of Life." How marvellous and manifold are its properties! It cleanses, but never pollutes; it aids to nourish, but never starves; it excites to normal action, but never irritates to fever and inflammation. Beyond all other agents, it absorbs heat and circulates it equably throughout the frame, and, in adapted quantity, is always retained until the function which needs it is fulfilled. Hence it wastes no force; makes no deduction from the sum total of organic power; but, on the contrary, aids the performance of every natural function.

Alcohol, then, contrasted in all its physiological properties with water, cannot rationally be regarded as *drink*, any more than food, since the one purpose of drink —

that of acting as a *vehicle* or *menstruum* of digestion and circulation — is counteracted exactly to the extent to which it is introduced into the system of any living thing, whether vegetal or animal.

62. When it is asserted that strong drinks are *nourishing*, the abstainer is strictly logical in replying, that such an opinion is fallacious, *because*, in the first place, it does not contain the elements of the living tissue; and in the second, it is speedily cast out of the body, in greater or lesser quantities,— in fact, is treated as an *intruder*. To this Dr. Lankester has unwisely objected: "*Both* water and alcohol are *equally* eliminated from the system, unchanged"! Very well, we reply, the objection would be a sufficient refutation of anybody who asserted that "water *nourished* the body *in the sense* of food." But nobody does say that of water, though many assert it of alcohol, which is lighter and more volatile! But even from the bare objection two clear inferences arise: (1) that it is absurd to call either alcohol or water *food;* (2) that to destroy genuine food wholesale, in order to generate an article not only worthless but pernicious, is at least as gratuitously wicked as for an invading general to burn down the growing corn, or tear up the ripening vines. But after this evasion, the differences between the natural element of Water, and the artificial Alcohol, still remain. Water fulfils useful, necessary, and blessed purposes in the vital economy, and goes out of the body in the actual discharge of a beneficent sanitary mission; while Alcohol really creates an internal commotion, de-

---

62. What was the evasive objection of Dr. Lankester, and other advocates of tippling? What is the answer to it?

files the vital stream, lowers the temperature of the blood, wastes the nervous energy, impairs the nutrition of the structures, and is finally expelled by the "Police Force" of the Sanitary System.

63. Still another plea is put forth in justification of the use of strong drink by those who love it. "Spirits," they say, "may not be either nourishing or warming, but we do not drink *pure* alcohol; we drink *wine* and *beer*, and these contain other elements, which *are* food." This delusion, no doubt, is bolstered up by the venal testimonies so readily obtained, and so widely advertised, by pale ale and porter brewers, who live in riches upon the ignorance and demoralization of mankind. They audaciously advertise, for example, that their beer and porter is "highly nourishing." Now Dr. LYON PLAYFAIR, C. B., Professor of Chemistry in the University of Edinburgh, has analyzed a specimen of this drink, and reports that of blood-forming matter it contains exactly *one* part in 1666 parts! Baron Liebig, in his "Chemical Letters," states that the whole purpose of brewing is to get rid of the nitrogenous, blood-forming elements of the grain, and to transmute the useful sugar into alcohol. "We can prove," says he, "with mathematical certainty, that *as much flour as can lie on the point of a table-knife is more nutritious than eight quarts of the best Bavarian beer;* that a person who is able *daily* to consume that amount of beer, obtains from it, in a whole year, in the most favorable case, ex-

---

63. Are there other elements in alcoholic drinks that are nourishing? What is the proportion of *nutriment* in Porter, according to Professor Playfair? What in Bavarian beer, according to Professor Liebig?

actly the amount of nutritive constituents which is contained in a 5-lb. loaf, or in 3 lbs. of flesh!"

64. Dr. Hassal's analysis of "Old Pale Ale," from Burton, published by Allsop & Co. themselves, will enable a child to see through the impudent delusion. A gallon of it, containing 70,000 grains, and costing 2s., was found to consist of Water, 65,320; Sugar, 100; Vinegar, 200; Hop extract, 710; Malt gum, 2,510; Alcohol, 1,160 grains. Now, as we have seen, only that seventieth of a pound of sugar is food of any kind; not the alcohol; not the hop (which is a vegetable narcotic); not the vinegar; and not even the gum, since that substance passes undigested through the body.

65. As to Wines, the case is no better. The albumen of the grape *is* valuable nourishment, but in fermentation it becomes *yeast*, which is corrupting matter; while the sugar becomes spirit. Now even Dr. R. Druitt the great eulogizer of the Light Wines, is compelled to confess that "*Alcohol is a mere drug;* and although *a* constituent, is not *the* valuable one, in Wine."

The salts of wine are also the salts of grapes, and in the latter exist in a more assimilable form, and in greater abundance.

66. On looking at our bodies, we are struck with two kinds of work that are being done, both inextricably

---

64. What is Dr. Hassal's analysis of Pale Ale? How many elements in ale are food of *any* sort?

65. What is Alcohol in Wine, according to Dr. Druitt? What are the valuable constituents in Wine, and where do they pre-exist in greater abundance?

66. What are the *four kinds of work* done by the body? What is the meaning of the correlation of force?

associated with our life. (1.) The blood and juices within, the solid limbs and tissues we feel, the breath we exhale, the water we expel, and the perspiration which transudes from the skin, are all *warm*. Heat is *got up* in the system, and the thermometer tells us that, in the natural state, our external parts are at 98° F., and our circulating stream at 100°. (2.) This warm-blood is being continually sent from the heart, the beating *life-pump* whose strokes we can feel and count, through all the arteries of the system, to every cell and tissue of the living-house. With these two sorts of work, or power-in-action, we perform (3,) *external* work, with feet and hands, under the direction of the Will; and, therefore, (4,) *Mental* work, of sensation, feeling, thought, and volition. How these forces pass from one form to another, — become translated, as it were, — or how they are *correlated*, is only partly known, but of the fact itself there can be no doubt whatever. For example, a person whose heat has sunk several degrees, or whose body has not been nourished for days, or whose frame has been wasted by fever and inflammation, can neither work with his body, nor think or feel with his brain; and, on the other hand, a person who has been subjected to intense emotion of any kind, whether of pleasure or of pain, is incapable of much physical work. The great law holds good that *all* labor is exhausting; which simply means that *all organic force is transitory*, and is continually undergoing change or transformation; and the conclusion is, that we must *restore* the old conditions in order to realize fresh force or power.

67. The NATURE of the machinery or organism concerned in this fourfold work is plain enough, though it

has yet many secrets and processes hidden from the eye of human science. (1.) The stomach, for example, is a primary grate where are prepared the *fuel*-food for lighting, and the *nourishing*-food for building-up. The lungs are at once the bellows which (by *in*spiration) take in the fresh air (or oxygen), for oxidizing the carbon and hydrogen of the food and tissues, or burning it up; and which (by *ex*piration) send out the excess of carbonic-acid gas, or foul air, thus serving as a chimney for the perpetual ventilation of the house. The arterial system, where the oxygen meets with the transformed food and tissues, is the general *furnace* of the body; and, associated with this system, are liver, intestine, kidneys, etc., which, in conjunction with skin and lungs, are the drains and purifiers of the system for casting forth the waste, effete, or poisonous products of vital changes.

The heat evolved in these changes daily, in the body of a healthy, well-fed adult, is probably *equal* to the raising of 5½ gallons of water from the freezing condition to the boiling-point. (2.) The great central pump of the Heart is a congeries of *muscles*, with adapted valves, for forcing the pabulum of the blood through the whole body, aided by other contrivances. At each stroke of this living-pump, from 5 to 6 ounces of blood are thrown with great power into the arterial tubes; and in the 24 hours of the day, it pumps out a quantity, ranging in different persons from 14 to 20 tons! It

---

67. What is the machinery, and what the various organisms, *corresponding* to the four sorts of work? Which is the grate, and which the furnace of the body? What organs cast out dead and waste matter? What is the function of the Heart? How much blood does it pump out daily? What is the work of the Nerves? What of the Brain?

has been reckoned that this would be equal to carrying from 14 to 20 sacks of coal to the top of the London Monument! As the blood thus courses through the body, the various organs and tissues, by their special affinities, *select* the substances similar to themselves, and are thus renewed in their structure, — in other words, take up a *new stock of force.* (3.) With this renewed tissue, bone, muscle, and nerve, external work is accomplished. The bones *sustain* weight and carry force as levers; the muscles *contract* under a stimulus; the ligaments *hold* fast by the cohesive power of their structural affinity; and so internal, mechanical work is done, and (4) the Nerves illustrate the higher forms of force, associated with the soul. Like *telegraphs*, they receive messages and they transmit telegrams. They convey a stimulus to the muscles, and other organs, partly controlling them and partly enabling them the better to perform their function. The Brain is the great centre where the Sensory Nerves which receive messages, and the Motor Nerves that convey them, meet in a common sanctuary, where Emotion is engendered, and Thought emerges into consciousness.

68. Now it will be plain, on a little reflection, that as all *work* implies the expenditure of power, and as power is, like matter, always a fixed quantity, so the various kinds of power exhibited in the life of a human being must be mutually measurable; that is, a certain quantity or degree of one power can be changed into a certain

---

68. What does *work* imply and involve? Is power measurable, and how? What is the common standard to which power is reducible? What is the meaning of a *foot-ton*?

quantity or degree of another, *and no more.* Wood of a certain texture, for instance, or coal of a certain composition, are known to give out a fixed quantity of *heat,* which again creates a fixed quantity of *steam,* or elastic vapor, which in turn does a certain amount of *mechanical work,* and no more. Each condition or element measures the other. So with the body. The food (if used) measures the heat and nutrition; this the work done, or capable of being done, whether of heart or nerves, hand or brain. An important question now arises: *How can the very varied kinds of work that man performs, be measured by a common standard?*—A man weighing 150 lbs., for example, works for 3½ hours on the revolving tread-wheel of a Reformatory. Although, owing to the turning round of the wheel, he is always in the same spot of space, his ascending motion does the same sort and amount of work that would have been had he taken *so many steps* up a steep mountain side. That work, if taken to the foot of the Mont Blanc, would have carried him up to the height of 7,560 feet. Now this work can be referred to the standard of heat; being, in fact, chiefly done by that force. It has been found that so much heat as will raise the temperature of 1 lb. of water 1° F., if directed to the steam-work of an engine, will raise one pound weight of anything 772 feet; or, to reverse the illustration, will *lift* 772 lbs. weight one foot upwards. Hence the man who lifts his own body, weighing 150 lbs., 7,560 feet, has really done work equal to raising 506 tons of 2,240 lbs., *one foot;* or, in the language of science, he has done 506 *foot-tons* of work.

69. To take up the old illustration of the monument. The heat which would raise one pound of iced water to

the boiling-point is equal to 62 foot-tons, and that which would so raise 5½ imperial gallons, would, as steam, lift 3,412 "long" tons, one foot high; or hoist 170 sacks of coals of 200 pounds each to the top of the monument (202 feet).* So a man weighing 150 lbs., who ascends that Doric column, expends 13½ foot-tons of power; which, since a perpendicular ascent is twenty times harder than motion on level ground, is equal to a walk of three-quarters of a mile. Putting, then, all sorts of work together, the *force* daily generated in the adult body is probably, at its smallest, 2,000 foot-tons; in its medium, 4,000; at its greatest, 6,000, which is equal to lifting from 10 to 20 long tons of coal to the top of the monument!

70. Of course, the whole and sole proximate source of this POWER is to be found in our FOOD; into which this force was put by Divine Providence, that food which "cometh out of the earth," but which derives its energy from the sun's rays, interwoven with the cells and structure of plants during the natural process of "growth." Thus as the solar heat which passes into wood is given out as flame and caloric in the boiling of the kettle, and reappears as steam, or elastic vapor, which science now harnesses to her *work-carriages*, and compels to do the

* The floor of the observatory in Bunker Hill Monument is of almost exactly the same height.

---

69. How much heat would lift 170 sacks of coals to the top of the monument of London? How much power does a man of 150 lbs. weight expend in walking to the top of that column? How much is that work equal to in walking on a plain? What is the *total force* probably generated, daily, in the body of a man of ordinary size and activity? What is the *minimum*, and what the *maximum*?

70. What is the *ultimate* source of power? What the *proximate*? What

drudgery of muscle, so the solar forces fixed in the food, but liberated in the blood by the action of oxygen, reappear as the heat and energy of the human frame. A small proportion, say one-tenth, of food is required to be *nutritive*, containing some suitable combination of nitrogen, essential to all living structures; but the bulk of it must be matters of an oily, saccharine nature, or of starch convertible into sugar. The following tables, modified from those of Professor Frankland, will throw great light upon the actual worth of various kinds of food, and ought utterly and forever to dissipate the ignorant belief in the value of intoxicating liquors: —

## I.

WEIGHT AND COST OF FLESH-FORMING FOOD REQUIRED TO FURNISH HALF AN OUNCE OF NITROGEN, THE MINIMUM AMOUNT NEEDED IN HEALTH.

| | Weight in Ounces. | COST: London. | COST: Boston.* | Heat value in foot-tons. |
|---|---|---|---|---|
| | | s. d. | | |
| Pea meal | 15 | 0 3 | | 2,194 |
| Oat meal | 20 | 0 3½ | | 3,134 |
| Wheaten bread | 40 | 0 5 | | 3,236 |
| Good cheese | 9½ | 0 6 | | 1,627 |
| Lean beef | 12 | 0 7½ | | 667 |
| Potatoes | 120 | 0 7½ | | 4,709 |
| Rice | 50 | 1 0½ | | 7,304 |
| Milk | 100 | 1 0½ | | 2,446 |
| Cabbage | 328 | 1 8½ | | 5,563 |

* In gold, January, 1868, a shilling sterling is twenty-four cents, and a penny, two cents.

are the three cheapest sorts of food as *flesh-formers*? What the three dearest? What food is the cheapest source of power, or heat? What the second? What the two dearest foods for nutriment? What for fuel?

It will be observed, from the last column, that many substances which are of special value as *nutriment* are less so as *fuel*, or heat-generators, and the reverse. The next table concerns the total *force* value measured by the power of generating heat, when digested, absorbed, and oxidized.

## II.

### WEIGHT AND COST OF SUBSTANCES REQUIRED FOR DOING 4,000 FOOT-TONS OF WORK IN THE BODY.

| | lbs. weight. | COST: London. | COST: Boston. |
|---|---|---|---|
| | | s. d. | |
| *Oat meal* | 1⅝ | 0 4½ | |
| *Fat of beef* (or dripping) | ¾ | 0 6 | |
| Potatoes | 6½ | 0 6½ | |
| *Bread* | 3 | 0 6 | |
| Lump sugar | 1⅞ | 0 11¼ | |
| Butter | ⅞ | 1 2 | |
| Cheese (good) | 1½ | 1 3 | |
| Cabbage | 15⅜ | 1 3½ | |
| Boiled eggs | 2¾ | 1 6 | |
| Arrow-root | 1⅝ | 1 7½ | |
| *Lean of beef* | 4½ | 3 9 | |
| Isinglass | 1¾ | 28 0 | |

71. These calculations were based upon the experiment of *burning* these various substances in an *artificial* retort, and measuring the heat; but in ale and beer many things exist which are not absorbed by the body, or burnt in the blood, — such as gum, hops, and alcohol. But assuming, for the sake of argument, that the alcohol, narcotic hop, and gummy residue of the beers, are really

**71. What is the cost and value of beers? Is gum digestible?**

consumed in the body, and not eliminated,* what, according to the tables of Prof. FRANKLAND, would be the value of such hypothetical food as compared with natural sources of power?

| | |
|---|---|
| Guinness' Stout, 6½ bottles at 10d. each, would cost | 5s. 2d. |
| Bass' Ale 9 bottles at 10d. each, will cost | 7s. 6d. |
| And give out of heat | 3.28 |

So that, were the constituents of beers ever so digestible, a pound of dripping at 9d. would exceed in value 9 pints of Bass's best ale, costing 7s. 6d.; and 3d. worth of oatcakes or porridge would generate more power than 7 pints of "Guinness' Stout"! Though eating beef, ham, and mutton, for the production of "force," is a very wasteful method of living, it is economy itself compared with the extravagant and (after all) utterly *delusive* plan of gaining power from pale ale, or brown stout. This, surely, is a demonstration that the drinker "pays too dear for his whistle."

Sir BENJAMIN BRODIE, F.R.S., Surgeon to Queen Victoria, after a long life of experience, gives, in his "Psychological Inquiries," his final verdict thus: —

"Alcohol removes the uneasy *feeling* and the inability of exertion which the want of sleep occasions. But the relief is

* The authorities for the statement that *gum* is not food are the following: — Frerich's *Handworterbuch*, iii. Blondot's *Traité de la Digestion*, p. 297. Simon's *Archiv*. i. Gmelin's *Verdauung nach Versuchen*, ii. Boussingault, in *Annal. de Chemie*, 3d ser. xviii. Lehmann, iii. Of 50 grains of gum in mixture, 46 grains were found in the excrement, undigested. We know the old traveller's tale of persons in the Sahara living *for days* on gum; just as we know of the Indians, of Orinoco, living for weeks on *clay*. Neither case applies to the ordinary circumstances of man; for if the gastric juice *does* partly dissolve gum when men are *starving*, and it has nothing else to digest, experiments clearly prove that it will not do so when it has *anything better* to operate upon.

only temporary. Stimulants do not *create* nervous power; they merely enable you, as it were, *to use up* that which is left, and then they leave you more in need of rest than before." (I., p. 143.)

Baron LIEBIG says of the drinker: —

"SPIRITS, by their action on the nerves, enable him to make up deficient power *at the expense of his body*. He consumes his *capital* instead of his interest."

Prof. PEREIRA, in his "Treatise on Food" (1843), says: —

"Ales are not fitted for ordinary use, *on account of their* INTOXICATING and STUPEFYING qualities."

Dr. CHAS. WILSON, in his "Pathology of Drunkenness" (Edinburgh, 1855), says: —

"No circumstances of ordinary life can render even the moderate use of intoxicating fluids either beneficial or necessary, *or even innocuous.*"

Dr. E. SMITH, in his "Practical Dietary" (1865), says: —

"The proper place for these compounds is as *Medicines;* but not as Foods; and they should not find *any* place in mere dietetic arrangements." (p. 313.)

Dr. H. R. MADDEN thus expresses himself in an elaborate Essay on "Stimulating Drinks" (London, 1847): —

"Alcohol is not the *natural stimulus* to any of our organs, and hence functions performed, in consequence of its application, *tend to debilitate* the organ acted upon.

"Alcohol is *incapable of being assimilated*, or converted, into any organic proximate principle, and hence cannot be considered nutritious.

"The strength experienced after the use of alcohol is *not*

*new strength added* to the system, but is manifested by calling into exercise the nervous energy pre-existing.

"The *ultimate exhausting effects* of alcohol, owing to its stimulant properties, produce *an unnatural susceptibility to morbid action in all the organs*, and this, with the plethora superinduced, becomes a fertile source of disease.

"A person who habitually exerts himself to such an extent as to require the daily use of stimulants to ward off exhaustion, may be compared to *a machine working under high pressure*. He will become *much more obnoxious to the causes of disease*, and will certainly *break down sooner* than he would have done under more favorable circumstances.

"The more frequently alcohol is had recourse to for the purpose of overcoming feelings of debility, *the more it will be required*, and, by constant repetition, *a period is at length reached when it cannot be foregone*, unless reaction is simultaneously brought about by a temporary total change of the habits of life.

"Owing to the above *facts*, I conclude that the DAILY USE OF STIMULANTS IS INDEFENSIBLE UNDER ANY KNOWN CIRCUMSTANCES."

72. The author of "The Chemistry of Common Life," who was no physiologist, put forth the notion, that if alcohol was not direct food, it *aided* the digestion and absorption of food. But this is not the fact. As Professors Todd and Bowman justly state, in their great work on Physiology, the essential action of alcohol on animal tissue is such, that if a glass of grog were taken after a mutton-chop, and were *kept* in the stomach, the meat would never be digested. Luckily for the drinker, the spirit, by the law named in § 60, mixes with the water of the blood, and passes on with the current of the circulation, and thus, after delaying digestion, allows

---

72. Does alcohol *aid* digestion? Whose experiments show that it retards digestion?

fresh supplies of gastric juice to perform that function. The recent experiments of Dr. Henry Munroe, of Hull, published in the London "Medical Journal," may be here summarized, as showing that the same essential tendency to retard digestion is common to all forms of alcoholics.

| Finely Minced Beef. | 2d Hour. | 4th Hour. | 6th Hour. | 8th Hour. | 10th Hour. |
|---|---|---|---|---|---|
| I. Gastric juice and *water* | Beef opaque. | Digesting & separating. | Beef much lessened. | Broken up into shreds. | Dissolved like soup. |
| II. Gastric juice with *alcohol.* | No alteration perceptible. | Slightly opaque, but beef unchanged. | Slight coating on beef. | No visible change. | Solid on cooling. *Pepsine* precipitated. |
| III. Gastric juice and *pale ale.* | No change. | Cloudy, with fur on beef. | Beef partly loosened. | No further change. | No digestion. *Pepsine* precipitated. |

The *pepsine* is the digestive ferment, which is thus demonstrated to have its function obstructed so long as any alcohol remains in the stomach.

---

## IV.

## The Pathology of Intemperance.

73. A *poison* may be defined to be, "A substance, which, brought into contact with the skin, mucous surfaces, nerves, blood cells, or other organs of man, *alters their normal state*, by virtue of some special inherent *quality*." Such a disturbance means, first, some degree of altered *structure*, temporary or permanent; and, second, a consequent altered *function*, which may be either

73. Define a *poison*. Is it a notion of quality or quantity? What are the three classes of poisons? How are they distinguished? In which class do you rank *tobacco* and *alcohol*?

an increased, or a lowered action. Hence, 'Poisons' are usually classed under three general heads: as (I.) *Irritant*, or acrid poisons, which inflame and tend to destroy the living tissue; (II.) *Narcotics* or sedatives, which lessen the action of the nerves, and, if taken in sufficient quantity, destroy action and feeling; (III.) *Narcotico-acrids*, which possess the double action of both classes, according to their dose or concentration. Arsenic, Spanish-fly, jalap, and sulphuric acid are examples of the first class; opium, prussic acid, and chloroform, of the second; deadly night-shade, *tobacco*, strychnine, and *alcohol*, of the third. On this point, Orfila, Taylor, Christison, and all toxicologists are agreed.

74. The slightest thought will induce the belief, that the continued use of any one of these powerful agents, however disguised or diluted, so long as it produces a sensible effect at all (and who would take it if it did not?), must tend to alter the natural condition of the bodily organs, and to produce effects that, sooner or later, will tell sensibly upon human life. In the preceding part of this Text-Book, it has been shown, by a series of *facts*, that health, strength, warmth, endurance, and vital power, are all best upheld by abstinence from alcoholics, and that the moderate use of such liquors actually and sensibly increases mortality. This proves, by experience, that alcohol is not food, but *is* poison.

75. Drs. Simon and Thudichum, of London, have re-

---

74. Is it probable that *any* continued use of poisons can be harmless? What facts contradict the notion?

75. State the fallacy of the definition that alcohol is food. What does it *assume*, and what *omit*? Give the confession of Dr. Thudichum.

cently attempted, on theoretical grounds, to include alcohol in a partial definition of food. They assume that alcohol is decomposed in the body to some extent, and gives out heat. This is to beg the definition as well as the fact. For even if alcohol were burnt in the body, and made the body warmer instead of colder, it would still be true that, *before it was decomposed, it acted as a poison* upon blood and tissues. Now, true food must not only warm and nourish, but must do so without burning and destroying. Food must answer the end of food *innocently*, which alcohol does not. A true definition of food will give, not only the chemical action, but the physiological relation. After all his pleas and apologies, Dr. Thudichum is compelled to make the fatal concession concerning alcoholics: "Whether they are beneficially consumed, or otherwise, must remain for future research to determine." Science has reached no conclusion adverse to experience.

76. Some of the leading physiologists of the day — such as Prof. Lallemand, Dr. King Chambers, and Dr. Edward Smith — incline to the view that the main action of alcohol is to depress vitality by its narcotic action upon the nerves and brain. This view, however, should be held in connection with the fact, that all vital organs resist the first blows of a narcotic as truly as of an acrid agent; whence it follows that when a narcotic is given in small doses, the reaction will resemble the symptoms commonly ascribed to a "stimulant," or goad. It is of

---

**76. What views are held by some leading physiologists as to the *exclusive* action of Alcohol? Can a narcotic be also regarded as a stimulant? Do stimulants give "force," or "expend" it?**

little moment what the agent is called, so long as the fact is perceived that it does not *give*, but calls out and wastes power. A stimulant is not the corn that strengthens the horse, but the whip or spur that induces the animal rapidly to expend its strength. It is not the new cash which accrues to a man on the death of a rich relative, but the money which the lawyer has borrowed for you by mortgaging your old farm. It will all have to be paid back again, sometimes with interest and costs. It now remains to trace the chief pathological results of the use of alcohol.

Two series of experiments performed with Bourbon whiskey and sherry wine in April, 1867, and reported in the "Chicago Medical Journal," are instructive. The whiskey was mixed with sugared water, which was an error, because sugar tends to *raise* the temperature, and thus to confuse the experiment. We record the results:—

| | Temperature in mouth. | Pulse per min. |
|---|---|---|
| Before whiskey, drank at 10.30, P. M., | 98¼° | 83 |
| After 4 oz. " " " 11.00, " | 97¾° | 85 |
| ' " " " 11.30, " | 97½° | 89 |
| " " " " 12.30, A. M., | 97½° | 85 |

"The sphygmograph shows, that while the number of beats were increased from 83 to 89 per minute during the first hour, *the force of the heart and pulsations was weakened*, whence a congestion of the venous radicles would ensue."

77. This substance is so virulent a poison that it can be taken only in the diluted form of ardent spirits, a

---

**77. How does Alcohol produce *sudden death?* What relation does it bear**

teaspoonful of which has often destroyed the life of a child, and from half a pint to a pint that of men unaccustomed to its use.* It produces death in such cases by *nervous shock*, not very dissimilar to that of a blow on some susceptible centre, like the ganglionic nerves of the stomach. As consumed in wines, cider, and beer, the violent acridity of the poison is sheathed in ten or twelve times its bulk of water. The experiments of Dr. Ed. Smith, F.R.S., published in the "Philosophical Transactions" for 1859, prove that alcohol "interferes with alimentation" and "its power to lessen the salivary secretion impedes the due digestion of starch."

"When spirituous liquors are introduced into the stomach," says Dr. Aitken, in his "Practice of Medicine" (5th Edit.), "they tend to coagulate, in the first instance, all albuminous articles of food or fluid with which they come in contact; as an irritant they stimulate the glandular secretions from the mucous membrane, and *ultimately lead to permanent congestion of the vessels* and to *thickening* of the gastric tissues. In these effects it is impossible not to recognize the operation of an agent most pernicious in its ultimate results. The coagulation is very different from that effected by the gastric fluids, and tends to render the articles more difficult of solution by the gastric juice." "Even diluted, in the

* Oesterlin (*Handbuch der Heilmittellehre*, 1855) records the case of a child, 1½ years old, who had two table-spoonfuls of brandy (which is half water) given to soothe it. Bloody flux, convulsions, lockjaw, and death in nine hours, followed. Roesch (*Henke's Zeitschrift*, 1850) gives a case where two table-spoonfuls of brandy, taken at sips, proved fatal to a healthy girl of 4 years of age, in spite of medical aid.

---

to alimentation? Give Dr. Aitken's explanation of the effect of Alcohol

form of beer or wine," says Dr. Lankester,* F.R.S., "it is found to act injuriously on the delicate membranes of the stomach and other digestive organs." † "When taken in large quantities in any of the above forms, it acts most injuriously on the stomach, liver, brain, heart, and other organs of the body. . . . It is found to destroy the quality of the blood, to congest the membranes of the brain, to produce incurable affections of the liver and kidneys, and to effect changes in the muscular structure of the heart, the result of all of which are painful and lingering diseases, or sudden death." ‡

Another result, even when positive disease itself is not generated, is to *mask* the symptoms of disease produced by other causes, to frustrate the aims of proper treatment, and to set the physician's skill at defiance. "So destructive," adds Dr. Lankester, "is this agent, on the whole body, that large numbers of persons avoid its use altogether, and thus have successfully demonstrated that the use of this agent is not necessary to health." The consequence of this again is, that while the abstainer has not half the sickness of the moderate drinker, the diseases to which he is subject are much more amenable to treatment, and require less violent remedies.

* The inflammatory appearance of the drinker's stomach has been frequently exhibited in the plates published by Mr. E. C. Delavan, illustrating cases supplied by the late Dr. Sewall, President of the American Medical Institute. See Dr. Nott's "Lectures," and Dr. Lees' "Illustrated History of Alcohol."

† "School Manual of Health." London, 1868. ‡ Ibid.

---

upon the food and the stomach. What is the dictum of Dr. Lankester? How does Alcohol act in regard to disease?

78. Alcohol, in even moderate doses, if continued, sensibly alters the character of the blood. This has been shown by a series of experiments and microscopic observations, instituted by Schultz, Virchow, Boecker, and others. Prof. Schultz (Berlin, 1842) says:— "Alcohol stimulates the vesicles to an increased and unnatural contraction, which deprives them of coloring matter, and hurries them on to the last stage of development, i. e., induces their premature death,—not suddenly, but gradually, and more or less according to the quantity of alcohol used. The pale vesicles lose all vital resistance, less oxygen being absorbed, and less carbon being carried out, and the plasma itself becomes an irritant to the circulatory and secreting organs." This is the reason why alcoholized blood cannot suitably nourish the body, and how especially it is unfit to promote the healing of wounds and inflamed parts. Virchow (1853) describes, as the result of his experiments in the use of beer, "A decrease of water (the vehicle of vitality); an increase of fibrin, and of colored clot, which reddened much less rapidly on exposure to the air than normal blood, and contained many more of the pale blood-discs than is usual in perfect health, which may be regarded as defunct bodies, no longer capable of their original duty, that of absorbing oxygen." *

Boecker (1854) argues that this is evidence of partially effete matter kept in the blood. His experiments

* Dr. Moleschott (Müller's Archiv.) has shown that when the liver is cut

---

78. Whose experiments clearly show the influence of Alcohol upon the blood? State the results arrived at by Prof. Schultz; and the inference as respects *wounds*. Give the verdict of Prof. Virchow, as to effects of beer; of Dr. Boecker, and the inferences. What modifies, or limits, the evils of

with Rhenish wine had the effect of largely lessening the amount of carbonic acid breathed out, and stopping the excretion of earthy phosphates, thus retaining ashes in the living house and stopping ventilation. As Dr. King Chambers says, "There is a general resemblance between these experiments and those with pure spirit, modified apparently in close proportion to the smaller quantity of alcohol and to the amount of the antagonistic agent, water, therein absorbed." This is an im-

out of frogs they lose their power of breathing out carbonic-acid (foul air), and absorbing oxygen (fresh air), *in proportion as these cloudy blood discs increase.* For particulars of experiments, see "Works of Dr. Lees," vols. i. and iii. The following wood-cuts rudely show the alteration produced in blood by the action of alcohol, so far as *form* is concerned.

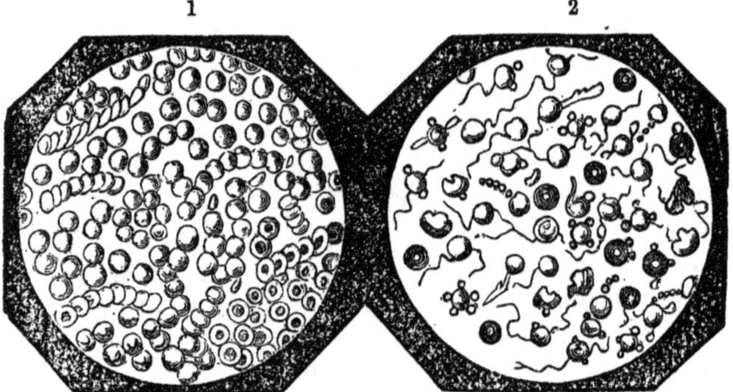


Fig. 1. Blood corpuscles: some with darkened centres, owing to the focal point at which they are seen; others in rolls indicative of slight inflammation.

Fig. 2. Blood corpuscles altered from their natural shape by the action of sherry wine or diluted alcohol (250 diameters).

---

alcoholic liquors? What is the latest alcoholic curse, and what constitutes its worst evil?

portant truth. All alcoholic liquors are bad *in the degree in which they contain alcohol;* the heavier or more concentrated, the worse they are. Wines, beers, or ciders, are but alcohol diluted and flavored differently. The last deadly agent of intemperance, madness, and disease introduced into France, *absinthe*, owes its worst effects simply to the strength of its alcohol. No possible drugs or adulteration can be so bad as this essential and characteristic element.

79. "It is shown by abundant testimony," says Dr. Aitken, "that from excessive drinking the blood becomes surcharged with unchanged and unused material, and contains at least *thirty per cent.* more of carbon than in the normal state. The order of events by which this comes about is somewhat as follows: Alcohol is directly absorbed by the blood-vessels without undergoing any change. Part of it is eliminated very slowly as alcohol by the lungs [and skin], by the liver, and by the kidneys, but appears to tarry in largest amount in the liver and the brain; * another portion is [supposed to be] decomposed. [If so] its hydrogen enters into combination with oxygen, which, with acetic acid [not yet detected, however, if produced], carbonic acid, and water are formed. Oxygen is thus diverted from its proper function, the exhalation of carbonic acid at the lungs is

* Dr. Percy, and the French experimenters, made this assertion on very good grounds, but Schulinus has recently performed experiments, in which he seems to have proved that *the blood* of drinkers contained as large a percentage of alcohol as any other part.

---

79. What is the result of excessive and continued drinking? In what order do the effects come? How does Alcohol *rob the blood of oxygen?*

diminished both absolutely and relatively, and less urea is excreted by the kidneys. All the evidence, therefore, points to alcohol *as causing the retention of substances which ought to be eliminated* [i. e., cast out]; and [the effect of] this retention of effete [or waste] matter is still more intensified by the stimulant action of alcohol [in] increasing for a limited period the frequency of functional acts, followed as it is by a *corresponding* depression of the nervous system." *

Professor Lallemand also observes, that "alcoholized blood contains, during life and after death, a great number of free fatty globules, visible even by the naked eye. The pathological alterations are: very vivid inflammation of the mucous membrane of the stomach; accumulation of blood in the right chamber of the heart and the large veins; congestion of the membranes (*meninges*) covering the brain; and especially of the lungs." ("Conclusions" J. K.) Lecanu found in a drunkard's blood as much as 117 parts of fat in 1,000 parts; the highest healthy proportion being 8¼ parts, and the usual 3 only! Hence, as Dr. King Chambers remarks, "Alcohol is really the most ungenerous diet there is. It impoverishes the blood, and *there is no surer road to that degeneration of muscular fibre so much to be feared.* Three-quarters of the chronic illnesses which the medical man has to treat are occasioned by this disease! In *Heart-disease* it

* "Practice of Medicine," 5th edition. London, 1868. This is the old doctrine taught by Dr. Lees, that "Alcohol robs the blood of oxygen."

---

Give Lallemand's testimony. Explain its relation to *fatty degeneration* and *heart disease.*

is especially hurtful, by quickening the beat, causing capillary congestion, and irregular circulation, and thus mechanically inducing dilatation of the cavities." In fact, alcohol seems to produce the peculiar condition of the tissues called "fatty degeneration," more than any other agent known.

80. The influence of alcohol upon the blood is strikingly exhibited in its effect upon the milk of suckling mothers. "Alcohols," says Dr. Ed. Smith, "are largely used by many persons in the belief that they support the system and maintain the supply of milk for the infant; but this is a serious error, and is not an unfrequent cause of fits and emaciation in the child." * The "Newcastle Express" (England) some time ago reported the proceedings at an inquest at Monkwearmouth, where the surgeon stated that the child "labored under chronic inflammation of the bowels, and the coroner said there was no doubt the child had died from convulsions arising from inflammation produced by taking the alcohol *in* the mother's milk." Sir A. Carlisle, the celebrated surgeon, said in 1814, of fermented liquors, "The next in order of mischief is their employment by nurses, a common occasion of dropsy in the brain in infants. I doubt much whether the future moral habits, the temper and intellectual propensities, are not greatly influenced by the early effects of fermented liquors upon the brain and

* "Practical Dietary," London, 1865, p. 162.

---

80. Does Alcohol pass into the milk of mothers? What are the consequences upon the sucking child? Give the testimony of Drs. Smith, Carlisle and Inman. How does it alter the constituents of milk?

sensorial organs," Dr. Inman, of Liverpool, in his "New Theory of Disease "(1861), admits that, "through the influence of lactation, children have suffered severely from diarrhœa, vomiting, and convulsions. I have known a glass of whiskey toddy, taken by the mother, produce sickness and indigestion in the child 24 hours thereafter" (p. 44). On the analysis of the milk of the same woman, a few hours before and after the use of a pint of beer, it has been found that the alcohol increases the proportion of water, and diminishes that of the *caseine* or curd, which is the nourishing element; and that the alcohol is very perceptible in the milk.

81. Among the conclusions from the experiments of Lallemand, Perrin, and Duroy (*Rôle du Alcool*, 1860), are some which show the results of the action of alcohol both upon the blood and nervous system, and prove that moderate excitement is *simply a lower degree of the same kind* of abnormal stimulation which is known as *inebriation*, and that alcohol never *gives force*, but merely wastes it.

"B. The ingestion of alcohol produces upon animals an intoxication that is marked by a *progressive series of functional disturbances and alterations*, the intensity of which corresponds with the *quantity* of alcohol absorbed.

"C. It manifests itself at first by a general excitement; but, by and by, the respiration and circulation are relaxed, and the temperature lowered.

"D. *Muscular power is weakened and extinguished;* beginning at the extremities.

---

81. What celebrated Frenchmen made experiments on Alcohol? State their chief conclusions. B. C. D. K. R. T. U. V. X; what is the inference from this last? What from the whole?

"K. The pathological alterations are: very vivid inflammation of the mucous membrane of the stomach; the accumulation of the blood in the right chamber of the heart and the large veins; congestion of the *meninges*, and especially of the lungs.

"R. *We never found, in either the blood or tissues, any of the derivatives of alcohol.*

"T. Alcohol is rejected from the vital economy by divers systems of *elimination:* by the lungs, the skin, and the kidneys.

"U. *These organs are found to eliminate alcohol after the ingestion of* doses very small.

"V. The elimination lasts many hours, *even after an ingestion very moderate.* The kidneys continue the longest to reject.

"X. *Aldehyde* [a derivative of alcohol], *when* introduced into the stomach, *is* readily found in the blood.

"These facts establish, from a physiological point of view, *a line of demarcation* between *alcohol* and *foods.* Foods restore the forces, without the organism betraying, by disturbed functions, or by outward agitation, the labor of reparation, *which is accomplished silently in the woof of the tissues.* Alcohol, on the other hand, immediately *provokes*, even in a moderate dose; an excitement which extends through the entire economy."

82. Dr. T. K. Chambers, Hon. Physician to the Prince of Wales, says:—

"It is clear that we must cease to regard alcohol as *in any sense* an *aliment*, inasmuch as it goes out as it went in, and does not, so far as we know, leave any of its substance behind it. It remains for some hours in the body, and exerts in that time a powerful influence. What is that influence, and over what tissues is it exerted? '*A stimulant to the nervous system.*' On

---

**82. What is a stimulant to the nervous system? Give the views of Dr. Chambers.**

the nervous system, doubtless and *especially on the mental functions of the nervous system, every experimenter, from the first patriarch downwards, would agree that its prime action is evident.* But what *is* a stimulant? It is usually held to be something which spurs on an animal operated upon to a more vigorous performance of its duties. It seems very doubtful if, on the healthy nervous system, this is *ever* the effect of alcohol, even in the most moderate doses, and for the shortest periods of time.* There is noticed, also, an increased rapidity of pulse; but that cannot be regarded as an evidence even of locally augmented vital action, for, of all patients, those specially exhibit it who have the weakest hearts, and are most enfeebled by disease. *A diminution of force is quite consistent with augmented quickness of motion.* Physiologists have always taught, as confirmed by all experiments, that large doses of alcohol immediately, and small doses after a time, depress the nervous centres; the primary action is anæsthetic, — *a diminution of vitality in the nervous system.*"

These facts enable us to realize the subtle and varied consequences of the use of alcohol, through the nervous system and brain, upon the mind and actions of men. The forms of mental perversion to which the use of this poison gives rise, from irritable temper to outrageous crime, — darkening the perceptions, exciting the passions, hardening the heart, blunting the conscience, and destroying the brain, — are infinitely various, and find their abundant illustration in the records of our legal tribunals. It is not a text-book but a cyclopædia

* "Renewal of Life," London, 1859; and "Clinical Lectures," London, 1865.

---

Does increased pulse or motion prove increased *force*? What is the *primary* action of Alcohol called? what does *anæsthesia* mean? What *mental* effects follow the use of Alcohol? Give two historical examples.

that can adequately exhibit them. The assassin Booth and the Emperor Theodore are two of the latest examples on the tableaux of modern history, which can never be forgotten.*

Dr. H. Munroe, of Hull, has published several cases where the maniacal tendency to set fire to houses and to steal (*pyromania* and *kleptomania*) were entirely due to the use of intoxicants. Plato, twenty centuries ago, recognized a fact in physiology, when he forbade the use of wine to the newly married. It perverts the brain of the unborn child; it strikes a blow at reason and virtue in the very womb. It is the real cause of so many ill-balanced minds, neither insane nor sensible; and in its higher use it is the teeming fount of the sad idiotcy which disgraces and depresses our boasted civilization. In Dr. Howe's reports to the Legislature of Massachusetts, he shows that nearly *one-half* of the idiots had drunken parents (145 out of 300). It is an undoubted fact, exemplified in the history of thousands of families, that the children born after their parents joined the

* Wilkes Booth, the cowardly murderer of the late President of the United States, when he saw his helpless victim in the box at the theatre, had not the cruelty to strike the blow; his human feelings overcame him, and trembling with suppressed agony at the thought of becoming an assassin, he rushed into the nearest *restaurant*, crying out, "Brandy! Brandy! Brandy!" Then, gulping down the hellish draught, it instantly poisoned his blood, fired up his brain, transformed his whole nature into that of a raging fiend; and, in this remorseless condition, he shot down that noble-hearted President, — the nation's great hope, the people's best friend.

---

State Dr. Munroe's cases. What was Plato's doctrine? What are the consequences of neglecting it? What proportion of idiots have drunken parents?

Temperance Society, are not only physically healthier but mentally *brighter* and *better* than those born before.

83. Dr. Ed. Smith, "London Phil. Trans." 1859, has published the results of experiments made upon himself and friends. After sipping a few spoonfuls of wine, the first thing in the morning, they noted down the following symptoms and sequences: —

"In from three to seven minutes, *the mind was disturbed.* Consciousness, the power of fixing the attention, the perception of light, and we believe of sound also, and the power of directing and co-ordinating the muscles, were lessened; whilst there was a very marked, peculiar, continuous, thrilling, not unpleasant sensation, passing down through the whole system, during thirty minutes. After this period the effect diminished, as shown by increased consciousness and the perception of light, *as if a veil had fallen from the eyes; nevertheless, the last power to be completely regained was consciousness.*

"SPIRITS made us very hilarious and talkative in ten minutes, and during twenty to twenty-five—so much so, that my friend was altogether a king. But as minutes flew away, so did our joyousness; and, little by little, we lessened our garrulity, and felt less happy, until at length, *having gone down by degrees,* we remained silent, almost morose, and extremely miserable. Then, indeed, we felt the horrors and the sorrows of the drunkard's lot, and saw, *with a clearness which can only be perceived by such experience,* how certain it is that he must again drain the intoxicating cup.

"In addition, *every mental perception was darkened;* and the dreaminess, which is not an unpleasant feature of it, is a condition in which neither thought nor imagination acquires power."

---

83. What were Dr. E. Smith's experiments? In what order were the effects produced on senses and mind? What was the sentient result that explains the *slavery* of the drinker?

An agent with such tendencies as these can hardly be regarded as a friend of man or God. By necessary law it is thus seen to be the *seed* of inordinate appetite, creating and fostering a passion for itself, which grows with what it feeds on. The sole issue of its use is sensuality and sin, ending in that frightful condition of moral slavery, confirmed drunkenness, when the rational *Will* is abolished, — a condition which forever debars its victim from reaching

> "That tranquil height
> Where wisdom purifies the sight,
> And God unfolds to the humble gaze,
> The bliss and beauty of his ways."

84. Power must plainly be stored up in some available form, before it can be expended. In the human body it exists as a concentration of cohesive, chemic, organic, and nervous forces, the sum of which is the actual *strength* or capacity of the Constitution (1,) for nutrition and excretion, i. e., health-power; (2,) for endurance and resistance of disease; and (3,) for voluntary work with the surplus. When people are recovering from illness, it is not until the nutritive functions are restored that the *strength* comes back for working with the hands or the brain. So, after long walks, the brain is not in a fit state for thinking, because the surplus, or *accumulated* power, has been spent. But the constitution and the food, in each case, expresses a fixed amount of power, just as does the mechanism of a steam-engine with its

---

84. Explain the *law* of the generation of power in the body, and its distribution.

fuel and steam. All these forces, as a little thought will show, are correlated, and many of them mutually convertible, — i. e., as one form disappears, it *becomes* another of exactly the same value. So much concentrated sun-power passed into wood or coal in growing, holding together its parts, does, when separated in burning, *reappear* as light and heat; the excess of heat above the boiling-point passes into steam-force, and that vanishes into mechanical action and attrition, etc., to become once more light, heat, and electricity. The forces of the sun interweave themselves into the texture of the golden grain, and become fixed as *cohesion* or chemical attraction; bread made from that grain is digested into blood, part transformed into muscle, part into oily and saccharine fuel in the circulation, to be at last decomposed *in the performance of the work* to which it was destined. Thus we return to our starting-point, for all this merely explains how force is *liberated* after being temporarily *fixed*, or stored up for use.

A little diagram of the Body and its essential parts — *Head*, *Trunk*, and *Limbs* — will make the application of this law very plain.

If, under normal action, of the whole measure of force coming from digested food, we have *less or more* used up by the Trunk, then there must be a corresponding alteration in the *surplus* force available for the uses of the Brain and the Limbs, i. e., for Thinking and Working. It cannot be used first in the body, and also in the brain, the nerves, and the voluntary muscles of the limbs Hence, if the SUM of a Man's *available force* derived from Food be represented as 24 degrees, of which 17 are needed for the healthy and vigorous working of the body itself, — there will be 7 degrees left for voluntary work, physical or mental. When alcohol is introduced, however, it evidently creates an *increased activity of the internal vascular system*, indicated by greater pumping of the heart, and quickened pulsation and breathing. Now, unless this work can be done *without expenditure of power*, which is absurd, *just so much force* as this increased internal work required *must have been abstracted from the surplus fund* destined for *voluntary* work, — the real end of the wonderful series of divine provisions revealed in nature; in other words, the Body, regarded as an instrument of voluntary action, is now *less strong* by 2 degrees, having only 4 units of energy available instead of 7.

This demonstration will explain the meaning to be put upon the remarkable words of Baron Liebig, in his "Animal Chemistry," (1843).

"The circulation will appear accelerated at the expense of

---

**Give the statement of Liebig as to the *force-wasting* action of Alcohol. Show *why* the stimulation of the vascular-system *robs* the voluntary nerves of useful power.**

the force available for voluntary motion, but without the production of a greater amount of mechanical force."

In his later "Letters," he again says: —

"Wine is quite superfluous to man. . . . It is constantly *followed by the expenditure of power.* These drinks promote the change of matter in the body, and are consequently *attended by an inward loss of power,* WHICH CEASES TO BE PRODUCTIVE, because it is not employed in overcoming outward difficulties, — i. e., in working."

In other words, according to this great chemist, alcohol abstracts the power of the system from doing useful work in field, workshop, or study, in order to cleanse the house from the defilement of Alcohol itself.

# V.

## The Medical Question.

**85.** Is Alcohol a curative agent? Were we to answer this question in the affirmative, it would really be, to the impartial mind, an argument against its common use. Why take a *cure* when we have no *complaint?* Medicines are not for the healthy, but the diseased, and that which makes them medicines at all is their peculiar power to produce *extraordinary* changes in the body. Physic and food are contraries, related respectively to disease and health. If alcoholics are ever really useful *as* medicines, or even as adjuncts to medical treatment, certain conditions must be observed in their use, which are generally overlooked.

(1.) The *disease* must be there and understood before the remedy, or supposed remedy, can be administered.

(2.) It must be known that the alcohol is the essential part of the remedy, and not a mere accident. For example, when brandy and hot water are given for spasm, the *real* remedy is the heat.

(3.) The nature and strength of the liquor must be known, which it rarely is. Besides, it is often adulterated with powerful drugs that may occasionally effect the benefit ascribed to the spirit.

---

85. Is Alcohol a medicine? What does this imply? To what are food and physic related? Is it physic for health and food for inappetence? What is the characteristic of all medicine? Is not all physic bad in health? What are the *five* conditions for a rational prescription of Alcohol? As to the

(4.) Above all, the exact condition of the patient, and the time for the administration, with all the proper tests, must be reduced to a system and science; otherwise the prescription is mere quackery. Where are these conditions fulfilled?

(5.) Lastly, careful and comprehensive experiments must be made in regard to the administration of alcohol for certain classes of disease, showing the benefit of the practice by the *lessened* mortality. Where are these?

As respects the *first* condition, alcohol is generally prescribed where the symptoms are obscure, or where other things have failed, with the mere chance or hope that the case may be hit. In some instances, the nature of the disease, and hence the remedy, has been entirely mistaken.* Dr. Aitken, in his great work,† supplies an illustration worth noting: "The term alcoholism is used to denote various symptoms of disease attending *morbid processes of various kinds* capable of being traced to the use of stimulants containing alcohol. The term is used in the sense analogous to that in which we use the terms mercurialism, ergotism, narcotism, and the like, the agents inducing these specific states *acting after the manner of a cumulative poison.* The progress of modern science has distinctly demonstrated the poi-

* For the showing out of the whole subject, see Dr. Lees' "Doctors Drugs and Drink." London, 1867.

† "Practice of Medicine," vol. i., p. 828.

---

***first***, **give Dr. Aitken's example of the huge mistake of treating *alcoholism* with Alcohol, on the supposition that it was evidence of exalted vitality. State the differences between the old and new method of treating *delirium tremens*.**

sonous action of alcohol. In 1828 it was theoretically advanced by Leovielle that *delirium tremens* consisted in an *exalted* state of the vital powers of the brain, excited by the molecules saturated with alcohol. . . . . But now it is [seen to be] a matter of fact, determined by direct experiment as well as by observation, that alcohol is absorbed directly into the circulation, and is capable of acting as a direct poison upon the nervous tissue through which the *infected* blood circulates." The old mode of treatment, with opium and drink, killed, in Edinburgh, 25 per cent., in Glasgow, 50 per cent., while now hundreds have been treated with warm baths, nourishing food, no alcohol, and no opium, and not one per hundred dies.*

86. As to the *second* condition, especially in ailments affecting stomach, liver, and kidneys, it has been found, on excluding the alcohol of porter and some wines, that the benefit has been increased. Accidental elements of cure are frequently overlooked, and the credit given to agents which really opposed the cure. Beer and porter are multifarious compounds.

* Mr. Hutchinson, of the London Hospital, however, reports some cases which did well with beer. This was owing, not to the alcohol, but the drugs. He "rarely employs opium or *spirits*. In private practice, he reports the best *narcotic* to be bottled stout, but for hospital use common London porter is *sufficiently stupefying*, if taken in quantity." — ("Medical Times," Nov. 21, 1868.) M. Gosselin, of Paris, observes, in a recent chemical lecture, that "one of the contra indications to the use of chloroform is the *inveterate use* of alcoholics *so common* in the *classes brought* to the hospitals. In these subjects, who have passed their fiftieth year, anæsthetics should either be abstained from, or employed with the greatest circumspection." — ("Gaz. des Hop.," Oct. 31, 1868.) This evinces again the lowering nature of alcoholic liquors.

---

86. As to the *second*, what is the fallacy of reasoning into which practitioners are liable to fall in reference to *compound* drinks and prescriptions? How can the true curative element be detected?

87. The *third* condition is rarely fulfilled. Dr. Aitken has some excellent observations in his second volume: —

"Although so extensively used, as yet little is *certainly known* of the action of alcohol when administered in the form of wine, beer, or spirits. *None* of the general statements so frequently met with as to the composition or effects of any particular class of beverages *can be relied on as a guide to the physician in prescribing;* and much error seems to prevail on the subject, not only in the popular mind, but also amongst medical men." . . . "Alcohol is the most potent agent for good or evil in all these beverages; and, therefore, its *amount* and its effects challenge attention in the first instance. A pint of beer (20 oz.) may contain *one*, or *two, or more ounces* of absolute alcohol, or *less than a quarter of an ounce!* This alcohol may be associated in the beer with an amount of *free acid* varying from *fifteen to fifty grains*, and with an amount of *sugar* varying from *half an ounce to three or four times that quantity.* A glass of sherry (2 oz.) may contain from *a quarter of an ounce* to *half an ounce*, or more, of absolute alcohol, with sugar varying in quantity from a mere trace to 20 or 30 grains, associated with a very variable amount of free acid, and other ingredients. It is impossible, therefore, for a physician to know what his patients are drinking, unless he is acquainted with the chief constituents and their amounts contained in the *identical* liquor which he may prescribe; and, of course, before sound conclusions can be arrived at, the *conditions* under which these beverages are administered, or taken, must also be very *precisely observed.*" . . . "The blindly empirical and routine mode in which alcoholic beverages are generally prescribed, in absolute ignorance of their constitution and genuineness, renders it advisable in a text-book to insist fully on these topics, believing that the physician cannot successfully

---

87. As to the *third*, give Dr. Aitken's protest. "Show how a pint of beer or wine may *differ greatly* as to the substances in it, — as to its Alcohol, its sugar, its acids, or its adulterations."

cope with diseases, and especially with *constitutional* diseases, and the ill-health with which they are associated, unless he learns judiciously to use the immense power at his disposal in the influence of *diet*, *water*, and *alcoholic beverages* as agents in the management of the system during the intervals between the paroxysms of these diseases." (p. 242.)

88. As to the *fourth* condition, in the case of fevers, Dr. Anstie, an opponent of temperance doctrine, lays down as the law, that alcohol cannot be scientifically administered until the urine of the patient has been analyzed, and the sphygmograph (or pulse-writer) has been applied for the course of many hours: otherwise, mischief, not benefit, will result. He says, "Even the slight and trivial symptom of *flushing in the face* is a sign of the first degree of the *poisonous action*, namely, a vaso-motor paralysis, and shows that at least we have touched the border-line at which the beneficial action of alcohol ceases, and its poisonous effects begin."—("Lancet," Jan. 25, 1868.)

But this does not express the whole truth, for we have to do with the *quality* of the drink as well as its quantity, and the precise purpose it is ordered for. On both these points the ordinary practitioner is deeply ignorant. In the chemical section (p. 10), we referred to *three* sorts of alcohols — methylic, ethylic, and amylic — the boiling-point of which is, respectively, 151°, 172°, and 270°. In drinking the compounds generally sold as wines and whiskeys, no man can detect the actual kind of alcohol he is consuming. Of the

---

88. As to the *fourth*, give Dr. Anstie's test and testimony. Is "flushing in the face" a sign of alcoholic poisoning? State the warning of Dr. W. B. Richardson.

physiological difference, however, Dr. W. B. Richardson, F.R.S., thus discourses: —

"The scientific physician ought never to attempt their use except as alcohols, *the precise nature of which he understands.* Does he want a quickly acting stimulant which eliminates rapidly, *taking out little force,* he has it in *methylic* alcohol. Does he want an alcohol that shall create a more lasting effect [draw out more power], he has it in *ethylic* [wine] alcohol. Does he want to *reduce the body,* to prostrate it for many hours, he can do that with *amylic,* or butylic, or caproylic alcohol. But when he is ordering alcohol by the general loose names of gin, brandy, rum, wine, he has no conception of what he is prescribing, nor of the effect of his prescription." *

89. As to the *fifth* condition, all facts run counter to any such conclusion, and condemn as worthless or pernicious the old routine practice. The statistics of the London Hospital exhibit, over a series of years, a gradual advance in the quantity of alcohol prescribed, and a no less gradual increase in the mortality. From 1862 to 1864, the deaths rose from 7 to 10 per cent. In the *surgical* department, from 1854 to 1864, from 4.48 per cent. to 6.55 per cent., — an increase in both cases of nearly *one-third!*

90. On the other hand, every trial in the British hospitals, in the treatment of particular diseases without spirits, or with vastly reduced quantities of alcoholics,

* "Medical Times," March 7, 1868, p. 255.

---

89. As to the *fifth,* do facts run in that direction, and give any support to existing routine? What are the statistics of the *London Hospital?*

90. What do the trials in British hospitals tend to establish? What have Drs. Wilks, Rees, and Sutton shown at Guy's as to the treatment of

has been, without exception, succeeded by a largely lessened mortality. Cholera, rheumatic fever, typhus, and typhoid fevers may be taken as instances. Drs. Wilks, Rees, and Sutton have treated rheumatic fever extensively, *without drugs and stimulants*, and instead of the common frightful sequel of heart-disease, it has been cured in half the usual time, with less than *one* per cent. of that malady, which turns out to be rather a result of stimulant treatment than of any natural connection with the disease. So true is the remark made thirty years ago, by Dr. R. D. Mussey, that, "under the stimulant practice, trains of morbid symptoms are often aggravated, and *new centres of irritation established*, which, if not sufficient to destroy the patient, prolong the period of the fever, and frequently cause relapses, or a lingering convalescence." *

In regard to typhus and typhoid fevers, the unhappy influence of the late Dr. Todd's treatment has not only led to the sacrifice of the Prince Consort of England and of himself, but of tens of thousands of valuable lives besides. The mortality in his own practice in rheumatic fever was always very large; and, as Dr. A. W. Barclay observes, in his "Medical Errors," the cases contain, in themselves, a complete refutation of his theory. "The 18 cases reported, give 15 in which there was *heart-complication*, and in some of these the stimulating treatment was fully carried out.

* Mussey and Lindsley's Prize Essay on Alcoholic Liquors.

---

rheumatic fever? Give Dr. Mussey's evidence? What does Dr. A. W. Barclay allege as to Dr. Todd's treatment of fever?

In common fever again eleven deaths occurred among twenty-four cases."

91. The reports of fever-treatment without stimulants, by Dr. Henderson, of Shanghai, and Dr. Bishop, of Naples, which reduced the mortality from twenty-eight to seven per cent., attracted, several years ago, the attention of several English physicians. Dr. T. K. Chambers, who, under the ordinary treatment, lost one patient in five, under the new method, had only three deaths in 121 cases. Well might this physician say to his students, in his Clinical Lectures: "Above all, I would caution you against employing wine as a substitute for the true restorative treatment. It may be useful as an *adjunct*, but never in its place." (p. 61.)

92. Two uses have been imagined for alcohol as a medicine in fever, — the one, that of a *fuel* to keep up animal heat when solid food cannot be taken; the other, that of an *anæsthetic*, like chloroform, which will stop the destructive waste of the nervous system, indicated by low, muttering delirium, — the use, as it were, of a drag upon a carriage going too rapidly down hill. Our answer is, that this is altogether a matter of *fact*, not of theory; and the facts are dead against the fancy. What is here wanted to be done can be better accomplished by other agencies. Milk, unfermented wine, or fruit juices, are better fuel than alcohol, while the wet

---

91. Give the results of the treatment of fever, without stimulants, at Shanghai, Naples, and London? Does Dr. Chambers call Alcohol a "medicine," or an *adjunct*?

92. What are the two imagined uses of Alcohol as physic? What is the value of the fancy; and why must it be thrown away?

sheet, or ice applied to the head or spine, is equally potent, and infinitely preferable for soothing the nervous system and regulating the pulse. The error of the prevailing system was long ago pointed out by a practical and philosophic physician, Dr. Archibald Billing, who thus enforces the truth: —

"Tonics give strength; *stimulants call it forth.* Stimulants excite action, but action is not strength. On the contrary, over-action increases exhaustion. One thing necessary to the *recovery of the nervous* system (in fever) is *arterial blood.* To produce this of good quality, digestion and free respiration are requisite. The digestion having been disturbed, it is useless to supply other than fluid nutriment (I have found *milk* the best), until some renewal of nervous energy takes place. *This restoration will not be expedited by stimulants.*" *

93. The elaborate statistics published in March, 1864, as to the treatment of typhus fever in the *hospitals* at Glasgow, by Dr. W. T. Gairdner, professor of physic, are of the greatest weight, and must eventually settle the problem with the profession. It is only a question of time.

In many hundreds of cases (nearly 600), of all ages, *the mortality lessened exactly as the dose of alcohol diminished*, milk, or buttermilk, being given in its place. Wine, reduced from an average of 34 ounces to 2½, was followed by a reduction of deaths from

* "Principles of Medicine." 4th edition. London, 1841.

---

93. What was the most significant experiment ever made as to the treatment of typhus with and without Alcohol? What do Prof. Gairdner's statistics prove?

17 to 11 per cent. Of 209 children under 15 years of age, treated without any alcohol, *not one died*, though the very same class of cases, treated with alcohol in the *Infirmary*, had a mortality of *six* per cent. An inquest should have sat upon the six, and the just verdict would have been, "Infanticide by medical routine and obstinacy."

94. Dr. J. B. Russell, of Glasgow, commenting on the preceding facts, observes that, "*Alcoholic stimulants are a two-edged sword in the hands of the practitioner.* If employed within the range of their stimulant action, *which is variable in every case*, they are helpful; if pushed beyond into their narcotic action, they impair the vitality, which it is our duty to augment. Even as pure stimulants, they may be used unnecessarily, so as to *push and urge the laboring energies of the system*, maintaining an unnatural excitement in a journey, which could, with leisure, have been more easily accomplished."

Professor Lehmann, in his "Physiological Chemistry," observes, that, "when once the *fact* is admitted, that the first thing in many diseases is to furnish *a copious supply of oxygen* to the blood, which has been loaded with imperfectly decomposed substances, and to remove, as quickly as possible, the carbonic acid which has accumulated in it, these observations will have afforded us *true remedial agencies* which exceed almost every other in the certainty of their action. We should

---

**94.** Give the opinion of Dr. J. B. Russell, of Glasgow, as to the results of recent experiments? State Lehmann's great principle of cure. What are the latest conclusions of Dr. Gairdner, as stated by the "Medical Journal?"

forbid the use of spirituous drinks, and not even prescribe tinctures, which hinder the necessary excretion of carbonic acid." (Vol. III., on Respiration.)*

It is certain that the exaggerated notions of the therapeutic value of alcohol are giving way before inquiry and evidence, and that the old theories are being fast exploded. The "British Medical Journal" (June 22, 1868), for example, in reporting another of the admirable lectures of Professor Gairdner, "On the Limits of Alcoholic Stimulation in Acute Disease," remarks: —

"The author condemned the practice, and also the theoretical views leading to the practice of the late Dr. Todd. *It is as nearly as possible a demonstrated fact*, that much of what is spent in wines and spirits for the sick in hospitals, and, therefore, probably in private practice, *is unnecessarily, if not injuriously, spent.*"

There is no question that stimulants, prescribed for trifling ailments, have introduced intemperance into

* Public writers are always insisting upon the need of pure air and sanitary regulations, who yet fail to see the important fact that the use of alcoholics violates both conditions. "Excess of carbonic acid," says one of them, "is the most discernible injury inflicted by communities upon open air, — an injury revenged with fatal force upon the aggressors." In different air, taken from different parts of the same town, the amount may vary as from 9 to 29; "and in this latter district," says Dr. Angus Smith, "the deaths rose to 4.5 per 100 of the population." It is remarkable that this is *exactly the ratio* of mortality amongst our drinkers themselves, while it is only one per 100 amongst abstainers, who cannot, and will not, live in the bad districts. "Much of the *phthisis* [consumption] and *scrofula* [arising from defective nourishment] of town populations is, doubtless, due to an atmosphere *overcharged with carbonic acid.*"

---

What special reasons, as given by Prof. Laycock, impose a great *moral responsibility* upon physicians in regard to the prescription of Alcohol?

many families, and spread social and personal ruin all around. "I have seen," said Dr. S. Wilks, physician to Guy's Hospital, "*so many* cases of persons, *especially ladies*, who have entirely given themselves up to the pleasures of brandy-drinking, become paraplegic [half paralyzed]. From what we hear of our continental neighbors, it would seem that *that* diabolical compound styled *absinthe* is productive of exhaustion of nervous power in even a much more marked degree. It would seem that the volatile oils, dissolved in the alcohol, give additional force to its poisonous effects." *

Let us hope, however, that the members of a noble profession will speedily awake to a full sense of the great responsibility under which they labor in prescribing alcoholics, recollecting the fact, of which their daily practice gives them a perpetual proof, — the fact, as stated by Professor Laycock, M.D., — that "indigestion, being temporarily relieved by alcoholic stimulants, it lays the foundation for *an ever-growing habit* of taking them in women, and excites a more and more urgent desire in the drunkard," so that "*it is in this way* that many persons of position and education become irrecoverable sots." Forgetting this law, and pandering to fashion or appetite, the physician will fail in his true and holy mission, and, under pretence of healing physical disorder, will leave behind him, in many households, a demon more rampant and remorseless than ever tore the flesh of the possessed ones in olden time.

* "Lectures on Diseases of the Nervous System." — "Medical Times," Oct. 24, 1868.

# VI.

## Temperance in Relation to the Bible.

95. A Latin epigram written in an old Bible, says, "This is a book where every one seeks his *own* opinions, and every one *finds* them." And when it is recollected, that the Bible has been, in many ages and many countries, deliberately cited to justify despotism and drinking, slavery and sensuality, we can hardly wonder at the profane satire. The rebuke, however, really falls, not upon the Bible, but upon its *Interpreters*. The objective truth remains unaffected by the perversions of mankind, who, in behalf of their lusts and prejudices, do, as Cecil says, "labor to make the Bible *their* Bible." As looking at an object through a peculiar medium colors what we see, so our atmosphere of prejudice or passions, the limitations of our ignorance, and the obscuring media of versions or dead languages, will certainly tend to distort or darken our views of scripture truth. We must, *first*, honestly SEEK with single-eye for the genuine Truth of God; and, *second*, adopt EVERY MEANS for clearing away the haze which floats between the Truth and the Inquirer. Our aim must be to interpret the writers *in the sense of their own age*, not of ours; in short, to see with the eyes, hear with the ears, and under-

---

95. What was the meaning of the Latin epigram inscribed upon the blank page of a Bible? On whom does its censure fall? What are the two chief conditions for finding the Truth? What are the perverting media? What

stand with the hearts of the men of old, and, by placing ourselves in their situation, master the meaning of their thoughts and language. Unless our minds are pervaded with the *facts*, the *customs*, and the *opinions* of the ancients, misinterpretation of their writings is simply inevitable; but, purified and illuminated by such conditions, we may rest assured that the Facts of Nature, the Laws of Morals, and the Truths of Scripture, will be found in happy harmony.*

96. Among the *certain* facts, the following may be affirmed: —

1. That the Bible nowhere *condemns abstinence* from strong drinks.

2. That the Bible nowhere associates *God's blessing* with the *use* of strong drinks.

* A work conceived in this spirit has been brought to a conclusion, namely, "The Temperance Bible Commentary," by Dr. LEES and DAWSON BURNS, M. A., in which 637 texts are expounded and illustrated at large. Of this work, Professor Taylor Lewis, of Union College, himself an eminent scholar, says: —

"It is *unique* in its kind as a collection and fair presentation of everything in Scripture that can possibly bear on either aspect of the question. It sets before us the *whole* matter, — Hebrew, Greek, Latin, Syriac, Chaldee. It exhibits great research without parade of authorities, and substantial learning without pedantry. Its execution shows accuracy, conscientiousness, and fidelity. It is earnest, yet candid; very zealous, yet fair; truthful in its statements of adverse opinions; shunning no difficulties, yet manifesting everywhere the deepest reverence for the sacred oracles."

"The Temperance Bible Commentary," it is believed, not only attempts to solve the entire problem, but *does* solve it for all time. Every known, perhaps every possible objection, is there met or anticipated. In the text we have space only to point at certain broad facts and principles.

---

work has been conceived in this spirit? What is the characterization of it, given by Professor Taylor Lewis?

96. What are the six certain propositions, or points, which are made good in the "Temperance Bible Commentary"?

3. That the Bible, in various ways, *commends* abstinence from strong drinks.

4. That the Bible, in various and emphatic methods, exhibits the *manifold evils* of strong drinks.

5. That the Bible is the first book that proclaimed abstinence to be the *cure* for drunkenness.

6. That the great principle of the Bible — *philanthropy* — enforces the practice of abstinence.

97. Ignorance of a *fact* in history, and of a *principle* in language, has prevented men from seeing the truth of these plain propositions, which, nevertheless, stand out in bold relief from the sacred pages. The FACT to which we refer is, that there were in ancient times, as in modern, wines that were *good* and unintoxicating, as well as wines that were *evil* and inebriating.* Pliny, Plutarch, Theophrastus, and others, specially call the former, "wholesome," "innocent," and "moral," and distinguish them from those which inflame the blood and excite the passions. The PRINCIPLE to which we allude is, that where a *word* is the same, the *thing* is the same, in its species and qualities; whence the false and uncritical inference, that when *wine* is spoken of with approval in one text, and with disapproval in another, it must needs be *the same sort of wine!* The "Tippling-critic" says, "the same WINE but in different *quantity*;" the "Temperance critic" says, "the same word but

* For citations and translations from Latin, Greek and other authors, see the pamphlet by Dr. Lees, entitled, "Wines, ancient and modern."

---

97. State the *one fact*, and the one *principle*, ignorance of which stands in the way of the perception and acceptance of these propositions. First, — what is the *fact*, or distinction, concerning the thing, "Wine"? Second, — what is the *principle* concerning the word "Wine"? What does the tippling critic say, and what the Temperance man? *Note.* — What of the case

applied to wine of opposite *quality*." * On other words and questions, there could be no difference of opinion. Take, for example, the words man, woman, wife, spirit, angel, etc. The *generic* meaning does not imply that there is only *one kind* of men, wives, spirits, and angels; on the contrary, in each particular passage, it is for the context (if at all) to determine the goodness, badness, or other *quality* of the subject. So with the Hebrew, Arabic, Chaldee, Greek, Latin, and English words for "Wine;" from a *generic* term you cannot logically draw a *specific* inference.†

* The special implications of the evil quality of a particular wine cannot be got rid of by saying that the Bible warns against excess, and thus implicitly sanctions a lesser use. In reality, it warns against both the *use* and the excess. But the principle of the objection is false. It is the same as saying that if the decalogue prohibits from killing a man, we are allowed to maltreat him short of killing! Now, not only does the Old Testament commend abstinence, and condemn drink, but the New frequently and distinctly exhorts to it, while church history gives illustrious examples of it in the first ages. It was, as Prof. Jowett admits, ranked "amongst the counsels of perfection." The Bishop of Ephesus — Timotheus — was so extreme an abstainer, that he seemed to need an apostolic prescription to induce him to use "a little wine" even as a medicine. What sort of wine it was, we do not absolutely know; but we do know that Athenæus says of the sweet, unintoxicating Lesbian, called *protropos*, it was "very good for the stomach." (ii., § 24.)

† A citation from a distinguished British philosopher will serve as a sufficient example: "The business of a lexicographer is to explain *all the modes in which a word is used* by good writers, — tracing its derivation, assigning its radical import, and then subjoining passages from various authors, *in which the term is variously applied*," etc. — (S. Bailey; "Letters on the Philosophy of the Mind," p. 168, London, 1863.) He instances the absurdity of forcing the modern sense of *defalcation* (as defaltation, originated by an ignorant writer, and accepted by an ignorant public), upon the older and altogether different use of the word by Addison, in the sense of "cutting off" merely. It had no relation to "fault," but to *falx*, "a sicle." Yet

---

**of Timothy? Give examples of generic terms, and the ordinary inferences. What philosopher sustains this view of the *various applications* of certain words?**

98. The absurdness of the false principle exposed is enhanced by the fact, that in the Hebrew and Greek Bible a dozen words, with their special meanings, are all hidden under the English terms "wine" and "strong drink;" and that some of these words, clearly and undeniably, denote *unfermented* and *unintoxicating* wine.*

(1.) YAYIN is the generic term for wine, including the pure "blood of the grape," preserved-juice, and the juice after being fermented and drugged as well. It is applied in all these varied ways: "They wash their garments in *wine*." "They gathered *wine*." "Wine is a *mocker*," it "biteth like a serpent." "*Their* wine is the *poison* of dragons." Divine sanction is never associated with *yayin* where the context shows it to be intoxicating.

that is not so absurd as to put an exclusive, modern, and technical sense of "*fermented* juice" upon the ancient word "wine," by which a remote, derivative, and specific sense is made to override the broad and general meaning of "expressed juice."

* About 60 texts of the "Authorized Version" refer to wine (or what is supposed to be wine) with approbation, where the context shows or implies it to be a natural or unfermented product. Not more than 52 texts can be *proved*, by the context, to refer to *intoxicating* wine, and not one of these is connected with the Divine blessing. On the contrary, one-half of them describe it as evil, as a mocker, and a stupefier, or else *prohibit* it, either in general, or in special cases.

It is a remarkable fact, that an opponent of Temperance could at once go to the *Apocryphal* Scriptures,—Ecclesiasticus, to wit,—and by a ready and unambiguous quotation, confute the doctrine of the abstainer; but from the *Canonical* Scriptures no such passage is forthcoming. "Wisdom is justified of her children."

---

98. What augments the absurdity of forcing a specific sense upon a general term? (*Note.*—What is the noteworthy difference between the Apocrypha and the Canonical Scriptures? How many words in the original are translated, or hidden, under the one word "Wine"? (1.) What is the meaning of "*Yayin*"? Give texts where it is used for very different things. What

The derivation of the word, like that of the equivalent Chaldee term *Khamer*, probably points to the turbid, foaming appearance of fresh expressed juices; for certainly the Jews, in much later times, had no idea of the occult process of "fermentation." The Rabbis, in fact, had a theory that "the juice of fruit does *not* ferment!" The Targums speak of "the wine *Khamar* (=*yayin*), which Messiah shall drink, reserved in its grapes from the beginning." Thomas Aquinas, in the 13th century, decides that "grape-juice (*mustum*) is of the specific nature of wine (*vinum*), and may be used in the celebration of the Eucharist."

This word being general, necessitated, in the later age of Jewish literature, the use of two or three *specific* terms to indicate particular sorts of wine. As, for example, the following: —

(2.) Khamer: fresh or "*foaming*" wine in its first sense. But since the wine when it ferments becomes *red*, the idea of redness got associated with the Chaldee use of the word; and, perhaps, "thickness" also. It is a word used for the *foam* of the sea, and for the *bitumen* of pits.

(3.) Ausis, from *asas*, "to tread," signifies the same as the classic *protropos* — "first trodden" or "running" wine. "The mountains shall drop-down *ausis*."

(4.) Sobhe is "boiled wine," the *sapa* of the Romans, the *sabe* of the French and Italians. It was the luxurious drink of the rich; of course not intoxicating.

---

**is the Rabbinical equivalent? Give Aquinas's definition of grape-juice as "*wine*." (2.) What is the sense of *khamer*? (3.) Of *Ausis*? (4.) Of**

Other Hebrew words, translated wine, do not really signify wine at all, for example : —

(5.) TIROSH is a collective term for "the fruit of the vine" in its natural state, from the early "*tirosh* in the cluster" to the richer "blessing within it" of the full ripe grapes, ready for grateful consumption. Hence Micah's phrase, "Thou shalt *tread* vine fruit (*tirosh*), but shall not *drink yayin*," for the fruit shall be withered (vi. 15). It is associated, as a thing of growth, with *corn* and orchard fruit (*yitzhar* — not oil); dependent upon the dew and rain. In the Latin, French, German, Italian, and Spanish versions, it is generally, but wrongly, translated *mustum*, *mosto*, etc. It is nowhere implied to be either intoxicating or liquid. "Whoredom, wine, and new wine" does not make sense; but Idolatry, Inebriety, and Luxury does, — represented by Whoredom, Wine, and Grapes, which "take away the heart." The words in Prov. iii. 10, and Joel ii. 24, translated "bursting" and "overflowing," respectively signify no more than "abundance." (*See* "Bible Commentary.")

(6.) ÆSHISHAH is the word translated "flagons of wine;" but erroneously, as all scholars now concede. It denoted a *fruit-cake*.

(7.) SHEMARIM, from *Shamar*, "to preserve," means "preserves," well refined — not "dregs." *Wine* is interpolated; it only occurs *once* in the supposed sense of wine. The older translators regarded it as "sweet and

---

*Sobhe* or Saba? (5.) What is the true sense of *Tirosh*? Name the two texts, a mistranslation of which has deceived the commentators. (6.) What does *Asheshah* denote? (7.) Explain the sense and derivation of *Shema-*

dainty things." It corresponds in formation with *shemanim* (from *shemen*, oil), "fat things."

(8.) MESECH, "mixture" simply, which might be good or bad. The mingled wine of *wisdom* (boiled grape-juice mixed with water), or the wine of sensuality. "Who hath woe? They that are mighty to *mingle* sweet drink" (*shakar*), i. e., with inebriating drugs.

(9.) SHAKAR,* erroneously translated *strong* drink, comes from an Oriental root for "sweet-juice," and is the undoubted original of the European words (Greek, Latin, Teutonic, and Spanish) for *sugar*. It is used to this day in Arabia for *palm-juice* and *palm-wine*, whether fresh or fermented.

*In the Common Version of the Bible, there is just one text*, and only one, *that gives apparent Divine sanction to intoxicating wine*, namely, Deut. xiv. 26, where strong drink is named as a permissible element in a sacred feast. The answer is conclusive, — no word for "strong" exists in the Hebrew text. The term there used is simply SHAKAR, — the original of *saccar*, sugar. It denoted *Palm Wine* in various states, unfermented, sweet, and syrupy, as well as intoxicating and "bitter." Hence, as Bishop Lowth observes, the antithesis of Isaiah, —

* In Notes to Dr. Delitzsh's "Commentary on Isaiah" (Clarke, Edinburgh), we find a modified explanation: —

"The Arabic *sakkar*, no doubt equivalent to *sakchari*, 'honey of canes' (Arrian), an Indian word, signifying 'forming broken pieces,' i. e., *sugar* in 'grains or small lumps.'"

---

*rim*, falsely translated "*wine* on the lees." (9.) What is the meaning of *Shakar*? Is there any authority for adding "strong" to it? Of what European words is it the original? Which is the solitary text that apparently associates Divine sanction with *intoxicating* drink? What is the fallacy?

"Thy *shechar* (sweet wine) shall become *bitter*," — i. e., deteriorated, which it does when fermented.

(10). Oinos is the generic Greek word corresponding with the Hebrew *yayin;* and is applicable to *all* sorts of wine. The context alone can determine the specific nature of the wine to which the word points.

(11.) Gleukos only occurs once in the New Testament, and is not associated with any Divine approval. It is classically the name of *rich grape-juice*, or unfermented wine; perhaps, in some cases, for initially fermented wine, the preservation of which had been neglected.

(12.) Oxos was "sour wine," sometimes mingled with drugs.

99. Though the end of revelation is not to supersede experience and science, yet considering how drinking is connected at many points with morals and religion, *by way of hindrance to* the purposes of a progressive and Divine revelation, we may fairly expect that the subject would come under the observation of the inspired writers of the Bible. When we come to examine it, impartially, in the light of facts and reason, it will be found to have *anticipated* the ordinary wisdom of men and the developments of modern science. The great physicians of Europe express the last verdict of science when they affirm the old Temperance doctrine, that alcohol is

---

(10.) What Greek word corresponds with the Hebrew "*Yayin*"? To what is *Oinos* applicable? (11.) To what *Gleukos*? (12.) To what *Oxos*?

99. What *special* reason have we for believing that the subject of strong drink would be noticed in the Bible? What do we actually find? Does the Bible support the teachings of science? Give texts in proof that intoxicating wine is a *poison*, a *narcotic*, and a *demoralizer*.

simply a narcotic *poison*, and not *food* in any true or ordinary sense. The property of such a poison is to seduce, mock, deceive; to generate an ever-increasing appetite for itself; and to make the soul subject to the craving tyranny of the sensual nature. Now the express language of Scripture is but the echo of this conclusion: "Wine is a *mocker*" — "be not *deceived* thereby." The cry of the drunkard is: "They have stricken me, but I *felt it not* — I will seek it yet again." The voice of wisdom is: "Look not upon the wine, when it is red; when it giveth its eye in the cup" (or the marks of fermentation); "for, at last, it *stingeth like a serpent*." Nay, more, in three plain texts, the Hebrew for "poison" (Khemah) — the word six times so translated — is applied to this very species of drink which "stingeth *like* a serpent." The evil wine was like "the *poison* of dragons." — (Deut. xxxii. 33.) The princess made the king "sick with *poison* of wine." — (Hos. vii. 5.) And a woe is hurled against him who giveth such drink to his neighbor — who "putteth thy *poison* to him," — (Hab. ii. 15), — the consequence being that God's poisoned cup of wrath (Khemah) shall be turned to him. Is it not pure insanity to suppose that *such* an element is identical with the contents of any "cup of blessing"?

100. The New Testament *is not less explicit and comprehensive.*

(1.) Engkratia — self-control — is four times translated "temperance," twice *temperate*, and once *conti-*

---

100. How many distinctions has the New Testament on this question of Temperance? (1.) What is its word for "self-control"? Name the texts

*nent.* In 1 Cor. vii. 9; ix. 25, it has evidently a negative application equal to *abstaining.*

(2.) Epi-eikees — forbearing — translated once *moderation;* thrice *gentle;* once *patient.*

(3.) Sophroneo — sedate, discreet — translated *sober, sober-minded,* and *in a right mind.* This is mental "sobriety," — the state when we can obey reason, and resist appetite. This can have nothing to do with drinking, which, at best, is the gratification of a sensuous lust. Mental temperance being expressed by the preceding terms, we still need a word for *abstinence* in regard to the body. This is found in a compound formed from the negative particle *nee* (not), and *piō* to (drink) = neephō.

(4.) Neepho is found in the apostolic exhortations seven times; in its adjective form (*neephalios*) thrice. It occurs in such peculiar connections, that it seems absurd to put upon it any secondary or metaphorical meaning. The primary sense of the word, beyond all cavil, is that of ABSTINENCE; its secondary sense of "*wakeful*" expresses the condition in which people *are* who abstain from narcotics. "Without doubt," says Dean Alford, "the word signifies abstinence; but Dr. Lees is bound to prove that it means *total* abstinence!" Now, he is bound to prove no more than this, — that it means *not drinking*, and that the apostles use it, or ever *may* have used it, in that, its primary and proper sense. Josephus,

---

where it includes *abstinence.* (2.) What is the true meaning of the word translated "moderation"? (3.) What is the term for *mental* sobriety? (4.) What is the word for physical temperance or *abstinence*? How is it formed? What is its adjective? What does Dean Alford admit? How does Josephus, the Jewish historian, use the word? In what texts do the Apostles use *neepho*, in company with words for mental temperance and watchfulness? (5.) What is the fifth term?

one of their contemporaries, says of the priests "They *abstained* from wine" — (apò âkratou neephontes). Does this admit of doubt? Besides, Paul and Peter use the word *along with* the proper words for mental temperance and for watchfulness. Thus: —

1 Tim. iii. 2. Be (neephalion) ABSTINENT, *sound-minded.*

1 Thess. v. 6. Let us *watch* and DRINK NOT (neephōmen).

1 Pet. iv. 7. Be *sound-minded* and ABSTINENT unto prayer.

1 Pet. v. 8. (Neepsate) DRINK NOT, be *vigilant* . . . because your adversary seeketh whom he may *drink down* [kata-piē]. (So Dr. A Clarke, the commentator.)

To inquire why Josephus, Philo, and others should by this word mean "abstinence from drink," while the apostles signify "drinking a little," would be to follow perversity and appetite into the den of idols.

101. The objection that the deacons are not to be "given towards *much* wine," and the deaconesses (aged women) "not to be enslaved to *much* wine," falls before the fact that unfermented wine was allowed to women and to men after a certain age.* If it be said, Why warn against excess in what does not intoxicate? — we ask, Why Solomon informs us that "To eat *much* honey is not good," if no one ever did? This is the

* Titus, ii. 2, and 1 Tim. iii: 11, command that the *elders* and their *wives* shall be *neephalious* (abstinent), — i. e., no drinkers of ANOTHER SORT of wine — the bad.

---

101. What is the reference to "*much* wine"? Were "sweets" abused by the ancients? Give examples from Solomon and from Lucian. Were Bish-

fallacy of interpreting the language of the ancients by the customs of the moderns. Pliny and many other ancient writers show us that the abuse of syrupy and sweet wines was a *special vice* of their day. Lucian has this passage: "I came, by Jove, as those who drink *gleukos*, require an emetic," — before they drink again.

Josephus says of the Jewish priests, that, "on account of their office, they had prescribed to them a double degree of purity." So Paul deemed a *special* and *extreme* form of abstinence proper to be urged upon a bishop: just as the Law Book of the Ante-Nicene Church commands that a bishop shall not enter a *tavern*, except on necessity.

(5.) St. Paul uses a word which is equivalent to the modern pledge, — "*discountenance* the drinking usages," — namely, *nee* (not) — *par* (over, or in presence of) — *oinon* (wine). In 1 Tim. iii. 2, 3, and Titus i. 7, 8, in connection with being *no drinker*, sound-minded, and no striker, it is commanded that a bishop shall be *nee-par-oinos*, "nor near wine," — not in its company. (So Professor Stuart.)

The fact that teetotalism prevailed throughout the East for thousands of years; that it was a part of the discipline of the oriental priesthoods from Egypt to India; that it pervaded Judæa in the time of our Lord, and was manifested in the sympathetic sects of the Essenes and Therapeutæ, — are circumstances which *compel* the impartial critic to give a plain and literal sense

---

ops (or Ministers) subject to special restrictions? Name an example from the Law-Book of the pre-Nicene church. In what way did St. Paul enforce

to the language of the Scriptures, when it at once *corresponds* with historical practices and scientific verities. Language that would be understood elsewhere as inculcating *abstinence* could not in Palestine be regarded as teaching drinking.

Professor Murphy, of Belfast, asks concerning this text, "Is that the *form* a total-abstinence prohibition would take?" Certainly, it *is* the form which the Divine prohibition took. Does the form (or rather the *penalty*) get rid of the *essence* and *wisdom* of the law? If not, where is the sense of the objection? The Rev. A. Dobbin, in supporting Dr. Murphy, says, "It is no new discovery that the Bible is a temperance book; and that, in certain circumstances, it gives its *sanction* and *encouragement* to total abstinence. There is one thing, however, not *yet* admitted, — that the Bible IMPOSES total abstinence upon every Christian man as an obligation, as *morally* binding as the sixth commandment." Whatever notion may be attached to the word "imposes," it seems to us who are commanded to "be *perfect* even as our Father in heaven is perfect," that the Divine teachings, the Divine warnings, and the Divine example, *do* impose a very clear duty; and that what is reasonable and good, and the neglect of which fills the world with mischief and immorality, *murder included*, is entitled to be called a *moral* obligation as truly as any of the ten commandments. It is the *nature* of an action, not the *form* of an expression, that creates and constitutes our

---

this? Is there any other source of obligation, any higher sanction, than the Divine will, *so* expressed?

duty.* Plato "reasoned well," when he said that "many other cases one might mention, in which wine ought not to be drank *by those who possess understanding and a correct rule of action.*" — ("Laws," ii., 674.)

102. We can now go back to the *six* propositions laid down in § 94.

(I.) *The Bible nowhere* CONDEMNS *abstinence from intoxicants.* It nowhere teaches that it is either inexpedient or unlawful; hence abstinence cannot be *anti*-scriptural. No Jew breaks the old law, no Christian the new, by refusing to drink intoxicants. The New Testament law of "moderation" simply enjoins equanimity under persecution, and gentleness under provocation. There is no text that says, "To the pure all things are *proper.*" Timothy's case is conclusive as to the lawfulness of abstinence, for the apostle passes no censure, and limits the exceptional prescription by circumstances *personal* to the patient.

(II.) *The Bible nowhere associates God's* BLESSING *with* STRONG DRINK. We can only conceive of three

* It is still often objected that "*all* things are to be received with thanksgiving, and nothing to be esteemed *impure.*" It is a disgrace to modern scholarship, that texts having reference to obsolete and merely ceremonial distinctions of *meats* should be thus perversely applied, for the purpose of ignoring the *physiological* properties of an artificial *beverage.* The ancients were wiser, as the following extract from Justin Martyr, A. D. 148, will show: "Although we discriminate between green herbs, not eating *all,* we refrain from eating some, not because they are common or unclean, but because they are *bitter*, or *deadly*, or *thorny.* But we lay hands on, and take all herbs that are sweet, very nourishing, and good, whether marine or land plants." — ("Dial. cum Trypho." cap. xx.)

---

102. (I.) Does the Bible anywhere condemn Abstinence? Why cannot it be called *anti*-scriptural? (II.) What are the three most plausible examples of Divine sanction on strong drink? What is Dr. Wardlaw's comment on,

plausible objections to this statement. First, the text of Deut. xiv. 25, 26, already disposed of as a mis-translation and an assumption, since "*sweet drink*" is the proper representative of the original *shakar*. Second, the text of Prov. xxxi. 4–7, which, however, cannot be understood as anything but an *ironical* permission, a contrastive admonition, in fact, equal to saying that such liquors are *fit for nothing else* than to stupefy the brain and cause the soul to forget its duties, as the judge of life.* Third, the miraculous conversion of water into wine, at the marriage feast at Cana. But the presumption is against the idea that our Lord would transform innocent water into *intoxicating* wine, — an element that the cotemporary Essenes called "fools' physic," — which after Christians designated as the "invention of the evil one" — though, as Augustin witnesses, they readily drank the *juice of grapes;* which he very illogically condemns as inconsistent! In truth all our blessed Lord did, was to discountenance the dualistic mistakes of the Persian philosophy, with a foresight of the Manichæan revival of it, that there

* "I pity the state of that man's mind," says Ralph Wardlaw, D.D., "who can . . . allow himself to suppose that this passage contains an *inspired toleration of excess* — a permission and encouragement to seek relief in the insensibility of intoxication — to make wine the refuge from melancholy. Would it be fair to set this one passage against the whole Bible? — one text against its entire scope, and unnumbered positive, and pointed, and damnatory prohibitions? . . . But when men *do* take hold of a passage like this, and quote it with a leer while they are putting the bottle to each other's mouths, and drinking themselves drunk, they only discover the bent of their minds. . . . Let no such inference be drawn as that the Bible directs to wine as the refuge from cares. . . . It is the most wretched of all resources. . . . The Bible condemns every *approach* to excess." — ("Lectures on Proverbs." Glasgow, 1861.)

---

"*Give* strong drink to him that is ready to perish," etc? Explain the sig-

was essential evil in matter, and therefore in "marriage" and in "wine." Now, as his countenance of a pure marriage gives no sanction to a corrupt one, neither does his conversion of pure water into pure wine involve the slightest approval of that essentially impure and corrupt element which *is* "a mocker," and "*wherein* is excess." Here, again, the modern conception is anticipated by Divine Wisdom, in that miracle which, though the first in order of time, was recorded only in the last of the Gospels, when the error it meets was creeping into the church.

(III.) *The Bible, in various ways,* COMMENDS *abstinence.* 1. Paradise was not wrongly constructed; yet, amidst the perfect adaptations of food and drink to the wants of our perfect originals, alcohol found no place. To you "it shall be for meat," applied to grain and fruit, — not to that artificial and fiery product which results from their fermentative destruction. 2. The great host of the Israelites, under God's direction, wandered forty years in the wilderness, yet he, who sent them manna, never gave them inebriating drink. Who can doubt that, had such drink been *needed*, it would have been provided? How, then, can alcholics be required in the more genial circumstances of common life? 3. The Nazarites were a society of religious abstainers, whose pledge was drawn out by God, to do honor to him; and took rank with his prophets. The Rechabites were probably voluntary imitators of them, — outside Kenites or Arabians, — and were highly commended by the Al-

---

nificance of the first miracle of Cana, and why it was recorded last? (III.)

mighty for their fidelity to the pledge, and they assign an excellent reason for their practice,—"that they might live long in the land;" which they did. The Bible, then, implies that teetotalism is a physiological law or truth. The case of Adam and Eve involves this, as part of the best possible condition. The Nazarites, Daniel, etc., prove it by their experience, for they were "ruddier," "fairer," and "fatter in flesh," than the drinking Jews. But Samson's case is still more emphatic, since an angel was twice sent with instructions as to abstinence, before the birth of the strong one. Science shows the reason. Dr. Smith's "Experimental Researches" say, "*Alcohol greatly lessens muscular tone.*" Tom Sayers and Heenan, the well-mated champions of the prize ring, were obliged to *train* on teetotal diet. These, then, are but reverberations from a truth well known in heaven 3000 years ago. It cannot be supposed that the pledge was a mere whim, without any physiological significance or results. "In the beginning," as the Lord argued concerning marriage, the modern system was not. The first of men and the fairest of women were constituted teetotalers. Samson, the strong man, Samuel, the holy founder of the school of the prophets, and John, more than a prophet, were striking examples of God's favor upon the system. It could not be for no reason in the nature of things that teetotalism was made the antecedent to primitive perfection, to physical power, to mental intelligence, and to spiritual purity. 4. *Abstinence was taught as a necessary physical preparation for*

---

**In what ways does the Bible *commend* abstinence? Give Dr. Wardlaw's**

*moral purity and spiritual efficiency:* (*a*) In the cases of Samuel and of John the Baptist, the forerunner of the Lord. (*b*) In the case of the priests (Lev. x.) that they might *distinguish* holy from profane. (*c*) In the case of the Nazarites, that they might illustrate at once, and voluntarily, the virtues of self-denial and purity. The law of prohibition to the priests means this: "As men, do your own work your own way, but while wearing *my insignia*, and acting as *my servants*, the work shall be done in your natural state free from disturbing drink." * That to Nazarites implies, that "As I accept sacrifices only that have no spot or taint, so I accept your living sacrifice on condition that you are *unpolluted* with the poison and the mocker. (*d*) To this we may add the significant advice, "It is not for kings to drink wine."

(IV.) *The Bible, by various methods of teaching, exhibits the* MANIFOLD EVILS *of the use of* STRONG DRINKS. 1.

* It seems singular that the lesson has not been learned before, and yet commentators have sometimes been on the very verge of the truth. Dr. Wardlaw, of Glasgow, has this excellent comment on "Prov. xxxi., 1-5. The *principle* of the caution is applied to the priests, 'whose lips should keep their knowledge, as being messengers of the Lord of Hosts.' — (Lev. x. 10.) But such maxims and cautions *apply to all.* [Why not the Divine remedy?] In all, at all times, in all places, and in all circumstances, the mind ought to be in entire and undisturbed possession and exercise of its powers, for the transaction of business, for the discharge of duty, *for the avoidance of temptation.* In every instance in which, even in the slightest degree, the regular exercise of the powers of the mind is affected and impaired, *there is sin.* But let it not be even *thus* limited. Let it not be imagined that no sin is committed, unless, in some degree or other, there is the unsettlement of reason. There may be a large amount of sin, where there is nothing of the kind." — ("Lectures on Proverbs.")

---

comment on Prov. xxxi. 1-5. (IV.) State the *manifold evils*, under four

God uses *intoxicating* wine as the constant symbol of wickedness and punishment. *Khemah* is the poison of the cup of wrath, — the *maddening* element, — which is to the soul what physical poison is to the body. From Moses to John this expressive symbolism prevails. All the imagery of the prophets is pervaded with the idea of the evil of strong drink. 2. God shows us, in the biography of his people, how prophets, patriarchs, and priests fell into sin "through wine," and were "swallowed up" of strong drink. Solomon simply condenses history, and probably his own experience, when he says, "Wine is a mocker." That is its essence in relation to the soul. 3. God teaches us that the great cause of perversion in his people, as Church and Nation, after centuries of varied education and discipline, of unexampled laws and privileges, social, sanitary, and political, — was the love of drink. "What more could I do for you?" saith the Lord. "Why, then, when I looked for grapes, do I find poisonous (or wild) grapes?" The answer of the prophets is still the same. Amos sums up the whole in *four* transgressions; and the four resolve themselves into one cause. (1.) The judges passed unjust verdicts, to get fines *for drink* to be consumed in the holy places. (2.) They commanded the prophets to cease, unless they would prophesy of wine and strong drink. (3.) They tempted the Nazarites to break their pledge, because their sobriety was a standing rebuke to themselves. (4.) They cared not for the "affliction of Joseph," but drank wine in bowls — (Compare Amos ii.

---

**heads, ascribed to strong drink. (V.) In what way does the Bible proclaim**

6; Micah ii. 11; Isaiah v.) For these sins, it is said, "Therefore shall they go into captivity;" and it is remarkable that they learned sobriety at last in the court of Cyrus, the magian teetotaler, — royal fashion and Persian philosophy doubtless co-operating to that end. In this sublime history we see *evil* constantly associated with intoxicating drink; and exhibited as the *hindrance* to God's own teaching. How vain, then, to expect that our laws and crotchets will triumph over this sin, where his distinctly failed! The lesson to be learned is, that the church can only cure intemperance by banishing its *causes*.

(V.) *The Bible* PROCLAIMS *abstinence to be the* CURE *for drinking*. By approved examples, by advice, blessing, warning, and exhortation (as we have seen), the wise Jews might have clearly known the Divine will on this subject. But they despised the lesson, and would be taught only through *suffering* and *captivity*. Yet there was one invincible example, which nothing but stolidity could misunderstand. God interfered not with the ordinary life of his people unless in matters which transgressed not only the ends but the *channels* of Revelation. But in Leviticus, the 10th chapter, a case is recorded where strong drink having threatened the continuance of the Mosaic economy, it must be *effectually* and *instantly* dealt with. Within the limits of the priesthood and the work of the tabernacle — in brief, the sphere of the Divine service, both as to time and place, — the *end* desired is absolute sobriety. What did

---

abstinence as the *cure* for intemperance? Answer an *objection*.

Jehovah? Issue a mere warning against excess, like modern moralists, priests, and preachers? No, but an absolute mandate, *interdicting the use of strong drink in his service and in his temple forever*, guarded by the terrible penalty of death. And this seems to have answered its end, during all the ages of the Jewish dispensation. The wonder is, that a nation so afflicted with the degradations and depravities of drinking could not save itself by extending the remedy to its entire social and religious life. What was neither *needless*, nor *unwise*, nor *extreme* in God's plan, could hardly be folly and fanaticism in man.

It has been objected, that the priests were free to drink at other times, and only prohibited the use of wine going into the tabernacle. True, they were left "free agents" as regards their own work, and they abused that freedom sadly; but the wisdom of prohibition, and the reasons for it, remain unchanged. The *occasion* for the display of the Divine wisdom is not the guiding and binding element, but the *fact* and *nature* of its display; and thus the "specific command" may become a "general commend."

All historical teaching must be limited by time, place, and circumstance; but that fact, surely, cannot erase the universal truth within it. It is the express business of reason to separate the accidental from the essential, and hence the folly of attempting to evade the foregoing argument by reference to Ezekiel xliv. 18, where, along with the renewal of the prohibition of wine, the priests are commanded to wear linen garments and to cut their hair short! No doubt, as a means of physical cleanliness, in a hot climate and in the confined and heated labor of their special services, this, also, was a wise provision addressed to "the messengers of the Lord." But while the symbolism and peculiarity of that part of the law have passed away, and so do not *apply* to the modern minister, *the reasons for the prohibition of wine are as imperative as before.* Man is as weak, and wine is as strong as ever. Alcohol, as a brain-poison, disturbs and deceives the Christian professor exactly as it did the Jewish priest; and therefore the obligation of this part of the Levitical law as truly abides as any portion of the decalogue itself.

(VI.) *The Bible principle of* PHILANTHROPY *enforces abstinence.* The first condition of doing good to others is to strengthen and purify ourselves. It has been seen that abstinence, both as a dictate of self-denial and a regimen of reason, not only does good to the individual, but is a means to moral and social ends of vast importance. The prudential maxims of the New Testament confirm it. "Abstain from all appearance of evil." The Lord's prayer almost enjoins it. "Lead us not into temptation." The Apostle Paul implies that discipline of temperance was needful even to him. The Divine favor is promised to those who keep themselves from all temptation and sin, save such as may cross them in *the path of duty.* But that duty is often made very plain in the course of life. The Divine rule is, "Do good *as ye have opportunity.*" If eating meat, or drinking wine, *or anything*, threatens evil to our brother, or our neighbor, then we must abandon the pleasures of sense for the diviner joys of philanthropy. If not, we sin against

---

**(VI.) In what way does the Bible principle of philanthropy enforce absti-**

our brother and against Christ. "He who *knoweth* to do good, and doeth it not, to him it *is sin*." In obedience to this higher law, and to the light which Providence casts upon it, ought not strong drinks to be abandoned by Christian professors? The good that needs doing, the evil that needs destroying, wait upon the adoption of teetotalism. Mrs. Wightman, of Shrewsbury, who has reclaimed so many drunkards, and achieved so much good, was for years prejudiced against abstinence, in favor of a pre-formed and self-formed religious theory. But human nature was stubborn, — the FACT remained; her hopes and prayers were unavailing, and her theory had to give way. The gospel *and* drink failed to effect a social reformation; but the gospel and abstinence achieved, and still achieves, marvellous and manifold results of the most blessed kind. So must the right agency ever do.

Thus it may be seen, even from the bare summary of our case, how the varied language of the Old and New Testament, and the known facts of antiquity, conspire to establish every portion of our critical theory; how each separate fact and phrase finds its fitting place in the temple of truth; and how it is made manifest that Holy Scripture concurs with moral and physical science in teaching abstinence from narcotic poisons, — a doctrine which needs to be reiterated afresh from the pulpits of Christendom, until the torpid conscience is aroused, and the great obstacle to the progress and triumph of the gospel is removed out of the way.

---

**nence? What is the higher law? What held back Mrs. Wightman?**

# VII.

## The Historical Question.

103. Were the subject of intemperance, as it interweaves itself, not with the multiplied and minute circumstances of social and domestic life, but with the more public and memorable events of National History, to be treated in detail, it would swell into one of the largest volumes ever written. Here we can only record the leading facts of history as they bear upon the problem to be solved, — first, those that point to the nature and spread of the evil; second, those which indicate a partial or a perfect cure.

And, first, no idea can be further from the truth than that which explains intemperance, either as a matter of *race*, or of *climate*. It is one of those hasty generalizations which shallow intellects grasp at, and interested persons propagate. Pretending to be a philosophical induction, it is in reality contradicted by the most varied facts of history, which clearly show that the very same races, at different periods, have been the alternate subjects of drunkenness and of sobriety, and that the vice of intemperance has prevailed equally in the torrid, the temperate, and the frigid zones. The facts of which we shall now give specimens, — selected from regions,

---

**103. Has race or climate much to do with the prevalence of intemperance? Why must the hypothesis be discarded?**

epochs, and conditions most widely apart, — also show, that (*apart from abstinence*), no variations of social life, no diversities of civilization, no forms, or development of religious faith, have secured an *exemption* from the wide-spread curse of intemperance, — a malady and a vice which have penetrated alike the hut, the mansion, and the palace, the wigwam of the savage, the tent of the Tartar, and the home of the European, and desecrated, with equal stain, the tabernacles of Judaism, the pagodas of paganism, and the shrines of Christendom.

104. It is a curious fact, that amongst the few fragments of lost historical books and antique literature relating to the "world's gray fathers," which have been preserved to us, several striking notices of *intemperance* and its *remedy* are found. A page of Megasthenes' "History of India," cited by Strabo, shows that the highest, most religious, and cultured *castes* of Hindostan were then, and from time immemorial had been, abstainers, — "the Brachmans, the Germanas, and the Hylobious," or physicians.

The fifth and last of the "Pentalogue of Buddha" (B. C. 560) runs thus: —

> "Obey the law, and *walk steadily* in the path of purity, and [to do this] drink not liquors that *intoxicate* and *disturb the reason*."

105. A celebrated work by Porphyry contains a page of a lost work, by Chæremon, librarian in one of the sacred temples in Egypt, which has a very instructive

---

104. Was teetotalism an ancient doctrine? State two remarkable examples concerning India.

passage, enouncing a doctrine, both substantially and verbally identical with that of the book of Proverbs (xxxiii. 30, 31). He says of the priests: "Some of them [the higher] *did not drink wine at all*, and others [inferior] drank very little of it, *on account of its being injurious to the nerves, oppressive to the head, an impediment to invention, and an incentive to lust.*" Plutarch informs us, that even the priests of inferior deities "were strictly prohibited its use during their most solemn purifications;" that "wine was wholly forbidden to the kings," who were also high-priests; and that Psametik, 600 B. C., was the first of the regal line that drank it.

In the Hieratic Papyri (*Anastasi*, No. 4), Letter xi. contains a very singular and instructive passage, written, nearly 4,000 years ago, by an Egyptian priest and tutor, *Amen-em-an*, to his young pupil, *Penta-our*, who, afterwards, becoming steady and reclaimed, rose to the dignity of court-poet to one of the Pharaohs: —

"It has been told me that thou hast forsaken books, and devoted thyself to sensuality; that thou goest from tavern to tavern, smelling of beer (*henk*) at eventide. If beer gets into a man, it overcomes thy mind; thou art like an oar started from its place; like a house without food, with shaky walls. If thou wieldest the rod of office, men run away from thee. Thou knowest that *wine is an abomination;* thou hast taken an oath (or *pledge*) concerning strong drink, that thou wouldst

---

105. Was abstinence known in ancient Egypt? What does a certain librarian say? Does Plutarch mention it? Who mentions *beer* in ancient times? What was "wine" esteemed? Did taverns have a bad reputation then, as now? Give the testimony of a certain letter. Were temperance *pledges* known? Give the proof.

not put such [liquor] into thee. Hast thou forgotten thine oath?" *

Shortly comes another letter, from this Egyptian bishop, resuming the allusion to the temperance pledge: —

"I have heard it said, thou goest after pleasure. Turn not thy face from my advice! or dost thou really give thy heart to all the words of the votaries of indulgence? Thy limbs are alive, then, but thy heart is asleep. *I, thy superior, forbid thee to go to the taverns.*† Thou art degraded like the beasts! But *we see many like thee,* — haters of books; they honor not God. God regards not the breakers of *pledges,* — the illiterate. When young as thou, I passed *my* time under discipline; it tamed my members. When three months had ended, I was dedicated to the house of God. I became one of the first in all kinds of *learning.*" ‡

In contrast with the ancient Egyptians, it may be stated that the modern Copts are a *sober* people, whatever the explanation may be.

106. Persia was, no doubt, the primitive seat of the

* There was a sort of Burton-upon-Trent even then. In a letter following the one just cited, we find these passages: "The way up to Dja is covered with palms, yielding nothing fit to eat save their dates, not yet ripe. . . I shall walk like one strong in bone, traversing the marshes on foot. Then let the barrels be opened, which are full of *Beer* (*hek* or *henk*) of *Kati.*" Or was this *Gath* of the Philistines, and the liquor palm-wine?

† See Heath's "Exod. Papyri." (Pl., cxi., § 3.)

‡ How wonderful to see the present in the past! It is the old, old story! Man and drink! drink and man! evermore the same in their mutual relations; yet each generation as stupid as the one that went before, always renewing the lesson, but never coming to a *conviction* of the truth! The Egyptian priest says: "'wine' is an abomination," and he commands that a moral person should *abstain* from it, and not even go to the *tavern* where it is sold and drank. Solomon and the apostles use exactly similar language; but modern critics, looking at it through modern tastes and customs, actually transform their words into an apology for sipping "wine," and sitting at feasts!

Aryan, or European and Hindoo races. One of its ancient religions regarded wine as an instrument of the evil power. When history opens it up to us, the people were very temperate. In the words of Herodotus, "Strangers to the taste of wine, they drank water only." On this regimen, Cyrus conquered the East; with a departure from it, began the decline of that great empire. It is singular that the deviation commenced with the medical deception. According to Anquetil, in the reign of "Jemsheed, a cure performed on a lady of the court rendered the use of wine common. Until then it had been considered *only as a remedy*." * Thus, by a fallacy of appetite, common in our day, what was adapted to disease came to be consumed daily in health. On this change of manners and morals, Professor Rawlinson, says: —

"The Persians, even of the better sort, were in the earlier times noted for their temperance and sobriety. Their ordinary food was wheaten bread, barley cakes, and meat simply roasted or boiled, which they seasoned with salt and with bruised cress-seed, — a substitute for mustard. *The sole drink in which they indulged was water.* Moreover, it was their habit to take one meal only each day. The poorer kind of people were contented with even a simpler diet, supporting themselves, to a great extent, on the natural products of the soil, as dates, figs, wild pears, acorns, and the fruit of the terebinth tree. But these abstemious habits were soon laid aside, and replaced by luxury and self-indulgence, when the success of their arms had

* "Universal History," vol. i., p. 300.

---

106. What was the condition of the ancient Persians? Give the testimony of Herodotus and Rawlinson.

put it in their power to have the full and free gratification of all their desires and propensities. . . .

"Instead of water, wine became the usual beverage; each man prided himself on the quantity he could drink; and the natural result followed,— that most banquets terminated in general intoxication. *Drunkenness even came to be a sort of institution.* Once a year, at the feast of Mithras, the King of Persia, according to Duris, was *bound* to be drunk. A general practice arose of deliberating on all important affairs under the influence of wine, so that in every household, when a family crisis impended, intoxication was a duty." *

107. The Arabs, like the Jews, were, at one time, addicted to shameful excess in drinking. Mohamed found them so besotted that they worshipped sticks and stones. Yet, from a perception of the enormous evils of strong drink, as Warnerius observes, "the more devout pagan Arabs totally abstained from wine long before the birth of Mohamed." That great lawgiver, in words almost parallel with the injunction of the apostles, gave forth a law, which has more affected for good the millions of the Eastern populations, — Tartars, Turks, Persians, Hindoos, Arabs, Egyptians, and Moors, — than any other institution which was ever set up amongst them: —

THE KORAN, v. 7.

"O true believers, surely *wine* and lots are an abomination, A SNARE OF SATAN, therefore avoid them. SATAN *seeketh to*

* "Ancient Monarchies," vol. iv. Amongst the later Jews, at the Feast of Lots, a similar practice prevailed as at the feast of Mithras. The Rabbis held that they were "bound to be drunk." The connection is historical.

---

107. What was the state of the Arabs before Mohamed's day? What did he decree?

sow dissension and hatred by *means of wine* and lots; will ye not, therefore, *abstain* from them?"

2 TIM. ii. 26.

"And they *becoming sober again* out of the SNARE OF THE DEVIL, who are taken captive at his will."

1 PETER v. 8.

"*Drink not*, be watchful, for THE DEVIL walketh about *seeking* whom he may *drink down*."

108. The Nabathæans named by Diodorus, of Sicily (B. C. 60), lived in Central Arabia, and their vow closely resembled that of the Rechabites, who were probably a portion of the aboriginal tribe. Doubtless these, and the Pythagoreans and Persian magii, after the captivity, had great influence in modifying opinion and practice in the region of Palestine. The Apocrypha and Secular History indeed make certain the *fact* of the influence amongst the pre-Christian Jews, and the early Christians, — so much so, that unless we read the New Testament in the light of this fact, many of its allusions, even its words, will fail to yield up the truth to us which was patent to the minds of those to whom the original was addressed. Mr. Jowett, M. A., the Professor of Greek at Oxford, may be cited as an impartial authority: —

"Such examples (as Daniel and Tobit) show what the Jews had learned to practise or admire in the centuries immediately preceding the Christian era. So John the Baptist 'fed on lo-

---

108. How was this influence felt, and where manifested? Who witnesses to the temperance opinion and practice in the early church?

custs and wild honey.' A later age delighted to attribute a similar abstinence to James, the brother of our Lord (Hegesippus *apud* Euseb. *H. E.* ii. 23); and to Matthew (Clemens Alexandrinus, *Pæd.* ii. 2, p. 174); heretical writers added Peter to the list of these *Encratites* * (Epiph. *Her.* xxx. 2; Clemens, *Hom.* xii. 6). The Apostolic Canons (xliii.) admit an ascetic abstinence, but denounce those who abstain [like the Magi and Manichees] from any sense of *the impurity of matter.* (See passages quoted in Fritshe, iii. p. 151.) Jewish, as well as Alexandrian and Oriental, influences combined to maintain the practice in the first centuries. Long after it had ceased to be a Jewish scruple, it remained as a counsel of perfection."

Theodoret (A. D. 172) remarks of Tatian, that "he abhors the use of wine." Augustine reproaches "the Manichees with being so perverse that while they refuse wine (*vinum*), and call it the gall of the Prince of Darkness (*fel principiis tenebrarum*), they nevertheless eat of grapes."

Epiphanius, Bishop of Salamis, says of the *Encratites*, "They did not use wine at all, saying, it was of the Devil; and that drinking and using it was sinful." This was evidently said of *intoxicating* wine, not of the natural juice of the grapes, which they are foolishly charged with inconsistently sucking.

Photius observes of the Severians, "They were averse to wine *as the cause of drunkenness.*"

From this doctrine, propagated to the Eremites of the desert, and the later monks of the Arabian border, there can be little doubt that Mohamed borrowed his famous dictum: "Of the fruit of the grape ye obtain an *inebriating* liquor, and also good *nourishment.*" He

* This is the New Testament word for "Temperance," yet applied by the ancients to *abstainers.* Surely, they understood their own language.

issued an interdict against the one, but never against the other. The hostile spirit of controversy, in the early ages, however, led to the doctrine being repudiated *in toto* by the triumphant party, and thus the association of a practical truth with real or supposed errors was, for want of logical discrimination, the unhappy cause of great subsequent corruption of life in the Christian Church. The dark ages set in, followed by the sceptical, and it is only in our day that men are rising above the mists and looking once more at the original and abiding *facts*.

109. The most remarkable of all the religious communities of antiquity, were the ESSENES and THERAPEUTÆ, with their kindred associates. We are indebted for our knowledge of them to two writers, — namely, Josephus, the Jewish historian, and Philo, another Jew of the Alexandrian school. Their tenets and practices, in many curious particulars, bore so great a resemblance to those of the early Christians, that some learned writers have contended that they *were* Christians, protecting themselves from persecution and probable extinction under the veil of a secret orthodox sect.

Josephus thus writes of them in his "Jewish Antiquities" (xv. 11), — "These men live the same kind of life as do those whom the Greeks call Pythagoreans." . . .

In his "Wars" (ii. 8), he further says : —

"The Essenes are Jews by nation, and a society of men friendly to each other beyond what is to be found among any other people. They have an aversion to sensuous pleasure in the same manner as to that which is truly evil. Tem-

---

109. Who were the Essenes and Therapeutæ? Give Josephus' description of them. What do these facts *evidence* in the background?

perance (*teen enkrateian*), and to keep their passions in subjection, they esteem a virtue of the first order. *They are long-livers*, so that many of them arrive to the age of a hundred years; which is to be ascribed to their simple and plain diet; and the *temperance* and *good order* observed in all things."

Behind these facts concerning ancient teetotalism, there rests a deep, dark shadow, lit up anon with a lurid glare, the evidence of a still more ancient intemperance. Far as we go back, — beyond the verge of history, into the dim twilight of tradition, — we still find the traces of that ruin and wretchedness which ever follow in the track of strong drink. The precautions and protests of prudent and holy men, the prohibitions of the All-wise, the associations of mankind upon the basis of a common bond of union, a protective pledge and badge of brotherhood, point to a terrible background of *antecedent mischief and misery*, to a long experience of sorrowing hearts, of broken hopes, of blighted homes. When shall the cup of instruction be full?

110. Nor is modern history less significant and conclusive than ancient. If Oriental nations and tribes have been cursed by drink, — Kalmuck and Chinese, Hindoo, Persian, Arab and Copt, Syrian and Jew, — so have all the peoples of Europe, Greek or Roman, from the southern Sclavonian to the Hibernian Celt, from the Muscovite and the Lap to the Scandinavian tribes of many lands and names, Norwegian or Swede, Dane, Norman, and Anglo-Saxon, or Anglo-American.

---

110. What is the lesson of modern history? Name some of the nations, where amidst, vast varieties of social and physical conditions, intemperance still riots.

In this experiment races may mingle, climates may change, social conditions may be revolutionized, but the old *nexus* remains, — drink, drunkenness, and riot, — drink and degradation, drink and sensuality, drink and disease, madness, crime. Italy, with its happy climate, Norway, with its comfortable homes, France, with its wine, Bavaria, with its beer, Prussia, with its education, Ireland, with its poverty, England, with its wealth, Scotland, with its whiskey and religion, our own American States, with their schools and freedom, are, one and all, examples of the inefficacy of *all* these conditions even to arrest the growth of intemperance, much less to suppress and extinguish the vice.

111. A passage or two from Schlosser's "History of the Nineteenth Century," in relation to Prussia and Sweden, will be instructive. In Prussia, "The Council of Education, according to Büsching, who was a member, used every possible means to prevent non-commissioned officers, *addicted to brandy*, or incapable invalids, from being appointed teachers. . . The king (Frederick II.) insisted that his invalids should be provided for. . . What, however, is more melancholy than all, is, that in order to support a military school for nobles, he suffered recourse to be had to *lotteries*, which, as is well known, *are as ruinous to the morals of the poorest classes of the people* as brandy-drinking." (Vol. v., p. 7.) "In Sweden, the higher estates had, by law, diminished the enjoyment of brandy to the peasantry; the peas-

---

111. What curious legislation is recorded concerning Prussia and Sweden? What was the effect of extending free licenses in Sweden? Has that policy been reversed, and with what result?

ants, therefore, were desirous of avenging themselves by insisting upon the prohibition of coffee. . . The noble Hanoverian oligarchs decreed that the *peasants* should no longer drink coffee!" (p. 12.) Thus the government made it easy to do wrong and hard to do right.

"Gustavus (1775) had recourse to the Russian principle respecting the distillation of spirits, and introduced it into Sweden. This new privilege proved ruinous to the country, because *the income of the monarch increased just in proportion as the morality, health, and prosperity of the people declined.* The ruin and corruption of a nation, which had been, for ages, distinguished for the vigor and simplicity of the people, were effected by *converting the corn necessary for their subsistence,* and which was even partly imported, *into liquid poison,* and that too to increase the revenues of the crown." (Vol. iv., p. 370.) Of late years, the old bad policy has been discarded, especially in Norway, in consequence of the earnest agitation of the temperance question; and, now, the corn grown is found to be, not only adequate to the subsistence of the people, but affords a large surplus for *exportation.*

Sweden furnishes yet another example. It has a full and active machinery for instruction; yet, excluding offences against the forest laws, there was, in 1830, one criminal to 320 of the population; and one crime in 11 was *committed in drink.* From 1785 to 1825, the population increased 20 per cent., but the consumption of brandy 400 per cent., notwithstanding the education.*

* "Swedish clergy highly educated and intelligent (p. 303). A great variety of educational establishments exist, both private and public. The order of the peasants (yeomen) number 2,500,000, and own *double the property* of all other classes put together." — ("Scott's Travels," p. 322–3.)

Hence "it is well that we should guard ourselves against undue and extravagant expectations of the amount of good to be derived from school instruction. *Centuries of education will not remove the evils of bad and mischievous customs and laws*, which form, in fact, an indirect education of another kind, often more powerful and lasting in its influence than any series of lessons taught within the walls of a school-room." *

112. Prussia, notwithstanding her unexampled education, is a striking example of the essential *tendency* of alcoholic liquors to create an ever-increasing demand for themselves, and thus to perpetuate the evils of intemperance. The following facts were stated at a public conference, by Dr. Wald, of Konigsberg:—

"The Zollverein consumed 122 millions of dollars' worth of alcoholic liquors. Berlin in 1844, compared with 1745, had one church less, and 1,500 taverns more. Out of 60 children under 6, in the Orphan Asylum, 40 had been taught to sip drams, and 9 had a depraved desire for them. In the vale of Barmen,—renowned for its religious character or profession,—with a population of 80,000, not less than 13,000 were habitual dram-drinkers. In the conscription of that year (1852) for a district of Western Prussia, out of 174 young men, only 4 were admissible, the rest being physically incapacitated by dram-drinking. From year to year, prisons and lunatic asylums became more crowded, while thousands became permanently mad through delirium tremens (of which disease about 100 persons die annually in the hospitals of Berlin alone). Drink-

* "Westminster Review," vol. xxxiv. p. 69.

---

112. What is the actual condition of many parts of Prussia, as respects the effects of drink? What is the mortality arising from excess, in Laibach?

ing, by promoting domestic misery and discord, occasions nine-tenths of the increasing divorces of the country. Finally, one-half of the entire corn and potatoes grown in the north of Germany are converted into spirits, the use of which had increased *ninefold* since 1817." *

Maltè-Brun, the geographer (edition of 1827), had spoken of the Northern Germans as "being robust, frugal, and *intelligent*," as "deprived of beer and spirits,"—"while the Southern Germans, accustomed to wine, are given to drunkenness and superstition." Within one generation, then, the government *temptations* had altered the very character of the people. Lippich calculates, from the mortality returns in Laibach, that 120 of the whole population perished *annually* from excess, and that a *fourth* of all the adults who died there might have been saved by abstinence. The conclusion is irresistible, that Germany has not discovered the cure for drinking.

113. The philosopher and statistician, Quetelet, in his great work on human development,† explodes the fallacy that France is a temperate country. "Of 1,129 murders committed during the space of four years, 446 have been in consequence of quarrels and contentions in taverns." It is true that in large districts, and chiefly the most ignorant, there is little drunkenness and crime (a fact to which Quetelet refers); but that is owing to the fact of the extreme rarity of wine-shops, and to the

* See Report of Bremen Conference. Hertz, Berlin, 1852.

† "Sur l'Homme et le Développement de ses Facultés;" liv. iii.c. 3. (Bruxelles, 1829.)

---

113. What does Quetelet record as to French crime and its cause? What

extreme poverty of the people. In the rich and manufacturing parts, intemperance and its resulting evils abound. Dr. Morel, of the St. Yon Asylum, says, in his work "On the Degeneracy of the Human Race," that "there is always a hopeless number of paralytic and other insane persons, in our hospitals, whose disease is due to no other cause than the abuse of alcoholic liquors. In 1,000 patients, of whom I have made special note, at least 200 owed their mental disorder to *no other cause.*" (p. 109.) Many more, therefore, would be indirectly affected or aggravated by drink. M. Behic, in his "Report on Insanity," says, "Of 8,797 male, and 7,069 female lunatics, 34 per cent. of the men, and 6 of the women, were made insane by intemperance. This is the most potent and frequent cause." * French journals note, that years of plenty in the wine-districts are years of disorder and crime for the country at large. The "Annals of Hygienne," for 1863, observe, that, "in wine-growing countries, *delirium tremens* and alcoholism are most frequent." (Tome xxvii., p. 203.) The plain fact is, that, though partly owing to the temperament of the people, and partly to the better arrangements of the police, outrageous and besotted drunkenness may be less frequent, or less apparent, yet the serious and essential evils are as great there as in any other country. Sensuality pervades their life, crime is very prevalent, suicides are in excess, population is arrested, and extreme longevity is rarer than in almost any other

* "Medical Times," Jan. 1867, p. 37.

---

**does Dr. Morel say of insanity and drink? What M. Behic? What quan-**

land. In France everybody drinks, young and old, male and female, and we find one centenarian amongst 360,000 persons; in the United States of America, one in every 9,000. Sixteen years ago, Dr. Bell estimated the whole of the alcohol drank in France in the shape of spirit, wine, and cider, as equal to four gallons of proof spirit per head *annually*, for all ages, men, women, and infants. It is certainly not less now. Statistics obtained by Mr. E. C. Delavan, from the French government, in 1867, enable us to say that the production of wine in 1865 was rated at 1,089,000 gallons, and of distilled spirits and other drinks, 427,746,000. Of this enormous quantity, of which only a small proportion is exported, 77,000,000 gallons of wine are consumed in Paris alone, which is 42 gallons per head yearly! The *cost* of all this to the retail consumer, after deducting one-third for drinks exported, cannot be less than *one billion* of dollars,—one thousand million of dollars spent in what is not food, but which vitiates the morals, poisons the brain, and destroys the happiness of the people! *

In France, in 1856, there were 360,000 drink-shops, besides inns, cafés, etc. Over all France, one drunkery to 100 persons of all ages. De Watteville, the economist, puts drinking *third* in order among the fifteen di-

* A. Husson, of the Hotel de Ville, in his "Consommations de Paris" (1856), states that previous to 1830, each Parisian took 9 litres (quarts) of *brandy* per head annually; now 14 litres (or 3½ gallons).

---

tity of Alcohol, estimated as proof spirit, is consumed in France, per head? How many gallons of wine, per head, in Paris? What number of mere drinking-houses are there in France?

rect causes of pauperism. To this we have to add nearly five millions of pounds of tobacco, in smoking which the emperor and empress set the fashion! With such habits and temptations and examples can we wonder that every third birth in Paris is illegitimate, and that there are 60,000 criminals permanently residing in the prisons of the Seine? Mr. Dickens' "Household Words," while defending the beer-shop at home, thus discourses of its counterpart abroad: —

"*The wine-shops are the* COLLEGES *and* CHAPELS *of the poor in France.* History, morals, politics, jurisprudence, and literature, *in iniquitous forms*, are all taught in these colleges and chapels, where professors of evil continually deliver these lessons, and where hymns are sung nightly to the demon of demoralization. In these haunts of the poor, theft is taught as the morality of property; falsehood as the morality of speech; and assassination as the justice of the people. It is in the *wine-shop* the cabman is taught to think it heroic to shoot the middle-class man who disputes his fare. It is in the wine-shop the workman is taught to admire the man who stabs his faithless mistress. It is in the wine-shop the doom is pronounced of the employer who lowers the pay of the employed. The *wine-shops* breed — in a physical atmosphere of malaria, and a moral pestilence of envy and vengeance — the men of crime and revolution. *Hunger is proverbially a bad counsellor, but drink is a worse.*"

114. Even in benighted France, however, there is here and there a temperance oasis, — a green spot in the waste. In the little, quaint city of Villaneuvette, there

---

**How much tobacco is consumed? What does Mr. Dickens' periodical call the wine-shops of the poor?**

**114. What two little towns in France prove the benefit of prohibiting the**

is only one café and one hotel, both closed at nine o'clock. There pauperism, beggary, and illegitimacy are all but unknown; and the people live long and happily. At St. Aubin d'Ecronville, in Normandy, is an establishment for the production of those beautiful anatomical models which have made M. Anzoux so well known. He educates boys to this artistic work, and has generally about 70 persons in his employment. Neither smoking nor drinking is allowed. The *ouvriers* of St. Aubin never enter a wine-shop, nor waste a sou in smoking. Their hands are always steady, their heads always clear. The consequence is, that they economize and put money in the bank. What was formerly a beggarly, dirty village is now a thriving and beautiful little town.

In European Turkey, amongst another race of people, and in a beautiful climate, we have an example which should be instructive to America, and especially to the patrons and producers of Catawba wine.

Mr. Schauffler, American Missionary at Constantinople, thus wrote in 1827:—

"The prevalence of drunkenness upon *pure wine* has been on the increase for some ten years past. *Before*, it was *checked* by the high price of wine. It is a matter of regret that the poor German farmers [settled in Moldavia] should have entered upon a field of industry [wine-growing] promising in pecuniary respects, but so ruinous in its moral bearings. The number of *wine houses and cellars has been on a most alarming increase* since wine has become indigenous. It has often been said that

---

**traffic, and shunning the public house? Give the particulars. What is the result of wine-making in European Turkey? Give Mr. Schauffler's testimony.**

pure wine did not produce that *artificial appetite* for more. This is certainly incorrect."

Of course it is, for alike in America, Normandy, and England, experience proves that cider (which is apple-wine) is simply a stepping-stone to stronger drinks; not a preventative but a provocative.

115. Great Britain, however, perhaps, provides more varied illustrations of the whole subject of intemperance and its remedy than any other modern country, owing to the diversity of its laws, institutions, and peoples. In Scotland, with a lowland Saxon and a highland Celtic population, was seen the prevalence of drinking in all ages, from the most barbarous to the most refined, — drinking in peace and in war, in castle and bothie, — drinking amongst the pious and profane, with highland cateran and chief, with town bailie or lowland laird, and amongst the learned and polished circles of modern Athens. No place clean. It was the frightful results of pauperism, impiety, disease, madness, and crime, which, a few years back, led to the enactment of a measure for abolishing the selling of drink at toll-bars, and for the closing of dram-shops and public houses on the Sabbath, — a measure which has effected, according to the verdict of the Royal Commission, a vast benefit for the country, and, in conjunction with higher duties upon whiskey, sensibly arrested the growth of drunkenness, pauperism, and crime. Notwithstanding the occasional failure of town councils to do their duty, and see

---

115. What country well illustrates the entire question of Temperance, and why? State the facts concerning *Scotland*. What measures have conferred great benefit upon the country? What was the effect in Edinburgh?

the law *enforced* by their police, it is a measure which evinces the power of repression in a very striking way. *Before* it passed, the prison at Edinburgh was about to be enlarged at great expense; *after* its enactment, a large number of cells were found to be superfluous. If one day's suppression of the traffic can do so much, what might not seven days' suppression accomplish?

116. Ireland, again, has a peculiar people and a strange history. Its Celtic and impressionable race has at times been sober, and at others dissipated and intemperate to an excess, but during the lifetime of Father Mathew rose to a height of enthusiasm and sublime self-abnegation which attracted the attention and sympathy of the whole civilized world. At one time, we ourselves saw the secretary of this Apostle of Temperance, enrolling members amongst the *sixth million* of his disciples. One great error was committed, however, — that of not preventing the future inroad of the traffic by erecting a legal bulwark while the inspiration was upon the nation. Failing this, however, the temptations returned, the enthusiasm waned, the disciples fell away, and now the monument to Father Mathew, in the city of Cork, is desecrated by a perfect circle of whiskey-dens, where the people drink to their own degradation, and defile the precincts of a statue which should be sacred to purity and temperance.

All the bad laws and influences that have made Ireland a byword and a reproach to England have been aggravated by drink. Much of her agrarian outrages could

---

116. What is remarkable about *Ireland*? How many disciples did Father Mathew enroll, and what was the issue of the reformation? Why did it

not have existed save for that. Her poverty has been transmuted into pauperism and famine by the same vile agent; her industry has been paralyzed, her morals corrupted. A leaf or two from her history will at once demonstrate the curse of drinking and the blessings of temperance. In Ireland, failure of crops has several times proved a blessing, by leading to the suppression of distilling. The natural *loss* has suspended the self-inflicted *curse;* the gain has been the lessened evil.

For example, in 1757–8, 1760–1, the average balance of *loss* between corn imported and corn exported was £78,282. But in 1759, when, owing to a bad harvest, the distilleries were stopped, there was a balance of *profit* of £4,584. "The salutary effects of which," says a contemporary observer, "*were the restoring new vigor to our languishing manufactures*, and a visible reformation in the morals of the people." *

117. In 1808–9, 1812–13, again, for parts of those years distillation was prohibited. Of oats, the grain mainly used by the distillers, the total quantity exported in 1808–11–12–15 is given from the averages of the Customs returns,† and the quantity of corn spirits *paying duty* is added: —

* "Earnest Addresses to the People, against Drinking Spirituous Liquors," by W. Henry, D.D., F.R.S. Dublin, 1761.

† Vide "Parliamentary Papers," vii., 1823.

---

decline? What great omission was there? What was the result of closing the distilleries? Give the testimony of Dr. Henry, in 1761.

117. What was the pecuniary effect of partial prohibition of the distilleries in 1808–9, 1812–13? What was the *moral* and *social* effect of stopping the distilleries in those years?

| Oats in barrels. | Value. | Spirits in Gallons. | |
|---|---|---|---|
| 4,299,567 | £4,080,806 | 9,647,091 | *Years of Dearth and Prohibition.* |
| 3,033,831 | 2,267,225 | 22,419,197 | *Years of Plenty and Distillation.* |
| 1,265,736 | £1,813,591 | *Gain in four years, by bad harvests.* | |

Thus, even in years of dearth, the prohibition of distilling increased the oats exported nearly *two millions of pounds* in value; so that, making allowance for the parts of years during which the distilleries were in operation, the capital of the country was increased by half a million annually, with a positive gain in all social and moral aspects besides.

Mr. Sergeant Lloyd, before the Lords' Committee on the state of Ireland in 1825, assigned "the easy access to spirits" as the chief predisposing cause of the peasant disturbances in the county of Limerick.

Under the prohibition from June to December, 1808, and from March to December, 1809, whiskey rose from 8s. to 18s. the gallon, and *at once* sobriety and order supplanted riot and debauchery. In 1810, when the prohibition ceased, "*the commitments increased nearly fourfold;*" and the Lord Mayor of Dublin directed public attention to its cause. So, again, when the distilleries were stopped from February, 1812, to September, 1813, crime also stopped; and when they revived to their work of destruction, crime revived with them.

| Years. | Prisoners. | Years. | Prisoners. | 1 3-4 year's decrease. |
|---|---|---|---|---|
| 1811 | 10,737 | 1812 | 9,908 | 2,093 |
| 1814 | 10,249 | 1813 | 8,985 | |
| | 20,086 | | 18,893 | |

Thus, even in years of want, a partial measure, merely rendering drink dearer, was attended with a reduction in crime of *one-sixth*, when under ordinary circumstances it would have increased largely.

118. Another illustration is derived from a comparison of the years of Father Mathew's great success with *ordinary* years of intemperance. Lord Morpeth declared in the commons that "the heaviest offences, such as homicides, outrages upon the person, assault with intent to murder, aggravated assaults, cutting and maiming," had been greatly diminished.

His triumphs were from the year 1839 up to the culminating era of 1845, when the movement began to decline, in part owing to emigration, in part to the natural subsidence of *all* mere enthusiasms, but in 1847, 8, 9, to the desolation of the famine and the exodus.

Take convictions for OFFENCES AGAINST THE PERSON, as those most likely to arise from excitement, and to be least liable to fluctuation from varying social influences of an ordinary character, and of course, excluding the famine years, as subject to a disturbing influence.

---

118. What was the effect of Fathew Mathew's reform in respect to crime in Ireland? In what proportion was crime lessened? State the facts as to

11

| Six *ordinary drinking years*, during which, exclusive of *much* illicit whiskey, 70,913,546 gallons of British spirits paid duty.* | | Six *less intemperate years*, during which, with *little* illicit distillation, 42,506,190 gallons of spirits paid duty.† | |
|---|---|---|---|
| 1834......5,902<br>1835......5,832<br>1836......6,099<br>1837......2,631<br>1838......2,710<br>1839......3,156 | Total crime of the first class.<br>.......26,330 | 1840......2,584<br>1841......2,324<br>1842......2,128<br>1843......2,172<br>1844......2,093<br>1845......1,869 | Total crime of the first class.<br>.......13,170<br>A reduction of one-half. |

Take, now, two quinquennial periods, and see what they establish in regard to "Convictions at Quarter Sessions and Assize," compared with the years ***remarkable for diminished consumption of whiskey.***

| | Spirits charged duty. | Serious crime. | Executions. |
|---|---|---|---|
| *Ordinary drinking years*, 1835–39.......................... | 59,770,892 | 64,520 | 59 |
| *Partially temperate* 1840-44... | 33,766,525 | 47,027 | 21 |
| Difference .............. | 26,004,367 | 17,493 | 38 |

The prison returns for Ireland, compared with the revenue returns, show that a legal *check* to drinking is also a check to crime.

* Taken from the returns of the Inland Revenue Office. See "Report on Public Houses," 1853, p. 656. At the beginning of this period, 1,296 persons were confined in prison for illicit distilling; in 1840 only 175, and in 1841 only 171.

† In several counties during this period, there happened the unprecedented circumstance of the *presentation of white gloves* to the Judges.

six contrasted years. As to the increase or decrease of consumption. As to the decrease by means of increased duties.

| | Duty. | Gals. Spirits. | Cases of Imprisonment. |
|---|---|---|---|
| 1854. | 3s. 4d., and 4s. ........... | 8,440,734 | 73,733 |
| 1855. | Duty, 4s., 6s., and 6s. 2d.. | 6,228,856 | 54,431 |
| | | 2,211,878 | Decrease......19,302 |

It follows from these figures that to license drink-selling is to license felony, and breed crime. So true is the saying of the jurist Mittermaier, that "all his investigations led him to the same sad truth, that *society prepares the crime.*"

119. England, again, with her mingled races of Frisian and Saxon, Dane, Norman, Fleming, and Welsh, with her gentry habituated to wine, her city populations to gin, her shopkeepers to brandy, her southern and western peasantry to cider, and the bulk of her laborers to ale and beer, — has earned for her citizens the unenviable notoriety of being "drunken Englishmen." Not that they are in reality greater drinkers than the Dutch, the Germans, the Russians, or the French, but they display less reticence and self-control in the *manifestation* of their propensities. The whole history of this country is a comment upon the maxim, that *as are the facilities for the sale of strong drink so is the proportionate drunkenness, pauperism, and crime of the people.** The evil of drinking is all pervasive; it finds

* See Dr. Lees' "Condensed Argument for the Legislative Prohibition of

119. What is the *law* of the spread of intemperance in England? How

its way into church and state, aristocracy and democracy; the seats of learning, and the homes of ignorance; and at the present time (1867), the expenditure upon liquor for Great Britain is as follows:—

| | |
|---|---|
| Home-made spirits charged duty (selling, retail, at 20s. per gallon), . . . . . . . | £22,516,336 |
| Foreign and colonial spirits (at 27s. per gallon), . | 7,978,885 |
| Malt liquors (2 bushels malt per barrel of 36 gallons, at 48s.),* . . . . . . . . | 60,261,393 |
| Wines (but chiefly the stronger ones), at 15s. per gallon, . . . . . . . . . | 9,995,937 |
| Cider and perry, home-made fruit wines, black beer, etc., . . . . . . . . . | 507,449 |
| | £101,260,000 |
| Or, in American currency, the enormous sum of | $506,300,000 |

120. Of this sum, Professor Leoni Levi calculates that the *working-classes* spend about *one-third*, or, in round numbers, the vast sum of £70,000,000, which equals the entire government expenditure of the country for imperial purposes! It is a self-imposed taxation very lamentable and leads, in the loss of time and health,—

the Liquor Traffic,"—a volume of 160 pages, founded on the larger Essay, to which the Alliance awarded the prize of 100 guineas ($500 currency.) The whole subject is exhaustively treated.

* There were in 1866, exactly 50,217,828 bushels of malt charged duty for *home* consumption, which would produce, with water adulteration, above 1,000,000,000 of gallons of beer for 30,000,000 of people; being at the rate of 33 gallons each person, exclusive of other alcoholics.

---

much in pounds is expended on Alcohol in Great Britain? How much in dollars?

120. What is the share of *working-men's* expenditure? What does this self-imposed taxation bring with it? Who are the channels for the distri-

the true capital of the worker — in deteriorated labor, in pauperism, disease, and crime, to a second loss, which cannot be estimated at much less than the first. The *channels* and *agents* for this wasteful expenditure are an immoral and demoralizing body of men, called publicans, who unblushingly avow that their politics are those of the *trade*, first and last, and who are everywhere, as a body, found ranged against such ameliorating agencies as schools, free libraries, and temperance societies, but in favor of races and betting, prize-fights and cock-fights, — whose literature, from "Bell's Life" down to "The Licensed Victualler's Guardian," is that of extremely "low life." These men are licensed by the law to carry on their debasing and deadly trade! They are always on the increase, and bring after them a proportionate increase of criminals and police. These crime-breeders have, for three periods, numbered as follows for England and Wales alone: —

| | 1860–1. | 1862–3. | 1866–7. |
|---|---|---|---|
| Publicans .......... | 67,145 | 66,695 | 70,457 |
| Beer-sellers only... | 43,986 | 47,212 | 53,971 |
| Wine-dealers ....... | 1,467 | 2,657 | 4,448 |
| Total Retailers..... | 112,598 | 116,564 | 128,876 |
| Wholesale dealers.. | 3,055 | 3,533 | 6,341 |

bution of this drink? What number of traffickers in England? In Scotland? In Ireland? What has been the result of this increase in the traders?

In Scotland, in 1866, there were 98 brewers only, and 12,472 licensed victuallers.

In Ireland, in 1866, there were 91 brewers only, and 15,541 licensed victuallers.

Scotland has, besides, 132 distillers; Ireland, 60.

As the *temptations* gradually increase, drinking as gradually and certainly extends, notwithstanding the unparalleled influences of a physical, social, and religious nature which, during the past half century, have been *counteracting* the tendency of the system. In 1857, each person in England averaged a consumption of nearly *two gallons of pure alcohol*, but in 1866, of $2\frac{1}{5}$. In 1857, each person in Scotland consumed on the average $1\frac{1}{5}$, but in 1866 nearly $1\frac{1}{2}$ gallon. In 1857, each person in Ireland had an average of three-fourths of a gallon, but in 1866 above four-fifths.

121. The third line is very instructive in the above table: that which shows how the *wine licenses*, chiefly granted to confectioners, grocers, and eating-house keepers, had quadrupled in a few years.* The Hon. W. E. Gladstone perversely adopted the theory that the love of heavy-wet and potent drams was to be eradicated by

* An action brought into the Court of Common Pleas, in November, 1868, for the recovery of a wine bill, elicited the fact, that at a banquet held in the preceding August, at the New Market, King's Cross, London, over which the Common Sergeant of the city presided, 521 bottles of wine were drunk by the 180 guests,—i. e., THREE BOTTLES EACH! The writer has seen the wine bills of aristocratic clubs, which show that the proportion of drinking in the city is not greater than that in the West end.

---

How much *Alcohol* is consumed, on the average, in England, in Scotland, and in Ireland?

121. What was the result of Mr. Gladstone's scheme of *wine licenses* for

favoring a taste for "light wines;" and so, in spite of temperance warnings, he obstinately persisted in his plan. The results have been disastrous in the extreme. Young people, servants, and married women, who could not be seen in a dram-shop, have been tempted to drink the new and fashionable liquor, falsely branded as "innocent." It has done its work, and created, in ten thousand instances, an appetite for stronger stimulants. In 1868, there was a great scandal — one of many — created by the fall of a distinguished and aristocratic clergyman; whereupon the newspapers, which support the *causes*, give a homily upon the *effects!* Notably so, the London "Daily Telegraph," — a bitter opponent of abstinence and prohibition, as well as a constant perverter of American affairs. We cite its exact words: —

"Drink may doubtless sap a man's brains, weaken his powers, and even convert, as if by a harlequin's wand, a gentleman into a blackguard. The tale does but once more point the moral that he who *begins* to yield can never know whither the terrible habit may carry him. So stern and so steady is the march of its evil influence, that insensibly a man dwindles down into the shadow of himself, and can never win back the strength and the courage he has lost. 'No one drinks nowadays!' says Mrs. Grundy. Well, people no longer get drunk in the middle of the day, or reel into a theatre in the state which was common during the old days of the legitimate drama; but *the doctors tell us*, and the doctors ought to know, *that within the last few years there has been a fresh outbreak of the drinking mania*, not amongst the frequenters of the public house, *but in good society — in the home.* We cannot flatter ourselves that the report is exaggerated. Such propensities

---

confectioners? Give the words of the "Daily Telegraph," describing the consequences. Give an example of middle-class "temperance."

commonly seize upon society by fits and starts; and just now the unhappy suspicion again prevails, that ladies themselves occasionally take rather more than is good for them, under the pretence of 'supporting the system.' It seems but too true that *a dark shadow is cast on many homes by the fatal habit of secret intemperance*, and that, in not a few cases, the victims of the degrading vice have the excuse neither of ignorance nor of poverty."

But what excuse, we ask, have the legislators, who create the temptations?

122. The moral work of England is set at nought, and its legitimate fruits blighted by the pest of the traffic. The seminaries of Satan far outnumber the schools of Christ. Take, for example, the Sunday-school system, and follow the pupils into life.

| No. of Prisoners in Jail at *Leeds*. | No. who have attended Sunday school. | No. who have been S. School Teachers. | No. under 18 years of age. | No. under 18 who have attended S. School. | No. who have not attended S. School. |
|---|---|---|---|---|---|
| 282 | 230 | 23 | 33 | 28 | 52 |
| Aug. 14th, 1854. | Or 81 1-2 per cent. | Or 10 per cent. | Or 11 per cent. | Or 84 of column 4. | Or only 18 1-2 per cent. |

The Rev. J. Kingsmill, in his official report on the Pentonville Penitentiary, 1849, says: "Of 1,000 convicts 757 had been scholars in the different day schools,

122. What does the traffic do in relation to Sunday-school scholars and teachers? Give the figures as to prisoners in Leeds jail, and the evidence

high and low, in the country; *and nearly half of that number, on an average, five years.*" (p. 14.)

While we write, there are in England, one million of paupers receiving relief from the public funds, and another million on the verge of pauperism, living, or starving on charity. About every eighth person is either beggar, or pauper, or criminal, or publican who creates him, or policeman who catches him, or judge who tries and condemns him.

Well-regulated minds are at the foundation of a nation's order, economy, and peace, but coextensive with the increase of the traffic has been that of idiotcy and insanity amongst the people. Upwards of 30,000 persons are now in the various lunatic asylums of England and Scotland, operating as a dead weight to civilization, and indicating a still larger number of persons, who, owing to moderate perversion, are either vicious, extravagant, or unreliable, the centres of domestic unhappiness, and the sources of social danger. Lippich found, that of forty children, born of drunken parents, *only six* were in possession of vigorous health, while *two-thirds* of that offspring were nipped wholly in the bud. When the muscular and vascular system is so palpably shrivelled, what must be the injury to the delicate and susceptible nervous system and the brain?

During the last ten years, a million and a half of criminals have been in the prisons, and let loose again. "We are now," says the "London Times," "in the unwonted case of having among us many thousands, taint-

---

of Mr. Kingsmill. What is the amount of pauperism in England? Cite the testimony of the "Times."

ed, stigmatized, corrupted by crime, its slovenly habits and horrid associations. We are surrounded by men, forming no inconsiderable per cent. of the population, asking for work or for charity, — conspiring against our property, and if need be, our lives; spreading the contagion and art of crime, waking while we sleep; combining, while we act each only for self; and forming an *imperium in imperio*, that may lead in time to the most disastrous consequences." There is, indeed, about the drinking system, a prodigality of mischief, — a seduction, virulence, and fermenting fecundity in the reproduction of vice and crime, which are without precedent or parallel.

123. The lives of the people, under a just and wise government, are the *wealth* and *strength* of the nation. It has been ascertained, with much approximate accuracy, from statistics of various kinds, that there are about 30,000 deaths annually in England, *directly* traceable to drinking, and the diseases and accidents it induces; and probably 30,000 more that have had more or less to do, *indirectly*, with the *use* of strong drink. It is certainly the greatest of all the causes of mortality in the army, the heads of which persist in distributing the grog or beer allowance, — a long-since demonstrated evil.*

* In Wales, the temperance and religious elements have prospered, and the drunkeries are greatly less, in proportion to the inhabitants, than in other parts of the kingdom. The consequence is, that crime, especially serious crime, is far rarer. In his charge to the Grand Jury at Denbigh, Lord Chief Justice Bovil said: —

"I have travelled thus far through *North Wales*, and have been able to

---

123. How many lives are prematurely sacrificed to drinking in England? How many die *indirectly*? What is the effect of the grog-rations in the

The reports of the English Registrar-General of births, marriages, and deaths, shall supply one final example of the deadly but untalked-of influence of alcohol in aggravating mortality, as compared with other agencies which excite universal notice, and compel to immediate legislation. What are the facts regarding *accidental* and *wilful* poisoning, which have induced the law-makers to prohibit the sale of poisons by chemists, except under the most stringent and special conditions? The signature of the buyer must be taken, and the poison must be distinctly labelled.

| | 1858. | 1859. | 1860. | |
|---|---|---|---|---|
| Cases of *accidental* poisoning, | 282 | 279 | 240 | 1,188 |
| *Suicide* by poison,* . . | 119 | 112 | 156 | |
| Murder and manslaughter † in three years, . . . | | | | 1,059 |
| Total, . . . . . . . . . . | | | | 2,247 |

congratulate all the grand juries I have met. At one place there was not a bill found for trial, and no cause on the list. In other places there were but few persons for trial, whose cases required little consideration at the hands of either jury or judge." (1868.)

In Caernarvonshire there is one public house to 188 people, and only one criminal to 2,452 inhabitants; in Anglesey, one public house to 216 persons, and only one criminal to 3,900 inhabitants, and *both* counties are low in education. But in Glamorgan (South Wales), though education is above the average, yet, *with one drunkery to* 120 *persons*, there is *three* and *four* times the proportion of crime—or one criminal to 909 of the population.

* The papers show that suicide is often caused by drink-perversion, leading to a loss of self-control; and that poisons are both given and taken in mistake, owing to the obfuscated condition produced by drinking.

† Most of these cases, again, are the direct results of drinking.

---

Army? How many cases of suicide by poison and accidental poisoning are recorded in three years? How many murders and manslaughters? How

These are sad, even terrible facts, to be found in the centre of Christian civilization; but they are in great part, only concomitants or consequences of another demoralizing agency, — *strong drink*, — of which its last fruits are worse for the victims and for mankind. Yet the figures next to be cited, from the returns of the same years, by no means tell the whole story, because false charity towards the dead, and *an unwillingness to hurt the feelings of relatives*, induce the medical attendant to put down *proximate* cause of death (*congestion*, or other disease) rather than the *real* one of drink.*

| | 1858. | 1859. | 1860. | | |
|---|---|---|---|---|---|
| Deaths from drink, . . | 288 | 345 | 318 | = | 951 |
| Deaths from delirium tremens, | 424 | 545 | 457 | = | 1,426 |
| Total, . . . | 712 | 890 | 775 | = | 2,377 |

Thus the whole number of cases of poisoning by arsenic, oxalic acid, and other drugs, was *less than one-half* of those arising from alcohol! — and the deaths, from this last form of poisoning, *exceeded by* 130 *cases the deaths from accidental and self-poisoning, and from murder and manslaughter all put together*. Yet the whole machinery of law and police is set at work to lessen the one set of effects, while the state lends its sanction,

* This is the same as though, to disguise the fact of a pistol-shot, or sword-thrust, the *result* of a duel, the attendant surgeon had certified that "the deceased died of a lesion and rupture of several arteries."

---

many deaths are there from drink and delirium tremens, in excess over those from *poisoning*? and how many in excess over poisoning, murder, and manslaughter combined? What contrast does North Wales present?

and society its silence, to uphold the *causes* of the other!

124. It has been objected, however, that though intemperance doubtless is the cause of many premature deaths, there are *some* diseases which the free use of alcohol prevents, or holds in abeyance, — consumption, to wit. Were this so, it would be no argument for drinking; because it is better that men should pass away in the course of a natural disorder, than with both impaired intellect and morals by a suicidal course of intemperance. Some years ago, Dr. Swett, of New York, stated as a fact, that of 74 cases of death from aggravated intemperance, in persons found in the dead-house, there was not a single case of tuberculous lungs. It may have been so; but it proves nothing against the great mass of contrary facts. Lippich, for instance, in his researches at Laibach, shows that 11 per cent. of drunkards died of consumption. Mr. Neison, the London actuary, found that of 357 drunkards, just 40 — that is, 11 per cent. again — died of phthisis. When we recollect, then, that two-fifths of the cases of consumption perish before their twenty-fifth year, when drunkards are beginning to train, and that 11 per cent. of the population is about the proportion in which persons of *all ages* die of consumption in England, — we have a clear answer to the fallacy; since, *taking equal ages*, while only 7 per cent. of adults perish of consumption, 11 per cent. of drinkers die of

---

* 124. Does the free use of Alcohol arrest or prevent any other disease? Has this been asserted, and in reference to what disease? Have not drunkards a much greater than ordinary proportion of consumption? How is this proved? Give the facts stated by Lippich, Neison, and Huydecoper.

that disease. Mr. Huydecoper, in his earnest address on the evils of strong drink, says: —

"I have, for a continuance of seven years, frequented, as one of the town clergy, the great military hospital at the Hague; and could I lay before you the number of those I saw expire there of *pectoral complaints* and consumption, and from whose dying lips I have heard the confession, that they saw in their sufferings the fruits of their excessive drinking, you would be astonished that so many, even in our father-land, should thus perish in the *bloom of life*." *

125. Mr. Neison, by a series of approximate calculations, reached the fact, that in England 1 in every 74 persons is a confirmed drunkard, and that, out of all the deaths between the three decades from 30 to 60, — which expresses the matured value of the man, — the proportions from drinking, were, 1 in 21, 1 in 16, and 1 in 22. Professor Huss, of Sweden, says that Eskilston, containing 4,000 souls, was so addicted to drink, that of the males 1 in 30, of the females 1 in 40, annually perished. He contrasts this town with the district of Jemtland, where the people were very moderate (though of the same race, and living in the same climate), where the annual mortality is but 1 in 78 of the males, 1 in 82 of the females. In the army, everywhere, the mortality is still more frightful. Dr. Forrey, in his observations on the records of the medical department of the United States army, ascribed to this vice more than half the

* "Een Woord . . van Sterken Drank." Amsterdam, 1853, p. 174.

---

125. What are the proportions of deaths amongst drunkards in England? What in Eskilstun? How does Jemtland *contrast* with this? What was the

deaths. Mr. Huydecoper says, that, among the Dutch, it is reckoned of their soldiers sent on service to the East, from 70 to 75 per 100 die from drink.

It is, therefore, no rhetoric to affirm that, of all the curses that ever visited this earth, intemperance is the most deadly. Fever and plague may visit us, but they do not tarry; famine may come, but it is followed by plenty; while drink, worse than pestilence, sits and broods amongst us, engendering a horrible offspring of sensuality and sin. Intemperance is an invited visitor, the provision for whose banquet is made under sanction of church and state, — whose *license* is pleaded by the victims, under a stolid delusion, from Holy Writ, and made *legal* by the crooked and corrupting policy of legislators!

Russia has been cursed for ages with intemperance, and, since the abolition of serfdom, drunkenness has become at once more common and more dangerous. The government had long made a point of raising a large revenue from corn brandy, not so much by heavy duties as by small licenses for distilling. The consequences were deplored by the late czar, Alexander, but his contemplated reforms were overruled. While we write, however (December, 1868), good news of wise efforts reach us. The taverns are as numerous in St. Petersburgh as anywhere, and are nicknamed "National Banks," for the double reason, that they yield a revenue to the nation, and absorb the money of their customers.

To put an end to the gigantic evils of the system, the

---

**former army mortality in the United States? What amongst the Dutch troops in India?**

government decrees: 1. That the *price* of corn brandy shall be trebled, by increase of duty. 2. That no tavern shall exist in any *main thoroughfare*, to tempt the people passing. 3. That every tavern shall be treated as an *inn*, and pay the customary license fee, — about $350. 4. That no tavern shall be open *within eighty yards of any of the government offices*, which *swarm* in the metropolis; so that this provision is a good stroke of prohibition. It is one virtue of despotic, as of democratic governments, that they are thus *able* to treat "vested interests" with contempt.

---

## VIII.

## The National Question and the Remedy.

126. The United States of North America have the unquestioned honor of originating the first systematic and organized plan for the suppression of intemperance; at least amongst the Western nations and in modern times. Here, as in the mother country, it had for ages been considered, that legal license and supervision of the traffic were all that could be done to repress intemperance, beyond the appeals of the moralist and the preacher. The people of the States, however, untrammelled by the conservative and conventional habits of

---

**126. Where did the first systematic endeavor to suppress intemperance originate? What conditions made America more favorable to its success than the old country?**

the old country, were not disposed to accept the great curse as a thing absolutely necessary and inevitable; but, on the contrary, as a practical people, engaged in hewing out a new form of society and civilization, set themselves to ascertain the *reason* of things being as they were, and then straightway began the work of reform. There were, of course, great difficulties in the way, — of interest, prejudice, appetite, and fashion, — but these were neither so inveterate nor so vast as in Great Britain, where a new truth has to fight its way over the social *debris* of a thousand years. Besides, what were difficulties to the genius of a people who had just emerged, not only safely, but triumphantly, from a long and terrible conflict for their political independence, and who had become a nation of sturdy Republicans in spite of English king and oligarchy? Hence the notion of a needed reform, of a *work to be done*, having once been fairly injected into the minds of the people, they pursued, and are pursuing it, with unfaltering purpose, and steady, invincible zeal. The occasions, rise, and progress of the remarkable movement we have now succinctly to record. The enterprise has had its five stages, and is destined to its sixth, ere it reach the culminating point which shall usher in the crowning epoch of civilization.*

## I.

127. There was the period of Chaos, when darkness brooded over the elements of social life in the States.

* Namely: 1. A confused perception of the EVIL. 2. Attempts at *regulating* the machinery of mischief. 3. Era of vague *Temperance*. 4. That of *Total Abstinence*. 5. The *No-license* agitation. 6. The epoch of *Prohibitive State Law*.

The freedom which the people exercised, at a period of great political and warlike excitement; the abundance of their means; the cheapness of liquor, with an almost open traffic, and other facilities for its purchase, — had produced their inevitable fruits. The country was overrun with intemperance, the cities were overflowed with disorder, the poorhouses filled with paupers, the jails crowded with criminals, — army, navy, and populace alike cursed with rum. Yet from the earliest period of the history of the States the sale of liquor had been looked upon with suspicion, and the worst forms of it absolutely *prohibited.*

In the town records of East Hampton, Long Island, for 1651, is an order of a town meeting, "That *no man shall sell any liquor but such as are deputed thereto by the town;* and such men shall not let youths, and such as are under other men's management, remain drinking at unseasonable hours; and such persons shall not have *above half a pint* at a time among four men." In 1655, the authorities "ordered, for the prevention of drunkenness among the Indians, by selling Strong Water, *First,* That no man shall carry any to them to sell, nor send them any, nor employ any to sell for them; nor sell them any liquor *in the town* for the present drinking, above two drams at one time; and to sell to no Indians but such as are sent by the sachem, and shall bring a written ticket from him, *which shall be given him by the town,* and he shall not have above a quart at a time."

---

**127. What are the *six* stages of the temperance enterprise? How did the old law treat the traffic? Give an example of prohibition. When did the business of distilling commence?**

Bancroft, under the date of 1676, has a summary of a new constitution for *Virginia*, in place of the tyrannical one of the aristocratic-proprietary. We quote the last sentence and the appended note from Hening.

"*The sale of wines and ardent spirits was absolutely prohibited (if not in Jamestown, yet otherwise) throughout the whole country.*"

Hening, ii. 361: "*Ordinances to sell and utter man's meate, horse meate, beer, and cyder, but no other strong drink whatsoever.*"

The business of making and distilling spirit commenced in Boston in the year 1700, when West-India molasses was converted into New England rum. In 1794, the distillation of *whiskey* from rye commenced in Western Pennsylvania. In 1815, the number of distilleries in the States had increased to 40,000, destroying 10,000,000 bushels of breadstuffs, to make 30,000,000 gallons of poison. Ten million gallons of *rum* were also manufactured annually at that time.

128. Shortly before the establishment of independence, the evil of *distillation* attracted the notice of the patriots, at one of their first Congresses. On the 27th February, 1774, the following resolution appears to have passed unanimously: —

"*Resolved*, that it be recommended to the *several legislatures* in the United States immediately to pass laws the most effectual for putting an *immediate stop* to the pernicious practice of *distilling grain*, by which the most extensive evils are likely to be derived, if not quickly prevented."

Dr. B. Franklin, Dr. Benj. Rush, and other signers of

---

128. What part of the system first attracted the attention of the early

the Declaration of independence, were members of this congress.

In March, 1788, an act passed the Legislature of the Empire State, entitled "An act to lay a duty on strong liquors, and *for the better regulation of inns and taverns.*" It provided that the Commissioners of Excise should not grant permits to any person to sell strong drink and spirituous liquors for the purpose of keeping a tavern, unless it should appear to them that such inn or tavern was *necessary* for the accommodation of travellers, and that the person applying for the permit was of *good character;* and that no person should sell strong drink, or spirituous liquors, *to be drank in his house, without first entering into a recognizance not to keep a disorderly or gambling house,*—and that if any person shall be convicted of any offence against this act, it should be lawful for the Court of General Sessions to suppress his permit.* It is clear, therefore, that the *old* laws acknowledge that the sale of liquor, without a *special permit* from the State, is a social offence.

129. About the year 1790, there was published in Philadelphia, a thin volume of "Sermons on Intemperance," apparently written by a physician,—we believe, Dr. Rush,—which seems to have attracted attention, and

* A similar act was passed *April 7th,* 1801, which *prohibited the sale of spirituous liquors by retail, or to be drank in the house of the seller,* and restrained and limited the power of the Commissioners of Excise in granting licenses; and contained a further provision, that all offences against any of its provisions shall be deemed *misdemeanors,* punishable by fine and imprisonment. This act was embodied in the New York Revised Laws of 1813.

---

Congresses? What prominent men took part in the discussion? On what basis was the traffic placed?

eventually to have led to a remarkable and most influential proceeding on the part of the medical profession of that city. The fact we refer to is explained in the following document: —

"DELETERIOUS EFFECTS OF DISTILLED SPIRITS ON THE HUMAN SYSTEM.

"*Communicated to the Senate, December* 29, 1790.

"To the Senate and House of Representatives of the United States, the memorial of THE COLLEGE OF PHYSICIANS in the city of Philadelphia, respectfully showeth: —

"That they have seen with great pleasure the operation of the National Government, which has established order in our country.

"They rejoice to find, among the powers which belong to this government, that of restraining by certain duties the consumption of distilled spirits in our country.

"It belongs more peculiarly to men of other professions to enumerate the pernicious effects of these liquors upon morals and manners. Your memorialists will only remark, that a great portion of the most obstinate, painful, and mortal disorders which affect the human body are produced by distilled spirits; and they are not only destructive to health and life, but they impair the faculties of the mind, and thereby tend equally to dishonor our character as a nation, and degrade our species as intelligent beings.

"Your memorialists have no doubt that the rumor of a plague, or any other pestilential disorder which might sweep away thousands of their fellow-citizens, would produce the most vigorous and effective measures in our government to prevent or subdue it.

"Your memorialists can see no just cause why the more certain and extensive ravages of distilled spirits upon life

---

129. For what is the year 1790 remarkable? Give the purport of the memorial of the College of Physicians.

should not be guarded against, with corresponding vigilance and exertion, by the present rulers of the United States.

"Your memorialists beg leave to add further, that the *habitual use of distilled spirits, in any case whatever, is wholly unnecessary;* that they neither fortify the body against the morbid effects of heat or cold, nor render labor more easy or more productive; and that there are many articles of diet and drink, which are not only safe and perfectly salutary, but preferable to distilled spirits for the above-mentioned purposes.

"Your memorialists have beheld with regret the feeble influence of reason and religion in restraining the evils which they have enumerated. They centre their hopes, therefore, of an effectual remedy for them in the wisdom and power of the legislature of the United States; and in behalf of the interests of humanity, to which their profession is closely allied, they thus publicly entreat the Congress, by their obligations to protect the lives of their constituents, and by their regard to the character of our nation and to the rank of our species in the scale of beings, to impose such heavy duties upon all distilled spirits as shall be effectual to restrain their intemperate use in our country.

"Signed, by order of the College,

"JOHN REDMAN, *President.*

"Attest, SAMUEL POWELL GRIFFITHS, *Secretary.*

"*Philadelphia, Dec. 27th*, 1790."

130. At last the enemy was fairly unmasked, and assailed in the stronghold of popular prejudice, by that very agency most likely to be successful. The ice once broken, Dr. Rush cast aside all reticence, and in 1794 issued his "Medical Inquiries" into the effects of ardent spirits, and announced the doctrine of *abstinence*, which ultimately became the basis of a radical reformation.

---

130. What celebrated physician published a book on the subject, and what *principle* did he announce? What ideas were coming into view?

After combating the errors of popular opinion, and enumerating some of the chief disorders engendered by the *use* (not abuse) of ardent spirits, he says: "It would take a volume to describe *how much* other disorders, natural to the human body, are increased and complicated by them. Every species of inflammatory and putrid fever is rendered *more frequent and more dangerous*, by the use of spirituous liquor." He thus struck boldy at the double superstition, — the virtue of alcohol as diet, and its prophylactic power as medicine. These papers excited inquiry, gradually attracted the attention of reflecting men in his own profession, and, finally, of the reading public. In 1805, he reproduced these views in a pamphlet, which procured a wide circulation. The formation of the first temperance society in modern times was the consequence. It was instituted in Moreau, Saratoga County, on the 13th of April, 1808, under the appellation of "The Union Temperate Society of Moreau and Northumberland." Dr. B. J. Clark was the originator of this idea of *social union* for suppressing the tyranny of *social custom*. The effort, however, remained local.

Philanthropists, senators, and the better part of the people, now began to see the danger which threatened the country and the State, and asked themselves the question, If this agent of disease, this physical, moral, and social pestilence, goes on unchecked, what will be the end? At last, the essential evil of the *drink* was perceived, and the "throne of iniquity" — the legalized machinery for disseminating the evil — rose dimly before the sight. Before, they had blamed the dram-*shop* rather than the *dram* — now, the more fundamental truth was being enforced, that it was the dram that characterized the shop and gave to it its peculiarity of seduction and sequence; while the correlated truth also emerged, that the shop was the centre and heart of temptation, — at once the hand that set the powder and fired the train.*

## II.

131. Out of these workings of light the second epoch had come, — that of systematic regulation. New social truths rose into view. It was seen that the licensed drink house is a licensed *snare*, and that "the more grog-shops the more drunkenness, pauperism, and crime," expressed a connection as certain as any other social law. In 1818–19, the authorities of New York largely reduced the number of *retail* grog-shops. In 1820, the report of the Society for the prevention of Pauperism in New York cites the testimony of the

* Hope, in the shape of prohibition, has at last come to the drunkard. The following was advertised in the papers of the day. We may hear in it the heart-voices of thousands of victims, crying to society, as all men cry to God: "*Deliver us from temptation!*"

"WHEREAS, the subscriber, through the pernicious habit of drinking, has greatly hurt himself in purse and person, and rendered himself odious to all his acquaintance; and finding there is no possibility of breaking off from the said practice *but through the impossibility to find the liquor, he therefore begs and prays that no person will sell him for money, or on trust, any sort of spirituous liquors*, as he will not in future pay for it, but will prosecute any one for an action of damage against the temporal and eternal interests of the public's humble, serious, and sober servant,

"JAMES CHALMERS.

"Witness, WILLIAM ANDREWS.
"NASSAU, *June 28th*, 1795."

---

131. What formula did the theory of regulation imply? In what city was it acted on, and with what results? Give the testimony of the Mayor of New York; and state the proof of a failure. *Note.* — Name a curious advertisement.

mayor: "The effect is very obvious; drunken people are much seldomer seen in our streets. It has had a very important influence on the morals of the community and lessened the number of crimes. Crimes have numerically decreased, and comparatively have very greatly diminished. This *great benefit to the community* is chiefly to be imputed to THE SUPPRESSION OF SO MANY OF THESE POISON-SHOPS, where a man might buy rum enough to make himself beastly drunk for *six cents.*" But such a mode of action depended upon the whim, the moral tone, and circumstances varying in various districts, and was itself so partial that it could not permanently stem the demoralizing stream which swelled up and swept on, carrying upon its fiery bosom the wrecks of home, health, and social prosperity. We find it officially stated, "that *three-fourths* of the assaults and batteries committed in the city and county of New York, and brought before the Court of Sessions, proceed from the degrading use of ardent spirits." In fine, the issue proclaimed that, nationally regarded, regulation was a nullity and a failure.

132. New York was no exceptional city at that time; it was a type of the whole country. The curse had eaten into every department of life; the church, the college, the camp, the change, the marine, the civil service, were alike infected.

President Jefferson said, a little before his death: —

"Were I to commence my administration again, with the knowledge which, from experience, I have acquired, the first

---

132. What was the state of the country as respects drinking? What did

question I would ask with regard to every public candidate for public office should be, *Is he addicted to the use of ardent spirits?*"

Mr. E. C. Delavan says: —

"I know of two bishops who fell, through wine, both brothers. I know of one drinking a whole goblet of sacramental-wine as his part, and then going from the communion table and disgracing himself with women; for which he was tried and unseated."

Prof. Leonard Woods, D.D., Andover, said, in 1836: —

"I remember that at a particular period, before the temperance reformation commenced, I was able to count up nearly *forty* ministers, and none of them at a great distance, who were either drunkards, or so far addicted to drinking that their reputation and usefulness were greatly impaired, if not utterly ruined. I could mention an ordination that took place about twenty years ago, at which I myself was ashamed and grieved to see two aged ministers literally drunk; and a third indecently excited." * "With the light now cast on the subject it seems to me incredible, that a minister of the gospel can be in the habit of using any intoxicating liquor, without injuring his own piety and diminishing the success of his labors. It tends to inflame all that is depraved and earthly, and to extinguish all that is spiritual and holy. *It is poison* to the soul as really as to the body."

133. The politico-economical relations of the question just before the birth of the present movement, in 1826, may be gathered from some calculations made and published, in 1827, by Judge Cranch: —

* Ninth Report of American Temperance Society, p. 47.

---

President Jefferson confess? What was the condition of the church? Give the evidence of Mr. Delavan and Prof. Woods.

UNITED STATES. — "Annual consumption of spirits 72,000,000 gallons; cost to consumers $48,000,000. The number of drunkards 375,000; at least 100 days of their work annually lost to the State, which may be estimated at $5,000,000. 37,500 drunkards annually die, their lives abridged by ten years on the average. Loss to the State (reckoning the profit of their labor, had they been sober at $50 a year) $13,000,000. The expenses of criminal justice amount to $7,000,000 a year. Drunkenness produces three-fourths of the criminals, hence $6,000,000 more to the debit of intemperance. Pursuing these calculations on the same principle as regards the poor, who become so through drunkenness, the loss of labor of the criminals shut up in prison, etc., a total of £100,000,000 sterling is arrived at as the total loss suffered by the country at that time in consequence of the use of strong drinks."

The population of the United States did not then exceed 12,000,000. Wine, cider, and beer not included in these estimates.

134. It may be well to compare these facts with the state of things *now*, after 40 years of temperance agitation, and 14 years of prohibition in several States Some districts may possibly drink as much as then, but others certainly consume far less.

THE STATES. — In 1860, there were 88,002,717 gallons of spirits distilled, and 5,115,140 barrels of fermented liquors brewed [excluding home-made cider], worth $739,020,579 at retail prices; while the value of all the flour, cotton goods, boots, shoes, woollen goods, clothing,

---

133. Who made some calculations, in 1827, as to the cost and consequences of making and using *ardent spirits*, in the United States? What is the total cost per head?

134. Describe the present condition of the States. How many gallons of spirits distilled in 1860? How many barrels of liquors brewed, and what the

and books, newspapers, and other printing, produced in the United States, was $610,000,000. The *time* lost by drinking, cost of crime, pauperism, litigation, etc., would make the total expense at least $1,000,000,000. The civil and diplomatic expenses for 1863 amounted to $11,066,138. Thus the people tax themselves $728,000,000 more for liquor than the cost of their government in ordinary times.

There are 180,000 licensed drink-sellers, which, at twenty customers each, make 2,807,200 tipplers. Hence, as one out of 30 every year finishes his training, and passes into the ranks of the confirmed sots, 93,574 drunkards are annually manufactured, who would form a column, in regular marching order, 26 miles long.

At a low estimate, there are 565,640 persons employed in distilleries, and wholesale and retail liquor stores, and only 146,176 ministers and school-teachers.

Railroads and Liquor. — Mr. Welles, in his report, gives us a table, "showing the aggregate sales" of liquors, at wholesale and retail, "in the several States and territories of the Union, during the fiscal year ending June 30th, 1867, as deduced from the receipts of internal revenue." The value of the retail liquor sales — that is, the first cost to the consumers — reaches, in a single year, the enormous sum of one billion four hundred and eighty-three million four hundred and ninety-one thousand eight hundred and sixty-five dollars ($1,483,491,865), that is, *forty-three dollars for every man, woman,*

---

total cost? How many tipplers annually pass into sots? What would they all number? What was the *total* cost of liquors in 1867? and what *per head*?

*and child in the country.* It is very nearly *one-eighth of the value of the whole year's merchandise of the country* (including liquors), by wholesale and retail dealers, auctioneers, and commercial brokers, — namely, $11,870,337,207. The sum of the wholesale liquor sales is something less than one-half of the retail sales ($600,278,950), which indicates the large profits of this traffic. The total present value of railroads is $1,654,-050,779, which only exceeds the annual cost of the liquor drank, by less than the worth of the railroads in the single State of Pennsylvania.

In the city of *Philadelphia* there are 7,600 rum-shops, 385 churches, and 245 school-houses.

600,000 kegs of lager-beer were brewed in *Milwaukee* in 1867.

135. Statistics of New York City, 1868. — The whole number of places where liquors are publicly retailed in this city is 5,203. Each rum-hole receives a daily average of 134 visits, making an aggregate of 697,-202 per day, 5,183,212 per week, or 218,224,226 visits in one year! Each visit averages at least 15 minutes. *This gives us* 5,455,605 *days of* 10 *hours each, or* 1,848 *years,* the whole value and life of a man from the birth of the Saviour to now! At present wages, each one, if sober and industrious, would earn $1 per day, or $5,455,605 in one year. But this is not all the lost time. The time of at least three persons is occupied by each grog-shop to do its work. This gives us 15,609 persons, — enough to make a large city. At $1 per day for each,

---

135. Give the statistics of New York city, in 1867, as regards the visits to the rum-holes. Express the loss of time by a supposed length of one life.

we have (excluding Sunday), $4,870,008, or an aggregate of $10,325,613 of wasted time by seller and drinker, — a sum sufficient to carry on all the Sunday-school, Missionary, Tract, and Bible societies in the land. But this is a mere fraction of the cost of rum. Each rum-hole *receives* in money a daily average of $141,53, making an aggregate of $763,280 per week, or $38,286,590, per annum, — to which add the value of lost time, and we have $48,612,192.

The total amount received for *licenses*, in 1866, was $1,-225,449.26; in 1867, $1,305,002.27; and in 1868, $1,447,-156.63, making a total in 31 months, of $4,047,608,16.

The total number of *arrests* by the police, for the year ending October, 1868, was 98,861, of which 50,844 were for intoxication and disorderly conduct.*

40,000 kegs of lager-beer are daily consumed in the city of *New York*.

NEW YORK STATE. — The carefully prepared statistics of the New York Prison Association show that there were, in 1863, 21,242 licensed liquor shops, and about 6,750 churches.

136. At the period referred to in §130 the social condition was gloomy enough, but still the friends of morality and order worked on. Trumpet notes were heard over wide districts of the country, indicating the

* Since the passage of the Metropolitan Excise Law, which *prohibits* the sale of liquor on Sunday, the Sunday arrests for drunkenness have been reduced nearly one-half, and about 3,000 of the worst rum-holes closed altogether. This is the result of *prohibition*, not of *license*.

---

The total loss of time *and* money. How many licensed liquor dens are there in New York *State*?

136. What were the indications of the coming enterprise? What accident

existence of a hope and a purpose, which only required to be known in order to become mighty by association. In 1813, the Massachusetts Society for the Suppression of Intemperance was formed, to discountenance "*the too free use* of ardent spirit and its kindred vices, profaneness and gaming, and to encourage temperance and general morality." Dr. R. D. Mussey, Dr. Torrey, and Mr. Jeremiah Evarts were concerned in this movement, and the last named, as editor, published six articles on the subject in the Boston "Panoplist" of that year. In 1822, the death of a teamster, crushed to death while under the influence of liquor beneath the wheels of his wagon, and the burning to death of another man, occasioned the delivery of two discourses (we believe, by Dr. Justin Edwards), which attracted attention by the remedy proposed, — "*abstinence from the use of intoxicating liquors.*"

This ultimately led to the formation of the American Temperance Society, of whom Dr. Edwards was the first secretary, and who wrote those early and most able reports, the reprints of which did so much in exciting attention to the subject in Europe, especially in Britain. In 1825, Dr. Edwards wrote "The Well-Conducted Farm," — (No. 176 of the Tract Society's Series), — exhibiting the results, to the workmen, of an experiment made upon an extensive farm in Worcester County, Mass., viz.: —

"They had a better appetite for food and were more nourished

---

led to the preaching of two sermons in 1822? To what did this lead? What celebrated tract was published in 1825? Who next preached six sermons? What medical man appealed to his countrymen?

by it than before; had greater vigor of body and mind; did more labor with less fatigue; got rid of disorders they had before; saved more money; were better tempered and happier; and so more useful to themselves and others."

In the following year, the Rev. Lyman Beecher, D.D., preached his famous "Six Sermons on Intemperance," at Litchfield; but they had merely a local influence, until republished afterwards by the American and the English societies, when they effected much good. John Ware, M.D., in an address at Boston, before the Massachusetts society named above, gave this testimony:—

"No impression can be more unfounded, no opinion more fatally false, than that which attributes to spirituous liquors *any* power of promoting bodily strength. Experience has in all quarters abundantly proved the contrary. None labor so constantly, so cheerfully, and with so little exhaustion, *as those who entirely abstain;* none endure so well hardships and exposure, the inclemency of weather, and the vicissitudes of seasons."

## III.

137. Thus, all these various influences rapidly gathered to a head, and the era of temperance organization was inaugurated,—an organization destined to confer untold blessings upon mankind. On February 13, 1826, the American Temperance Society was formed at Boston, and, in March, the Executive Committee, consisting of Dr. Leonard Woods, Dr. Justin Edwards, and Messrs. Tappan, Odiorne, and Wilder, issued their

---

137. When, where, and by whom, was the American Temperance Society formed? What were the results? What official action was taken in the

manifesto. *Distilled liquors were prohibited.* In the latter part of the same year, Professor Palfrey's "Sermons," Dr. Beecher's "Discourses," and Dr. Mussey's "Address before the Medical Convention of New Hampshire," successively appeared. *Total abstinence from ardent spirit* was the doctrine enforced, as interest and as duty, on the ground of health, social and individual safety, and religious feeling. The people accepted the teaching as a new gospel to them, — its necessity was felt, — and it speedily became regarded by the churches as immoral to drink spirits.

The triumphs of moral appeal were very great. The enthusiasm passed on far and wide. Thousands of drunkards were reclaimed, and the facts concerning drink as a source of pauperism and crime, attracting the attention of several of the presidents, and of leading statesmen, led to *official* action in the army and navy. One-seventh of the army (6,000 in all at that time) deserted through drink, and one-fourth were incapable of regular duty. The soldiers, in many parts, petitioned to have the grog stopped, which proposal General Jones and other officers supported, and on Nov. 2, 1832, General Lewis Cass issued the order from the War Department substituting sugar and coffee for grog. "Hereafter no ardent spirits will be issued to troops of the United States. No ardent spirits shall be introduced into any fort, camp, or garrison, nor sold by any sutler to the troops. Nor will any permit be

---

army and navy? What was the testimony of the churches? How many societies were formed, and drunkards reclaimed, by the year 1833? What amusing prediction as to the abstinence doctrine was falsified?

granted for the purchase of ardent spirits." A thousand ships went out of American ports without any grog, and this eventually led to its banishment from the navy. At a General Assembly of the Presbyterian Church, at this time, attended by above 500 ministers, it was declared that "among the means graciously blessed and owned during this year of jubilee, many of your reports specially commemorate the influence of temperance societies. In various places the reformation has been a harbinger, preparing the way of the Lord." In the next year a congressional temperance society was formed. Above 7,000 temperance societies were now in active operation, comprehending *a million and a quarter* of members, and including only 10,000 reclaimed drunkards. An able literary organ, "The Christian Examiner," published at Boston, thus records the results: —

"The greatest enterprise and the most hopeful omen of the age, perhaps, is the temperance reforn. Here is a moral miracle, — a nation, a world, fast sinking into the gulf of sensual perdition. How stupendous, almost hopeless, must have seemed to the first reformers, who stretched out their hands to stay that downward course, the work they had undertaken! But they entered upon it; they went forward; and what is the result? Within five years the entire conscience of the world, of the Anglo-Saxon world at least, is penetrated; a new sentiment, a new fear, a new set of moral maxims is wrought into the heart of nations; millions have joined in this work, — for we do not reckon the pledged men alone; new laws have been framed, new legal restraints devised, new domestic usages introduced; and it may be hoped that the plague is stayed. What most strikes our attention, and fills us with astonishment, is this, — that such an impression in behalf of morality could have been made upon *whole countries*, in so brief a space of time. It is altogether more surprising than the effect produced by the preaching of Peter the Hermit. The crusades to the Holy Land, which he recommended, were entirely in accordance with the warlike, chivalric, and superstitious spirit of the age. But here our reformers have made head *against* the settled habits, and often, too, the incensed *passions* of the people. If *this* could be done, anything can be done. The success of the temperance cause is a signal and glorious pledge for anything reasonable and just that good men may desire to undertake." *

138. The unwonted intelligence from America naturally excited great interest amongst the philanthropists

* Respect for the memory of a distinguished temperance reformer, induces us to record the fact, that, after Dr. Cheyne, of Dublin, the next most distinct exposition of the physiological doctrine that alcohol is poison, whether in fermented or distilled liquors, appeared in May, 1830. We give the title of the work to which we refer:—

"Dispepsy Forestalled and Resisted; or, Lectures on Diet, Regimen, and Employment; delivered to the students of Amherst College, spring term, 1830. By Edward Hitchcock, Professor of Chemistry and Natural History in that institution. Amherst: printed and published by J. & S. C. Adams, 1830."

In the following year a second and enlarged edition was published, with a "Reply to the Reviewers," especially to "The Christian Examiner," for November, 1830, that had ably reviewed the book, but which, nevertheless, fell into many of the blunders that still linger in our literature. A passage in these lectures shows how unfit even good men are to judge of the effect of proclaiming truth; how they violate duty when they timidly hold it back out of fear that it will not be acceptable! "I should consider it *extremely injudicious*, and *even Quixotic*, for any temperance society to require *total abstinence from the milder stimulants*." Yet, this very doctrine, two years later, spread like wildfire throughout Great Britain.

When the "Examiner" selected the professor as the representative of "over-zealous partisans," our author thus mildly disclaimed for the societies (as, indeed he had done in his original lectures) all responsibility on their part.

"At the time they were published, *I knew not that one individual* in the United States would *coincide* with me in my views, because I had not consulted an individual."

Yet these views were *not singular;* they were, in fact, truths which had ripened in many minds in many distant places,—views so ripe that they could not fail to drop down upon the social ground prepared for them, and be *eagerly* accepted.

of Europe. Between 1828 and 1830, — chiefly through the earnest efforts of the Rev. G. Carr, of New Ross, the Rev. John Edgar, D.D., of Belfast, Mr. John Dunlop, of Greenock, Mr. W. Collins, of Glasgow, and Mr. Thomas Beaumont, surgeon, of Bradford, — this new agency of reform was introduced into various parts of Ireland, England, and Scotland. A certain amount of good was done, especially amongst grog-drinkers of the middle class, but few drunkards were reclaimed. It was soon perceived, that, owing to the fact of English drunkenness arising mainly from beer, the American pledge was deficient and nationally inapplicable, besides involving, in the permission of the use of wine, an inconsistency which destroyed the moral power of its advocates. "The rich can drink their strong wines," said the people; "why cannot the poor man enjoy his gin?" It was felt that the pledge must be extended to every agency of enslavement, and include abstinence alike from spirits, wine, malt-liquor, and cider. This social necessity led to inquiry into the chemistry of the question, which revealed the fact that "alcohol" was the real agent of mischief in all these drinks, however disguised under various mixtures, adulterations, and names.*

* In 1828, the late Dr. Cheyne, physician to the forces in Ireland, in a "Letter on Wine and Spirits," announced the injurious character of *all* fermented liquors. The Rev. W. Urwick, D.D., in his "Remarks on the Evils, Occasions, and Cure of Intemperance," laid down total abstinence from *all* intoxicants as the only effectual cure for national intemperance.

---

138. Who introduced Temperance Societies into Great Britain? What followed, and *why* did they fail at a certain point? Under what circumstances was the pledge enlarged? Who originated the name *teetotal*, in

At a meeting in Preston, Lancashire, early in 1832, a reformed character and working-man, named "Dicky Turner," using an emphatic provincialism for "entire," said that he would go in for *tee*total, for "moderation" was "botheration." Mr. Joseph Livesey, adopting this "teetotalism" as the name of the new society they had formed on the principle of abstinence from *all* intoxicating liquors, afterwards carried this novel doctrine to the chief towns of Lancashire and Yorkshire, and later on to Birmingham and London. Thousands of earnest spirits took it up, and the old temperance societies, founded upon the American pledge, fast went out of existence. Drunkards were reclaimed by thousands, and by the agency of a band of lecturers, such as James Teare, Edward Grubb, Gray Mason, and Thomas Whitaker, the new doctrine spread from Cornwall to Caithness, and became very popular amongst the working-classes. In Ireland it engaged the notice of Mr. Martin, a Quaker, of Cork, who ultimately induced Father Mathew to become an abstainer, and commence that reformation which from 1842 to 1847 drew the attention of all Europe to the subject, and effected such a wonderful change in the habits of the Irish people.

Both these tracts were published by the Dublin Temperance Society, and influenced the movement in England and Scotland. [In 1832, Dr. Lees, then a young man, joined the movement, and, in 1835, signed the abstinence pledge, and immediately brought the question, by oral discussions, and through the press, before the notice of the nation, in its physiological and biblical aspects.]

---

application to abstinence? Who were the earliest advocates of the new principle in England?

## IV.

139. We return to the United States. Five more years passed away, and behold another change! Where were thousands of their reformed drunkards? Where their promising young men? Drawn partly into the vortex of the old traffic, and partly into a new form of social drinking. Both in private circles and in public houses, artificial mixtures and wines, but especially. cider and lager beer, were supplanting rum, *but doing rum's work.* The temperance army, then, must move up higher, — must outflank the enemy, — must establish all round him the lines of investment. In very truth, this was attempted; nay, the friends fancied they had *done* it, in hoisting a broader banner, and in altering the watchword of the old one.

The *teetotal* pledge was adopted from England, and the system made solid and consistent. *Total abstinence from* ALL *that intoxicates* became the motto, and once more, with renewed hope, the temperance army commenced a fresh campaign, as they imagined, with all the appliances and the munitions of war that were needed. It was a mistake; they fought the enemy, indeed, but they fought him with unequal weapons, for they did not even assault his *legal* entrenchments, and so, after every victory, they really left the enemy *garrisoned* in the country. Now it is certain that *enthusiasm*, which is not a normal state of any society, cannot possibly destroy an established and permanent *interest.* But the campaign was nobly

---

139. (IV.) What was the next step in history of the temperance enterprise? Describe the origin and progress of the *Washingtonian* movement.

fought from the year 1833 to the year 1845. The plan was fairly tried, and it failed only from essential defect. The noblest leaders of the movement in church and state gradually opened out the *immorality* of the traffic, and an irresistible public opinion was formed in the right direction. In 1840, the *Washingtonian* movement was inaugurated at Chase's tavern, Baltimore, by a few earnest spirits, resolved on reforming themselves and their fellow-victims of the traffic by stirring moral appeal. John H. W. Hawkins, J. Hayes, of Maine, and, subsequently, J. B. Gough, were amongst the most celebrated and efficient leaders of this remarkable movement. For some years, the enthusiasm raged like a prairie fire. It was an inspiration of philanthropy to convert drunkard and drunkard-maker by "moral suasion" — and it had the fullest trial. Absorbing much of the energy, it diverted the attention of the States generally from "legal suasion." It was aided greatly, too, by Father Mathew's visit to the States in 1849; but it failed, for obvious reasons. It stirred up a desire for freedom, but left the *temptation* intact; it corrected the judgment and enlightened the conscience, but it did not remove the *seducing agency*, and the crop of evil grew rank and rapidly. Judge O'Neal wrote in 1845, as follows: —

"This year a Washingtonian, who sank into a drunkard's grave, said, — pointing to a grog-shop on the left, — 'If I escaped *that* hell, *this* hell' — pointing to another on his right — 'yawns to receive me.' This year has fully satisfied me that moral suasion has had its day of triumph: some other aids must now be sought, *to keep what we have gained*, and to gain still more." *

* Gen. S. F. Cary, of Cincinnati, says: "Ten years ago, there was a large

Gradually, however, the public mind veered around to the right point of the compass again. In 1844, the Temperance Union, after the triumphs of Washingtonianism, declared that,

"*Could the temptation now be removed*, and the rising generation be permitted to come up without the allurements of the bar-room and the grog-shop, our beloved country would soon exhibit to the world a spectacle of peace and prosperity, sublime and beautiful." *

V.

140. Thus true temperance men were forced into political action, and the era of *no-license* began. We give specimens of the reasoning which led to this course on the part of the wisest and most thoughful of the leaders.

The sentiments that were forming and gathering in the public mind, and destined to be hurled ere long upon the traffic, we exhibit in the order of their date, extracted from the reports: —

number of the Sons and Washingtonians in this locality who were violently opposed to bringing the subject of temperance into political conflicts. In an old volume of the 'Washingtonian,' we find accounts of these conflicts with the suasionists and legalists, and the names of the prominent actors. *It is a fact worthy of deep reflection, that nearly all the advocates of pure moral suasion have returned to their cups.* Some of them have died drunkards, and others are at this hour the most inveterate enemies of the temperance reform. Those, on the other hand, who were advocates of law, have *nearly all* kept the pledge, and are still reliable friends of the cause."— "Crusader," Nov. 1, 1856.

John Hawkins, who from 1840, to his death in 1857, did such excellent service in the movement, was a firm friend of prohibition, and again and again pointed out the inadequacy of mere "persuasion for the traffickers."

* Tenth Report of the American Temperance Union.

---

140. (V.) What was the *no-license* era? Explain the reasoning of Judge Platt and Senator Smith.

Professor Ware, of Harvard University, 1832: —

"The nature of his calling renders it inevitable, that he cannot be a dealer in spirits without becoming *accessory* to vice and ruin."

President Wayland, the moralist, 1832: —

"Would it be right for me to derive my living from selling poison, *or from propagating plague or leprosy around me?*"

The *Presbyterian Synod of Albany*, in 1833, declared, "That the traffic is an immorality, and ought to be viewed as such throughout the world."

In 1833, the question was publicly debated, in the city of New York, "What *right* have legislators to pass laws which enable men *legally* to injure their fellow-men, to increase their taxes, and expose their children to temptation, drunkenness, and ruin?" The answer was the denial of the right to ruin; and opinion rapidly ripened into the initial shape of *prohibition.*

"The law," said Judge Platt, in 1833, "which licenses the sale of ardent spirits, is an impediment to the temperance reformation. Whenever public opinion and the moral sense of our community shall be so far corrected and matured as to regard them in their true light, and when the public safety shall be thought to require it, dram-shops will be indictable, at common law, as *public nuisances.*" *

When the vendors charged the temperance friends

* Judge Platt, at a public convention in Clinton County, N. Y., in 1833, made a statement which gives significance to the passage cited: —

"It is a lamentable fact, that, upon a careful estimate, it is found, that of the tavern-keepers and retailers of ardent spirits in this State, during the last forty years, *more than two-thirds have become drunkards.*"

with departing from their original programme, Mr. Gerrit Smith (now Senator) nobly replied: —

"I admit that a grand object, within the scope of the constitution and labors of the society is that of *persuading* our fellow-men to refrain from ardent spirit; but I do not see why we might not also seek to *remove the hindrances* to this accomplishment. Now, the manufacture and sale of ardent spirit constitute confessedly a very great hindrance to the work of inducing our fellow-men to quit the drinking of it. Could a society that should require its members to abstain from purchasing lottery tickets be expected to preserve silence on the subject of lottery offices? Could a society formed to discountenance gambling be expected to look with unconcern on the licensed allurements of gambling-*houses?* No more can ours look with indifference on the attractions and snares of the rum-shop. As in the one case, the lottery office and gambling-house irresistibly invite thousands to purchase tickets, and to stake their money at cards or billiards, who but for the sight of these resorts would never have fallen into this folly, so is it in the other, that men drink ardent spirit *because of the inviting facilities* for getting it; and so it is, that whilst these facilities exist, our *direct* efforts to promote total abstinence will be measurably, *if not fatally, counteracted by them.* Such views we must certainly admit to be just, unless we deny what the Bible, our hearts, and daily observation alike teach us, of the power of temptation."

141. The cry of "No license" was first heard in the municipalities. The popular voice electing its rulers, this battle was attended with varying fortune, in various districts, and in many was annually renewed. The contest, however, was of immense service. In it, the

---

**141. What were the *results* of refusing licenses? Give the summary of the lessons taught.**

"Ironsides" of *our* Commonwealth were getting disciplined. Proof of the anti-social, pauperizing, crime-breeding character of the traffic became matter of clear arithmetic, and created that feeling and conviction which afterwards culminated in the State Law of Maine. In some parts of the country great success attended this preliminary agitation. Throughout the "Old Colony," where the Pilgrim Fathers first settled, the "*no-license*" principle triumphed so far back as 1832, — a district comprehending two counties and several considerable towns.

"*In Barnstable and Duke's Counties, in* 1835, *after vacations of three, four, and seven months, the judges had to preside over two criminals only, and these for a petty larceny of less than two dollars.*"

In 1834, the State of Georgia was greatly agitated on the subject of the traffic. She expelled it from the seat of her university, and tested in *two counties* the authority to grant or refuse licenses. In Liberty County, with a population of 8,000, not one drop could be purchased.

In the County of Suffolk, Massachusetts, licenses were reduced from 613 to 314; in Hampshire County, from 83 to 8. In Plymouth and Bristol Counties, and in numerous towns, *no licenses were given*, and in many of them no ardent spirits sold. "*In some of those towns*, however, men who love the poison have sent for it to Boston." *

In 1844, in Connecticut, temperance commissioners were elected in 200 out of 220 towns. On the 19th May, 1845, *four-fifths* of the cities and towns of New York

* American Temperance Documents, i., p. 34.

State gave a strong vote against license. The State votes collectively were, —*pro*, 111,884; *contra*, 177,683. In 1845, the effects of prohibition in Massachusetts were thus stated: —

"From more than 100 towns the traffic is entirely removed, and a reduction is already visible in the public taxation. In one town, with a population of 7,000, there were, four years since, 469 paupers; 'no license' has reduced them down to 11."*

In the County of Ontario, under the operation of *no license*, the inmates of the jail were reduced from 125 in the year 1845, to 53 in 1846. In 1847, licenses were again granted, and the inmates of the jail increased to 132. In the County of Genessee, a similar course of things, no license succeeding to license, produced similar issues.

In Potter County, Pennyslvania, the traffic has been for a considerable time suppressed, the judge refusing to grant any license.

"*The prison has become tenantless; there is not a solitary pauper in the county;* the business in the criminal court has ceased, and taxes have been reduced one-half."

It was eventually discovered that *local* experiments admitted of smuggling from neighboring districts, though the results of the law were still good. But its fault was its limitation, — they hadn't *enough* of it. It was with this measure as it has been with our laws for the *suppression* of the slave-trade. The league to put it down was not, at first, *sufficiently extensive*. Nevertheless, it

* American Temperance Documents, i., p. 398.

was a great boon. "*What are the facts?*" says an appeal of the day.

> "*Four times as many crimes are committed in places in which liquor is sold as in places in which it is not sold.* And, in a number of cases, after the sale of it had been abandoned, and the use of it had ceased, *the criminal docket had been cleared, and the jails comparatively empty.* It increases, then, the power of temptation, and it is thus a palpable violation of the revealed will of God."

Facts and opinions, of which the following are a sample, were at this period promulgated throughout the States: —

In Catskill, New York, Dr. Hoagland and other gentlemen made a minute examination and report of the condition of things. Though eight merchants had abandoned the trade in spirits, and though a large proportion of the best families, and one-third of the inhabitants, had joined the temperance society, these facts were elicited: —

38 persons were engaged in the traffic, — or 1 dealer to every 40 persons not abstainers. Some of these places, they say, are perfect schools of vice.

130 *habitual* drunkards were traced, — or 1 in every 17 of the whole population, — or 1 in every 11, excluding the abstainers. Many others are *free* drinkers and *occasional* drunkards.

Of those who are already inebriates, or advancing to that condition, there are 2 in every 7 of the drinking population.

Taking the whole of Greene County, it was shown that of 300 criminals who had been imprisoned in the jail during 7 years, all, save 3, were intemperate; of 60 debtors, every one.

Of those who had received aid at the county poorhouse, during 3 years, *one-fifth* were juveniles, of whom seven-eighths were children, often orphans of the intemperate. Three-fifths of the adult females were intemperate; one-fifth dependents on intemperate husbands, etc. Each year above 300 such paupers. But for intoxicating liquors, therefore, any *public* provision for the support of the poor would scarcely have been necessary. The whole cost of pauperism and crime, flowing from intemperance, amounted to $8,634.

In Columbus, Ohio, of 44 persons found dead, the coroner's inquest was, that 38 of them came to their death by drink.

The *Philadelphia Medical Society* testified, after full inquiry through a special committee, that out of 4,292 deaths, in that city, above 700 (*or one in seven*) were occasioned by drink.

## VI.

142. *State* action was the natural result of municipal, being the growth and extension of the same idea. State conventions were held all over the Union for many years, sometimes attended by 500 delegates, thus laying the foundation for a change which, some day, would astonish the mere politicians. Vermont went in for a State *no-license* law; in 1847, the votes for license were 13,707,

---

142. (VI.) What epoch followed "no license"? What were the first

for *no* license, 21,793; in 1849, *for* 11,205, against 23,884.

The State of Connecticut, since 1834, had made, "license" or "no license" one of its political issues; and frequently carried the negative by overwhelming majorities. She guarded herself against the traffic by erecting some additional fences around it. In May, the Legislature reported a fact of great moment, showing that *license* is vastly more easy of evasion than prohibition. "From a recent examination in New Haven, it was found to contain 60 *grog-shops where liquor was sold contrary to law.*" In other States the same battle, with the same weapons, — the ballot-box, — was waged with varying success. During the presidency of General Andrew Jackson, in 1834, the principle of a prohibitory liquor law was distinctly admitted by the government in reference to one portion of its subjects; and the precedent, at any rate, was established for its application to *all.* We allude to the law "*for the Protection of the Indian Tribes,*" which, prohibiting the sale of all strong liquors to the red men, enforced its commands by instructing and authorizing the Indian agents summarily to *seize* and *destroy* all such liquors introduced for sale into the Indian territory, — a provision which was rigidly and righteously enforced.

In February, 1837, an able *report* was made by a committee of the Legislature of Maine, founded on very numerous petitions which had been presented, claiming protection against the issues of the traffic. The com-

---

experiments in *State* law? What was the Indian law? Who inaugurated the first attempts at a State law in Maine?

mittee framed a *prohibitory* bill, which, though lost in the Legislature, was taken up by the people.* They clung tenaciously to the conception, carried the proposition to the ballot-box, and, three years later, elected a Legislature that passed the bill, only to be vetoed by the governor.

In 1838, Tennessee passed a stringent license-law, restricting the retail sale of drink to *one quart*, or more. A gentleman travelling there in 1839, writes: "A most happy change is already realized; taverns once disorderly are now quiet and comfortable places for the weary traveller." † In 1838, a convention of 400 delegates ‡ presented a petition to the Legislature of Massachusetts, which had these pointed questions: —

> "Is it right to give *authority* to sell insanity, and deal out sure destruction? If it *is* right, why should *any* be forbidden to do it? If *not* right, why should any be *permitted* to do it? Why forbid all but 'men of sober life and conversation' to do this, if it be right? Why allow such to do it if it be wrong? It may be too much to expect from human laws, that they protect the *morals* of society from corruption; but is it too much to ask *that they will not throw open the doors of temptation?*"

* It was in 1837 that Mr. Neal Dow became prominently connected with the prohibitory movement. This gentleman was born at Portland, March 20, 1804. His family were members of the Society of Friends, but he himself is a Congregationalist; by business, a supervisor of a large tannery; and a person of abundant means. Maine contains a very earnest and homogeneous population, intent on their own business, careful of their estates, sober, moral, and religious in their habits, and of great persistency of character. Mr. Dow is an excellent type of the men of Maine, and worthy of their confidence. He became a general in the war of the Rebellion, and has twice visited Britain, gratuitously, in the service of prohibition, effecting vast good.

† "Journal of American Temperance Union," Feb., 1845, p. 24.

‡ This convention founded a State Temperance Society, on *total abstinence* principles.

In March, the legislative committee reported, recommending *prohibition*. On the 13th April, a bill was passed prohibiting the sale of spirits in less quantities than 15 gallons.

In 1839, Mississippi enacted the one-gallon law; while Illinois granted power to towns and counties to suppress the retail traffic *on petition signed by a majority of adult male inhabitants.*

143. These laws occasioned the mooting of a legal point as to their "constitutionality," in the Supreme Court. In January, 1847, the license causes of *Thurlow* vs. *Massachusetts*, *Fletcher* vs. *Rhode Island*, and *Pierce* vs. *New Hampshire*, came on for hearing. It appeared that the town of Cumberland, Rhode Island, had refused license. *The judgment of the court below, in each case, was unanimously affirmed*, to wit, that these laws "were *not* inconsistent with the constitution of the United States, nor with any acts of Congress." The decision covered two points,— the *extent* to which licenses might be conceded, and the right to prohibit unlicensed sale.*

Chief Justice Taney, in delivering judgment, said:—

"Although a State is bound to receive and permit the sale, by the importer, of any article of merchandise which Congress authorizes to be imported, it is not bound to furnish *a market* for it, nor to abstain from the passage of any law which it may deem necessary or advisable to guard the *health* or *morals* of its citizens, although such law may discourage importation, or

* See 5 Howard's Reports, 504.

---

143. What legal point was raised? What was the decision of the Supreme Court?

diminish the profits of the importer, or lessen the revenue of the government. And if any State deem the retail and internal traffic in ardent spirits injurious to citizens, and calculated to produce idleness, vice, or debauchery, I see nothing in the constitution of the United States to prevent it from regulating and restraining the traffic, or from prohibiting it altogther if it thinks proper." *

And in regard to liquors brought in from other States: —

"The law of New Hampshire is a valid law; for although the gin sold was an import from another State, Congress has already the power to regulate such importations; yet, as Congress has made no regulations on the subject, the traffic in the article may be lawfully regulated by the State as soon as it is landed in its territory, and a tax imposed upon it, or a license required, *or the sale prohibited*, according to the policy which the State may suppose to be its interest or its duty to pursue."

Mr. Justice McLean concurred in the decision, and said: —

"If the foreign article be injurious to the health or the morals of the community, a State may, in the exercise of that *great and comprehensive police power* which lies at the foundation of its prosperity, prohibit the sale of it. The acknowledged police power of a State extends often to the *destruction* of property. A nuisance may be abated. *Everything* prejudicial to the health or morals of a city may be removed." †

Mr. Justice Catren also agreed with the Chief Justice: —

* See 5 Howard's Reports, 573. † Ibid., 592.

---

State the principal points in the argument of Chief Justice Taney. Of Justice McLean. Of Justice Catren. Of Justice Daniel. Of Justice Grier.

"I admit, as inevitable, that if the State has the power of restraint by licenses to *any* extent, she has the discretionary power to judge of its limit, and may go the length of *prohibiting it altogether.*"

Mr. Justice Daniel, in answer to the argument that the importer purchases the *right* to sell, when he pays duties to government, said: —

"No such right as the one supposed is purchased by the importer, and no injury, in any accurate sense, is inflicted on him by denying to him the power demanded. He has not purchased and cannot purchase, from the government, that which it could not ensure to him, — a sale independently of the laws and policy of the States." *

Mr. Justice Grier thus asserted both the right of prohibiting sale, and that of the seizure and destruction of property: —

"All the laws for the restraint or punishment of crime, or the preservation of the public peace, health, and morals, are, from their very nature, of primary importance, and lie at the foundation of social existence. They are for the protection of life and liberty, and *necessarily compel all laws on subjects of secondary importance, which relate only to property, convenience, or luxury, to recede when they come in contact* or collision. SALUS POPULI SUPREMA LEX. The exigencies of the social compact require that such laws be executed before and above all others. It is for this reason that quarantine laws, which protect public health, *compel mere commercial regulations to submit to their control.* They restrain *the liberty* of the passengers; they operate on the ship, which is the instrument of commerce, and its officers and crew, the agents of navigation. They *seize* the infected cargo, and cast it overboard. All these things are

* See 5 Howard's Reports, 616.

done, not from any power which the State assumes to regulate commerce, or interfere with the regulations of Congress, but because police laws for the prevention of crime and protection of public welfare must of necessity have full and free operation, *according to the exigency that requires their interference.*" *

144. The position and feelings of the temperance party, immediately prior to the passing of the Maine Law, were one of mingled disappointment, hope, and despondency. Notwithstanding a moral-suasion movement carried on for twenty years, with a machinery unprecedented for its magnitude, and with a success almost marvellous, — a movement that had gathered into its ranks the successive rulers of the republic, the highest teachers, the most distinguished popular leaders, the great organs of the press, and the almost universal church of the Western world, — a movement that had manifested its power in redeeming tens of thousands, in moulding fashion, in conquering appetite and interest, and in penetrating and permeating with its *opinions*, platform and press, pulpit and forum, the school, the college, and the halls of legislation, — notwithstanding this career of progress, which, amongst moral and social organizations, is peerless in the history of modern times, intemperance was scarcely visibly diminished, but, in the great towns, rolled in like a devastating flood. True, there was a mighty difference between 1812 and 1831, and, in sentiment, between 1831 and 1851. The fifteenth report of the Temperance Union says: —

* See 5 Howard's Reports, 632.

---

144. What were the feelings of the friends of the Maine Law? What was beginning to be the feeling in relation to moral suasion?

"The committee feel no disposition to pass lightly by the evil, or to overrate the work accomplished. Intemperance is most appalling in our land. Its enginery is tremendous. The capital invested in the traffic it is impossible to estimate. *Moral suasion has well-nigh done its work,*" — i. e., all that it is *competent* to do.

"*Little more could be done,*" said a veteran reformer, S. C. Allen, in addressing the legislative society of Massachusetts, "*without more efficient legal action.*" The Rev. T. Brainard, D. D., of Philadelphia, at the sixteenth anniversary of the Temperance Union, characteristically expressed the same truth: —

"*We have come to a class of men who love money better than the right. The present laws have never been executed. They never can be executed. We have used up the conscience of the community. The men that have a conscience have abandoned the traffic.*"

145. History shows the utter hostility of the traffic to *all* reform, and the folly of compromises. The following illustrations, which are to be found in the American law-reports,* show that the traffic is restless under every restraint, impatient and evasive under every regulation, — that it not only engenders defiance of law in its supporters and victims, but is inveterately defiant of control, — and that all concessions of confidence have been blunders of policy.

* Johnson's Reports, xiv., p. 231. Cowen's Reports, i., p. 77. Wendell's Reports, xiii., xv., xix. Hill's Reports, i., 55; iii., p. 150; vi., p. 58. Denio's Reports, i., p. 540.

---

145. What has always been the position of the traffic to *all* reform? What eight illustrations are given?

(*a.*) The demand of a "moral character" in the conductor of a grog-shop was sought to be evaded by an *assignment* of license! The judges properly ruled that "character" was not transferable.

(*b.*) The demand that sales of liquor should be in quantities of five gallons, and not for *tippling* purposes, was set at nought by selling altogether, and delivering by *instalments*. The judges ruled against the impudent fiction.

(*c.*) The decree that the distinct and double offences of *selling* intoxicating liquors in illegal quantities and at illegal times, and doing so *without a license*, had separate penalties, was attempted to be argued into *one* offence with a single penalty! — so that conviction on one point would be acquittal on the other. The judges ruled against this modest plea of the traffickers also.

(*d.*) The demand that liquor should be sold only under the authority of a license was sought to be ignored by calling upon the prosecutor to prove the negative,—viz., that the seller *had no license!* This was as if a sheriff's officer, when called upon to show his writ of arrest, were to answer, "You must prove that I have *not* one!"

(*e.*) The law that placed the *power* to license in the board of excise, on specified conditions, was attempted to be quashed by an application to the Supreme Court to *compel* by writ the granting of a license, — thus really vesting the power in the *applicant!* The judges of course overruled this plea, as well as the preceding.

(*f.*) When the community sued by its overseers, it was argued that, as the penalties went to the poor-fund, *nobody* in that parish could sue, because *everybody* was interested in the fine!

(*g*.) The traffickers at last declared that the restriction of the trade at all was *un*constitutional! In 1845, the overseers of Norwich, County Chenango, N. Y., sued the two INGERSOLLS for the penalty imposed upon the sale of rum in less quantity than five gallons. The publicans pleaded, 1st. That two persons cannot be sued jointly; 2d. That the statue conflicted with the constitution of the States, and was void. The judge decided against both pleas.

(*h*.) The law which calls for a license to sell "*the dangerous article*" was in 1851 made a plea for SUPPRESSING "*temperance taverns*," where only innocent refreshments were sold; with a view to secure to the traffic not only the monopoly of drink-license, but also the exclusive privilege of offering a safe accommodation to the traveller. The court decided that "no license is necessary to authorize the business of *tavern-keeping, the right to do so being common to all citizens*."

146. Maine, in 1846, after fierce struggling and legislative debates, had the honor of first placing a prohibitive liquor law upon its statute book; but, as might have been predicted, while the law was correct in its principles, its adversaries took care to mar it in its methods and sanctions. A law of the nature of the one in question — opposed to the interest, appetite, and custom of a large minority — could not be expected to escape evasion, unless it originated a new executive machinery, or had some peculiarly effective sanction; nay, even in the best of cases, such a law would have an ordeal to pass

---

146. What State had the honor of first adopting the prohibitory law? To what was it opposed? Would it escape evasion?

through, and to starve out the established forces of the old system. The prohibitory law of 1846, however, gave no power to arrest the real offender, — *the liquor*, — but sought to sustain its provisions by the old apparatus of fines. The rum-sellers sold secretly where they could, but at all events sold, and when detected *paid the fines out of the profits of the offence.* The law did not yet allow the liquor itself to be its own evidence, and so gave room for the immoral traffickers to evade conviction by perpetrating perjury. The law, it is true, was vindicated by penalties; but it did not secure respect; for the liquor was left entrenched within the borders of the traffic. *The law failed because it was not as thorough in its apparatus as in its principle.*

Was the case, then, hopeless? Must society, with the knowledge and sufferings of a prodigious evil, sit down in despair of ever removing it? Not so. "If this law is a failure," said the Hon. Neal Dow, of Portland, "there must be a reason for it." Like other prohibitory laws, he argued, it denounced the wrong — *but, unlike them, it tolerated the instrument of the wrong.* A parallel to such legislation would have been to *prohibit* lotteries, gambling, and forgeries,—and respect as "lawful" property, the lottery ticket, the gambler's dice, and the forger's die. Henceforth, with that directness and earnestness which distinguish him, he proclaimed CONFISCATION OF THE LIQUOR AS THE *practical* CORRELATIVE OF THE PRINCIPLE OF PROHIBITION, — a guaranty, without which any liquor law must ever prove a dead-letter.

---

**How did it differ from that of 1846? Why did the law fail? What was the peculiarity of the Maine Law?**

This, and no other, is the peculiarity of what is called, by way of eminence, *The Maine Liquor Law.* As pirated books are now summarily burnt by our custom-house officers, so confiscated liquor was to be spilt or otherwise destroyed by the State officers, whenever discovered. The "rummies," as they are called, struggled with desperation, and strained every nerve, but were utterly routed. The temperance party, under the leadership of Mr. Dow, carried the elections of 1849, and in May, 1851, by an average vote of *two to one*, the bill passed the Senate and House of Representatives, and on the second of June became law, by receiving the signature of the governor of the State.* This law permitted the apparatus of the traffic to be received as evidence, just as are the implements of the gambler and coiner, and conferred upon the officers the summary power of destroying the liquor.

Opportunity was allowed for diverting liquor to legitimate uses, or disposing of it beyond the State. This was embraced, and preparation made generally in the cities and towns to acquiesce in the demands of the law, showing that law is a potent instrument in *creating* as well as expressing public sentiment. Here and

* The law provides *for the sale of alcohol for mechanical and medicinal (including artistic and chemical) purposes, by the appointment of a district agent, under bonds, and with a fixed salary.* It does not concern itself with the private acts of home brewing, or importation (indeed, the laws of the Federal Union *protect* importation) in the "original package." It regards every man's home as his castle, and only seeks to meddle with the *overt act of sale*; confiscating all stores of liquor of which a part has been sold, just as revenue officers would seize a whole bale of goods on proof of any part of them having been smuggled.

---

What was the effect of the law upon public sentiment?

there, however, several publicans had the temerity to retain their stores of liquor, which became liable to seizure and destruction. The first seizure and confiscation was made at Bangor, by order of the mayor; and on the glorious 4th of July, 1851, the city marshal rolled out from the basement of the City Hall ten casks of confiscated liquor, and destroyed the whole in the presence of the people. Soon after, Mr. Dow, as mayor of Portland, a city where great wealth had been made by distilling, issued his search-warrant on accredited suspicion of sale, and $2,000 worth of liquor was seized and destroyed. On both occasions the populace witnessed the destruction in respectful silence. Other seizures followed, and nowhere did the law meet with any grave opposition. Liquors smuggled from neighboring non Maine Law States, by various and often ridiculous devices, quickly fell into the grasp of the marshals and sheriffs, and received their legal doom. Drunkenness rapidly diminished; disorder disappeared; almshouses grew desolate; houses of correction and jails thinly inhabited or entirely closed; while external signs of moral and social prosperity were everywhere visible. Evasions of the law suggested new clauses for meeting them, which were passed by votes of two to one. Farmers, it appears, were allowed to manufacture *cider*, and sell it in quantities of not less than twenty-eight gallons; but it, also, came under ban and forfeiture when found in tippling-shops.

147. Let us here finish the history of the law in Maine. Year after year passed away, during which it vindicated

---

What was done under the seizure act?

**147. Relate the further history of the law. What suits followed?**

its power for good, while faithfully executed. Its enemies attempted in vain to excite *disturbance* of any serious kind; and at last resorted to one of the vilest and most unscrupulous conspiracies against justice which history records. In May, 1855, libels on the character of Mr. Dow were privately circulated, and appeals made to the *jealousy* of the law's observance. The Portland board of aldermen appointed the mayor and two aldermen as a sub-committee to take steps for the establishment (pursuant to law) of a "City Agency" for the sale of alcohol for mechanical, medicinal, and chemical purposes only. The mayor took steps accordingly, and purchased a quantity of liquor, which he ordered to be deposited in the City Hall. His enemies immediately had it bruited about that Neal Dow had become a liquor seller on a large scale, in violation of his own law; and obtained a warrant against him "for having liquors unlawfully in his possession." The officer of the court which issued the warrant at once seized the liquors in the City Hall. The case was tried in a few days, and resulted in the following judicial decision: —

"From the whole evidence, the court finds that these liquors were ordered by a committee chosen by the board of aldermen for that purpose; that they were ordered for the city agency, and for lawful sale; that they were sent marked and invoiced to the city agency; that they were placed in the room which had been appropriated for the city agency, and found in the possession of the city agent, legally appointed previous to this complaint. From these facts the court decides, that they were not kept by the defendant with an intent to sell in violation of the law, and that he is not guilty of the charge made against him in the complaint. It is ordered, therefore, that he be discharged, and that the liquors seized by the officer be returned to the city agent, from whom they were taken."

Before trial came on, however, a mob of persons assembled in front of the City Hall, and became very riotous. They smashed the windows of the hall, burst open the door, threw stones and brickbats, and severely injured several of the police. To prevent them from breaking into the place, drinking the liquor, and committing frightful excesses, the mayor, after the riot act had been read, and blank cartridge fired in vain, ordered the military to fire with ball. Several of the rioters were wounded, one of them killed, and the riot effectually quelled. A coroner's jury returned the following just verdict: —

"John Robbins came to his death by a gunshot wound, a musket, pistol, or revolver ball, shot through his body by some persons unknown to the inquest, acting under the authority and order of the mayor and aldermen of the City of Portland, in defence of the city property from the ravages of an excited mob, unlawfully congregated for that purpose near the City Hall, on Saturday evening, June 2, 1855, of which he, the said J. R., was found to be one."

148. At the State election in September, 1855, the vote for the Maine Law candidate for governor was not only larger than any governor had ever before received, in the history of the State, but greater by thousands than any other single candidate. But a *plurality* of votes is requisite, and, by a vast expenditure of money, supplied from New York, by secret influences, and an unsleeping organization, the united prohibition party were defeated. The opposition, though having control of both branches

---

148. What reverse took place?

of the Legislature and the executive, after six months' procrastination, screwed its courage up to "*low-water* mark," and proposed a substitute for the world-famous law, but a substitute so stringent, that in Britain it would be deemed no better than its predecessor! Mr. Barnes — a Whig Senator — introduced and got passed a modifying bill which involved the principle of the Maine Law: viz., "*that no person shall keep a drinking-house or tippling-shop within the State*," though in his accompanying report he alleges that "a man may eat and drink what he likes, and that to interfere with his doing so is to go beyond the true province of government"! The distilleries were again at work, and drunkenness and crime rapidly increased; jailers returned to their abandoned occupations, and for a time a state of things prevailed which had not been witnessed in Maine for six years. This reverse, and the workings of the modified system, however, only furnished them with another lesson in political leadership, and with fresh weapons of warfare; their phalanx returned again to the conflict with a firmer tread, to realize a more complete and lasting victory.

The members-elect of the Legislature of 1857 were almost *unanimously* Maine-law, anti-slavery men, — the rum governor was defeated by an adverse majority of 20,000 votes. The legislators of *April* were indignantly rejected in *September*, and the law was replaced on the statute book, with still more stringent clauses.

149. The passing of the *Maine* Law inspired an immense and even surprising enthusiasm in other States.

---

**What was the result of the election of 1857?**

Synods and conventions rapidly succeeded each other; and their utterances were of the clearest description. The church saw and declared that the essential thing for its success was the removal of the impediment of the traffic; the citizen perceived that this measure was *the* measure of the time, needful to secure the fruits of every other. In Dr. Cheever's expressive language, "*Every interest of evil would go down, every interest of good would come up.*" They looked and prayed for its advent as the ancient Egyptian might watch and wait for the rising of the Nile, whose blessed waters should convert the parched earth into the fertile field.

On the 21st January, 1852, in the Tremont Temple, in Boston, the citizens assembled for the presentation of their petition, to which 130,000 *well-written* signatures were attached, including 60,000 voters. The Hon A. Huntington, of Salem, said: "God speed the enterprise! It is a great cause, and can do more for the welfare of the people than anything else." It was borne on a double sleigh to the State House, over a rich banner, on which was inscribed, "THE VOICE OF MASSACHUSETTS, —130,000 PETITIONERS IN FAVOR OF THE MAINE TEMPERANCE LAW." Seven days later, a "grand demonstration" was made at Albany, the legislative capital of "the Empire State." The artillery company, gorgeous sleighs filled with officers, guests, and ladies, monster rolls of petitions, with 300,000 signatures, and half a mile of teetotalers and Sons of Temperance, with splendid regalia, badges, banners, and bands of music, assembled

---

**149. What was the effect of the passage of the Maine Law upon other states? Give Dr. Cheever's language. What demonstrations were made?**

in the neighborhood of the Delavan House, and after passing through the chief streets entered by permission the Assembly Chamber, where the meeting was called to order by the veteran Colonel Camp, and the claims of the law enforced by Dr. Marsh and others. The law asked for was, "*a law to prevent pauperism and crime.*" The petitions were referred to select committees, which reported acceptable bills, and assigned reasons. The Senate reported that a greater number of petitioners had united in the request than had ever before been presented in behalf of *any* measure.

From Maine the impulse spread to Minnesota; this territory arriving *second* at the goal. The law passed both houses of the Legislature in March, 1852, with the proviso that it be submitted to the people. The people at once gave it their imprimatur, and it became the law of the territory. (Singular to say, the Supreme Court pronounced it to be *un*constitutional for its having been submitted to the people; but the Legislature did not repeal it.)

In Rhode Island, the spring election returned a Legislature that (March 7th) enacted the law in the Senate without a count, and in the Assembly by 47 votes against 27; being the *third* in this race of social redemption. In Providence, a Maine Law mayor was returned by a majority of a thousand votes. This gentleman, the Hon. A. C. Barstow, at the 17th anniversary of the Temperance Union, held May 12th, 1853, in New York, said:—

"He was proud to represent Rhode Island, which, first of the States, elucidated the principles of religious liberty.

---

**What was the action in Minnesota? In Rhode Island?**

Though not the first in *this* cause, he could claim for her the honor of having, if not the genius to lead, at least the humility and virtue to follow. A prohibitory law has existed *for six years*, under which 26 out of 32 towns have steadily refused to give license."

150. The struggle continued in the Legislature of Massachusetts,— a State destined, however, to be *fourth* in the race. Petitions poured in. 180,000 petitioners prayed for the law, and the select committee to whom the matter was referred gave the petitioners a hearing, and were addressed in public by the Hon. Neal Dow, the Rev. O. E. Othman, Dr. Lyman Beecher, Rev. John Pierpont, and C. W. Goodrich. The committee reported a bill containing the essential features of the law, but stipulating for the manufacture and use of alcoholic liquor for all *necessary* and *useful* purposes. The debates were remarkable for eliciting brilliant appeal and important facts. Though this State is, perhaps, the *best-educated* one of the whole federation, and possesses great industry and wealth, it had not, *by these social means*, even aided by the most remarkable temperance movement the world has ever seen, succeeded in preserving the Commonwealth from a frightful sum of intemperance, pauperism, and crime. Above $8,500,000 were annually expended on the *retail* traffic, which involved a further cost for pauperism, of $2,000,000. Nearly a thousand *idiots* were found in the State, the children of the intemperate.

---

150. How many petitioners in Massachusetts for the law? What statistics are given in relation to the traffic?

*Committals for Criminal Offences, in Massachusetts, in* 1851.

| | | | | |
|---|---|---|---|---|
| To Jail for crime,....... | 6,666, | of whom 2,261 | were intemperate | = 34 per cent. |
| To Houses of Correction, | 3,175, | " 1,588 | " | = 50 " |

The Hon. Mr. Pomeroy ably replied to several objectors: —

"The principle had always existed in legislation; it was nothing new here. Ring the changes on 'human liberty' if you intend to rope and confine your victims! If we deprive any man by this bill of his liberty — *it is of his liberty to do wrong*, for which he never had the right."

It finally passed both houses by large majorities, and was signed by the governor, May 22, 1852.

In January, 1855, the Massachusetts law was amended, a section relating to the seizure of liquor made "constitutional," and some stringent penalties added, including a clause making the seller liable to be sued by the *wife* of the drinker, when damages could be proved to be the result of the drinking.

Four victories won within the year, and still the tide of battle rolled on. The cry was set up, notwithstanding twenty years' agitation for *no license*, of "premature action." By the doubting, the season for preparation is never used, as that of success never comes. Certainly we would not wed

"*Rash haste*, half-sister to delay."

Neither would we counsel worse marriage with the *whole*-sister,

"*Procrastination*, — the thief of time."

---

Has a man a *right* to do wrong? Why not? How many victories were won this year? How was the law amended?

Hear the instructive answer of Rev. Dr. John Marsh, on behalf of the American Temperance Union:—

"Vast multitudes said they *were* prepared for it; and what would another generation be without it? What were we fast becoming under our present license laws, with the waves of a foreign population rolling in upon us? *Nothing better, but continually worse.* They wish to impose no law upon the people by force; but when a people demand a law for *protection* against the traffic, they *do* require that it shall not be holden from them, because that, by the craft to be destroyed, distillers, brewers, and venders have their wealth. In demanding protection, they relax no effort of moral suasion. The vast influx of a foreign population; their deep sensuality; their readiness to engage, in all towns and cities, in the liquor trade; the ease with which they procure a license, and the corrupting influence of their liquor shops, *are viewed with much anxiety by all who love their country.* In five years, 1,041,238 immigrants arrived in New York alone,—persons who knew nothing of our habits,—who look from afar upon this as the land of license [and these, at least, are *prepared*]—prepared to be the pillars of this Temple of the Demon of Blood. *As one of the results, notwithstanding millions of teetotalers,* we are vast consumers of intoxicating drinks,—an average of *six gallons a head* of ale and spirits to all our population above childhood! For the year ending June, 1850, there were 27,000 criminals! On *the day* of the completion of the census, the whole number in prison was 6,702, of whom 2,460 were foreign. Of the *paupers* fed by us, 68,538 were of foreign birth; only 66,434 Americans."*

Gallant Vermont, the "Green Mountain State," in De-

* In Philadelphia, out of 5,000 tenants of the *almshouse* in 1851, 2,709 were *drunken men*, and 897 *drunken women*. Total pauper-recruits FROM HOUSES APPOINTED TO REGULATE THE TRAFFIC in one single city, 3,606. In Albany, out of 775 liquor dealers, not 100 are *native* Americans.

---

What was the fifth state? When did Vermont adopt the law?

cember, 1852, came *fifth* in the realization of this prohibito-protective law, — the Legislature submitting the time of its action to the decision of the people. On the 5th January, at Ruthland, in a State convention, the people expressed their *viva voce* satisfaction in the law with immense enthusiasm, and on the 6th February, 1853, affirmed the law by their *votes.*

Michigan came *sixth;* and on the law being submitted to the people as to the time of its operation, they voted, by overwhelming majorities, for its immediate action. The liquor party, of course, made what resistance they could, — feed the lawyers, bribed the legislators, and appealed to the judges. Nevertheless, justice was finally done. In 1856, *seven* out of the eight judges of the Supreme Court affirmed the "constitutionality" of the law.

151. On the 10th March, 1853, in answer to attempts made by the traffic to misrepresent the law, the people of Massachusetts held the largest temperance convention which had ever assembled in Boston, and passed some expressive resolutions of approval without a single dissentient. One was, "that this law is to be regarded as the *total abstinence pledge of a whole State*, — [in regard to the sale and purchase], — and that it is a duty to God and humanity, for the State, as for every individual, to keep the pledge unbroken; and we believe in the manifest destiny of this law to spread, ultimately, with the spread of the Anglo-Saxon race."

In some of the larger commercial towns, owing to that

---

**Which came the sixth? What was the action of the people?**
**151. What resolutions were adopted in Massachusetts?**

foreign influence and "trade connection" which sustained the prohibited *slave-trade*, the law was not enforced. In Boston, for example, things went on much as before; though a strong protest against the neglect was drawn up by a large minority of the council. In fact, just prior to the passing of the law, above 700 licenses were granted for a year by the city government. Citizens in the interior had only to visit Boston, in order to discover the merits of the law by the logic of contrast.

Thirteen years later, we find a vast improvement, the State having now got its own constabulary, wholly independent of local influences. In 1867, a license law was passed. Men of the most opposite creeds and parties coalesced here.

The beautiful State of Ohio had been strongly moved by the prohibitory question; and amongst the agitators we may name General Cary, — a man of eloquence and power; a lawyer by profession, but, by good fortune, able to devote his talents and energy to a "cause" which involves the wholesale prevention of broils and disputes, — the rectification of the wrongs of a nation. Petitions, with 250,000 signatures, were presented to the Legislature of 1852-3. Ohio subsequently suppressed the sale *for use on the premises.*

In Wisconsin, this year (1853), the Maine Law was lost by a single vote; while Indiana passed a law bordering upon it in stringency. The old law in Wisconsin made the vender responsible for damages; while, by another law in Iowa, every dram-shop is declared a nuisance, which may at once be broken up and exter-

---

What action did Ohio take? Wisconsin?

minated. But these enactments all *spared the liquor;* and hence not one of them has answered its end, or superseded the necessity of a Maine Law. All other laws allow the vender to *transplant* his machinery and material of mischief, which is the same folly as if a victorious general should *liberate his prisoners* as fast as they were made, — a course that, in recruiting the forces of the enemy, would speedily put an end to his own victories.

152. In March, 1854, a prohibitory law passed the New York Legislature with large majorities, but was unexpectedly vetoed by Governor Seymour. This created great excitement, and lost him his office at the fall election, Myron H. Clark being triumphantly carried by the temperance party. In various States sharp remedies were attempted for abating the evils of the traffic. In Greensboro', Alabama, the liquor license was raised to $1,000; in Marion, Alabama, to $3,000. In Pennsylvania, the question was submitted to the people, and lost only by a majority of 3,000 votes against, in a poll of nearly 300,000.

After a reign of two years in Old Connecticut, the new license system was abolished; and on the 16th June, 1864, a Maine Law was carried by a vote of 148 to 61 in the popular branch of the Legislature, and 13 to 1 in the Senate. The law was fixed to go into operation on the 1st of August, and was sure to be executed, for at the head of the State was Governor Dutton, a good lawyer and stanch temperance man. Thus a single

---

152. When was the prohibitory law passed in New York? What was the license fee in some States? Give the history of the law in Connecticut.

year satisfied the people that the legalized sale of strong drink is an evil that cannot be borne. The State election on the 3d day of November, 1868, resulted in the triumph of prohibition. Of the 220 members of the House of Representatives above 160 were prohibitionists. So that party can carry two votes to their opponents' one in the House, and three to one in the Senate. Doubtless the license law will be repealed, and the old prohibitory law restored.

Connecticut became the *seventh* State, which had adopted a prohibitory law, — the sixth which had been fired to emulate the wisdom of Maine in three years.

The governor, in a letter dated New Haven, October 20, 1854, says: —

> "The law has been thoroughly executed with much less difficulty and opposition than was anticipated. In no instance has a seizure produced any general excitement. Resistance to the law would be unpopular, and it has been found in 'vain' to set it at defiance. The principal obstacle in the way of complete success consists in the importation of liquors from the city of New York into this State, in casks and demijohns, professedly for private use."

Thus we again see that the drawbacks arise, not from too much, but too little law, as regards its *extension*.

The "New Haven Advocate" says: —

> "From all parts of the State the tidings continue to come to us of the *excellent workings* of the Connecticut liquor law. The diminution of intemperance, the reduction of crime and pauperism, the better observance of the Sabbath, etc., are the theme of rejoicing from every quarter. Men who voted against the law, and who have heretofore been its bitter opponents, are now its firm friends."

On the 8th February, 1855, Indiana placed herself *eighth* in the race of prohibition, by overwhelming majorities, appointing the law to commence from the 12th June. The decision was welcomed in the capital, Indianapolis, by rounds of artillery, the ringing of bells from every steeple in the city, and other tokens of public joy. Indiana has had the full operation of the law arrested, through the indecision and imbecility of her courts.

On the 16th of the same month, the Legislature of Illinois prohibited, with Maine Law sanctions, all tippling-houses, but allowed the manufacture of cider and wine, and their sale in not less than five gallons. The people, however, vetoed the measure.

On the 20th of February, 1855, little Delaware (by a vote of 11 to 10 in the House) promptly passed a protective law, the *ninth* star in the banner of prohibition: the *Dirigo* to the tardy South.

In July, 1856, Mr. T. B. Coursey, in announcing that the judges had unanimously sustained the law, says:—

"Our law, which has not been more than *half* executed, has *greatly diminished drunkenness*, and almost entirely stopped the sale."

153. On the 12th April, 1855, completing protection to the four great free States of the West, came Iowa. Though *tenth* in the race of prohibition, Iowa was one of the first to declare the traffic a nuisance. The constitutionality of the law has been sustained by the

---

When did Indiana adopt the law? What reception did it meet with? What law was adopted in Illinois? What and when in Delaware?

courts. It has been vigorously enforced in Keokuk. Mr. Kinbourne, when mayor, said there was not a physician, lawyer, or merchant, who partook of intoxicating beverages.

North Carolina, in February, passed a prohibitory measure through the House by a vote of 11 to 10. Restrictive measures were adopted in Texas and Mississippi, and in other States the initial agitation was commenced for the law of Maine. On the 10th March, 1855, the Assembly of Wisconsin passed the law by a vote of 42 to 23 ; the Senate concurred, but the governor vetoed it. The political party which had been dominant for forty years in New Hampshire was this month totally annihilated for its opposition to the law, good men of all parties (including some of its own) uniting in the defeat.

*Eleventh* in the race was the territory of Nebraska, which, about this period, passed a Maine Law, fearing lest the tipplers and traffickers of Iowa would be induced to cross the line, and overrun their territory.

154. Next, not least, the four years' labor of the Maine Law party in the Empire State was now to be consummated. In April, 1855, a prohibitory bill (somewhat marred from the original model) passed the Senate by 21 votes to 11, and the lower house by 80 to 45 ; and on April 7th received the signature of the Hon. Myron H. Clark, the governor. New York State, therefore, arrived *twelfth* at the goal. An idea may be formed of

---

153. What peculiarity was there about the Iowa law? What other States followed?

154. When was the law adopted in the Empire State? How many States did this make which had adopted it?

the inveteracy of the opposition, from the fact that on the day of the bill passing the Assembly, points of order were called to for nearly three hours in succession, in order to exhaust the patience of the House; motions being made to commit to select committees, committees of conference, and to a committee of the whole House. When the vote passed, the last move was a motion to "reconsider the vote," which was lost by 31 to 84. The day selected for the law coming into effect was the 4th of July, — the anniversary of the day on which they declared their emancipation from foreign rule, — a day than which none could be better for inaugurating a legal campaign against the tyranny of the traffic.*

155. On the 13th of August, 1855, the last of the New England States, New Hampshire, placed herself *thirteenth* in the race of prohibition. This was a crowning victory, which tended at once to sustain the law in the adjoining States, and to temper the reverse of the following year, to which we shall presently allude. Governor Metcalf, elected for a second time, in his annual message to the Legislature, 1856, said that

"The act is having a salutary effect. *It is more fully regarded and practically sustained* than any license law we ever had in

* In England, the event was celebrated on that day by the "Grand Alliance" Fete in the beautiful grounds of Elvaston Castle, near Derby, a seat of the Vice-President, the Right Honorable the Earl of Harrington, on which occasion two fine young trees (an American and an English species) were planted in the presence of 10,000 persons, called the "Alliance Oaks," and the record of the event literally graved upon the rock forever. The Hon. Neal Dow, Dr. Lees, and others were present on the occasion.

---

155. What was the "crowning victory"? Give the testimony of Gov. Metcalf.

the State. In many towns the sale of intoxicating liquors is wholly abandoned, and in others liquor is *sold only as other penal offences are committed, in secret.*"

The Rev. E. W. Jackson, writing in October, 1856, says: —

"The law *works like a charm*. It will be an easy matter to close up the last grog-shop in the State."

There was also a prohibitory law in force in one of the States south of "Mason and Dixon's line." The Gallatin "Argus" contains the copy of "An act to prohibit the sale and gratuitous distribution of liquors within Police District No. 1, of the County of Copiah," Mississippi. No more licenses shall be granted, and only druggists and apothecaries may sell, "for strictly medicinal purposes." The penalty for the first violation of the act is $100 fine, and ten days in the county jail; second offence, $200, and imprisonment in the county jail not exceeding thirty days. *This prohibitory law was approved on the sixth of March, and took effect on the first day of May*, 1856.

156. It is important to understand that the legislative opponents of the *Maine Law* never propose reverting to the old system *of irresponsibility*. The "New York Herald," a widely circulated paper, thus records a debate in 1853: —

"The temperance excitement has nearly reached its zenith. The friends and opponents of the Maine liquor law have each

---

What was the testimony of Rev. Mr. Jackson? Give the provisions of the law adopted by Mississippi.

156. What was the position of the "New York Herald" in 1853? What

presented their reports. Mr. Dewey commenced reading the report, and the manner of his reading, and the *classical language in which the report is couched,* very soon attracted the closest attention of every member of the House, and the whole immense auditory. Messrs. Dewey and Odell propose to regulate the sale of liquor by electing a Board of Excise, with power to issue licenses; retailers in towns and villages containing over one thousand voters shall pay for license the sum of *one hundred dollars;* in places containing two thousand and upwards, *two hundred dollars,* — to sell nothing but liquor, and that to adults only — *in taverns; not to be sold to any citizens, but to travellers alone,* — retailers to be subject to pay *all damages* which may occur from intoxicated persons, — and punishment to be inflicted for selling to *minors.*" *

It is clear, that these penalties, if inflicted, would ruin the business. After the passing of the law in New York in 1856, the rum party are *known* to have paid $10,000 to two leading journals for space to oppose the law, and lawyers were employed to carry liquor cases to the minor courts. When the verdict was in favor of the law, the case was moved to the "Court of Appeals." In all localities where such appeals were made, the law virtually ceased. Yet, such was the public opinion in its favor — such the respect of the genuine American population for "the States' collected will" — that over *two-thirds* of the vast area of New York State the law was implicitly

* Gov. Pollock, in his message to the Pennsylvania Legislature, 1856, shows that no one believes in the old system. "That the laws (previously) in existence were imperfect, and *failed to check or control the evils* of intemperance, is a proposition too plain to be doubted."

---

would be the result of the penalties if inflicted? Was the law obeyed in the State? How much of the State?

obeyed and honored.* What the state of things was in the fall of 1855, the journals of the day witness. The "NewYork Reformer" says: —

"This law has done a wonderful deal of good since it went into effect, notwithstanding the *Herculean efforts of its foes to render nugatory its beneficent provisions.* We advocate a 'fusion' of the virtuous and order-loving of all parties to sustain it. Unprincipled political leaders may denounce the 'fanaticism' that labors to ameliorate the condition of humanity, and will seek by every means to chain the wheels of reform to the *jug*-gernaut of conservatism — in vain!"

The "Saratoga Helper" says: —

"It is true the law has not been properly enforced, but when, before, were there ever such *superhuman efforts made to oppose and break down the law?* When, before, has a class banded together, raised large sums of money, and openly defied the legal authorities? The resistance does not come from the people, — it is the desperate struggle of a bad business to maintain itself in the public regard. Against this bitter, unrelenting opposition, the friends of right have had to oppose the doubtful bulwark of *an untried law;* have had to feel their way carefully in administering it; and they are suffering all the inconvenience of the delay of the courts."

On the 16th January, 1856, Governor Clark, in his

* It is a significant incident, showing how the most respectable classes regard the sale of spirits for tippling purposes as a social *nuisance*, that when bands of women in the West, and even in Cattaraugus county, New York, — not drunken, noisy women, such as led the Exeter bread riot, but quiet, well dressed, persistent ladies, — have gone to the grog-shops, broken the kegs and demijohns, and poured out the liquor, a sacrifice to the household gods, juries have, upon prosecution, invariably acquitted.

---

What testimony did Gov. Clark give in relation to the law?

message to the Legislature at Albany, thus manfully referred to the law: —

"Notwithstanding it has been subjected to an opposition more *persistent, unscrupulous,* and *defiant* than is often incurred by an act of legislation, — and though legal and magisterial influence, *often acting unofficially and extra-judicially,* have combined to render it inoperative, to forestall the decision of the courts, wrest the statute from its obvious meaning, and create a general distrust in, if not hostility to, all legislative restrictions of the traffic in intoxicating liquors, — *it has still,* outside of our large cities, *been generally obeyed. The influence is visible in a marked diminution of the evils it sought to remedy.*"

The mayor of Albany intimated to his police, that if they meddled with the law at all they should be dismissed! The Recorder of New York told the Grand Jury not to entertain any complaints! Yet the parties who initiate such proceedings publish to the world the failure of a law which they never tried! — wishing the people to forget that *a law can no more work itself* than can a physician's recipe. That some members of a family *prevent* the sick member from taking the physic is surely very absurd as an argument against the wisdom of the prescription!

157. At last came the anxiously looked-for decision of the New York Court of Appeals at Albany. This court is composed of four judges *elected* to it, and of four Justices of the Supreme Court. The judges on this occasion were, Denio, Alexander S. Johnson, Comstock, and Selden. The current justices were, Mitchell of

---

157. How is the Court of Appeals composed? Who were the judges? What was their duty?

the first district; Wright of the third; Hubbard of the fifth; and Thomas A. Johnson of the fourth. The cases were entitled "People *vs.* Wynchamer," and "People *vs.* Toynbee."

No doubt the New York act had several legal flaws in it; but its legislative OBJECT and PRINCIPLE was admitted to be constitutional, only requiring to be amended in its expression and process.

The duty of the judges was to carry out the obvious intentions of the law, under such *limitations of its generality* as constitutional rights might require and fix.* The only two points of importance, then, are these: —

(*a*) Can the Legislature "constitutionally" decree that *property on hand*, at a given time, is contraband *when used in a given way?*

(*b*) Did the New York Act *so* "constitutionally" decree liquor on hand to be contraband for certain uses?

To the first (*a*) the court UNANIMOUSLY answers, "It *is* competent." To the second (*b*) some of the judges reply, "The *act* does not *express itself* with *sufficient specificness* and *discrimination.*"

One thing, then, is very certain: *that the law is not*

* So T. A. Johnson, for the law, expressly argued: "If the language is *susceptible* of interpretation in harmony with the declared object of an enactment, courts are bound to give it that interpretation. They can only give a construction which will convict the legislator of absurdity or folly, in cases *where the language employed is so clear as to leave no alternative.*" We may add, that living judges are required chiefly for this purpose, — to make *specific* applications of the vague or broad principles of the law, *because* the law cannot alter or speak for itself. Some of these judges, following the reverse course, ignored a law because it cannot *discriminate* for itself.

---

State the only two points of importance. What did the Court answer to the first? What answer to the second? Why did they say the law was unconstitutional?

unconstitutional *because it is a Maine Law, or because it forbids the sale of liquor* (*on hand*, or otherwise *for certain purposes*), but BECAUSE IT DOES NOT DO THIS WITH SUFFICIENT DISTINCTNESS AND PRECISION. Let the friends of prohibition, then, marshal their forces anew, and march to the final victory in the old heroic spirit. They have succeeded in *getting* such a law; let them now turn their attention to perfecting its form and machinery, and to making the man that shall execute the measure.*

* Few persons, during the past two years, had labored more zealously for prohibition than the late B. F. Harwood, the beloved clerk of this same "Court of Appeals." He had often declared that the prohibitory law was his only chance of escape from that fatal propensity which has strown his profession with so many wrecks. When the time came for the assembling of the decisive tribunal, he visited Judge Comstock, and thus besought him to save the law: —

"Judge Comstock, you know that I am addicted to drinking; but you do *not* know — no living person knows — how I have struggled to break off this habit! Sometimes I have succeeded for a while, and then these accursed liquor-bars, like so many man-traps, have effected my fall. For this reason, I have labored for the prohibitory law at every stage. Great numbers of our Supreme Court judges, and others of our most learned and able jurists, have endorsed its constitutionality. For myself, I have no more doubt of its constitutionality than I have that I am now alive. So great and beneficent a measure should not be balked upon the mere *technicalities* of our profession. My last hope, Judge Comstock, is with you. Sustain the law for which I have labored, and my energy will be redoubled. Close the liquor-bars, even the respectable liquor-bars, and I shall be saved. *Your decision is with me a matter of life and death!*"

On the morning of Tuesday, the 25th March, amidst the most painful suspense, the eight judges took their seats. The vote of five of their number was handed to the clerk to be entered: *We declare the law to be void.* How did Mr. Harwood feel at that terrible moment? As a man feels who has to write his own death-warrant. Then the last hope of a noble heart gave way. During the week he fell before temptation and despair combined. On Saturday night he raved; four men could not hold the man who was so gentle when himself that a little child might lead him. By eight o'clock on the *Sabbath morning* the liquor-traffic had achieved one of its signal victories, and the city was startled at this swift and awful commentary upon the decision of Tuesday.

158. Let us now indicate, by some facts and figures, and by official, political, and professional testimonies, beginning with New York State, what have been the social results of an imperfect, because initial and impeded, prohibitory law.

We shall not, of course, in estimating *crime* lessened by the law, take account of the cases of violation of the law itself, — which are for acts that, in their relation to the public, *were precisely the same before they were treated as offences as now*, only vastly more numerous and mischievous. Sometimes, even, we shall not notice " drunkenness," — first, because we here treat of drunkenness, not so much on its *own* account, as that to which it leads; and second, because, in very many places, *before* the law was passed, simple drunkenness was left unheeded by the police, but *after* the law was narrowly watched and instantly pounced upon. In both cases, the *acts of offence* might be greatly diminished, while the *committals* were somewhat enlarged.*

The returns in the following table, illustrating the partial operation of the New York law, are, for the same period, save Utica, which is but for four months

* Some one quoted Judge H. W. Bishop, to prove that the law made bad worse. " Criminal business has very largely increased under the new law." Was this true? Quite true — for *one side* of truth. Turning to his charge, we find he goes on to explain. " I had, in my last term in the County of Middlesex, no fewer than 104 indictments, *under the new law*. I say, without fear of contradiction, that nine-tenths of all crimes of personal violence are committed in a state of intoxication, and if the source of the evil is dried up by the new law, judges by and by will have little criminal business to attend to."

---

158. What is now to be indicated? How is crime here estimated? How is drunkenness here treated?

instead of six, namely, from the 6th of July to the 31st of December inclusive of each year: —

| Committals for offences excluding drunkenness. | 1854. | 1855. | Decrease in favor of the law. |
|---|---|---|---|
| Cayuga County Jail . . . | 85 | 59 | 26 |
| Onondaga " . . . | 138 | 103 | 35 |
| Seneca " . . . | 75 | 28 | 47 |
| Ontario " . . . | 89 | 45 | 44 |
| Albany Watch House . . . | 1,974 | 1,278 | 696 |
| Syracuse (Police Record) . . | 778 | 515 | 263 |
| Auburn " " . . . | 104 | 50 | 54 |
| Rochester " " . . . | 1,552 | 740 | 812 |
| Utica " " . . . | 165 | 80 | 85 |
| | 4,960 | 2,898 | 2,062 |

R. R. Brown, hotel-keeper at Carthage, New York, says that *by abolishing the liquor-bar he is brought in contact with a better class of customers, and all the duties and associations of his business are improved to a degree* which affords him a fourfold compensation for the "unprofitable profits" which arose from vending "the drink of the drunkards."

New York State next illustrates the power of prohibition *by its absence.* There was an alarming increase of

What was the testimony of the hotel-keeper at Carthage?

crime both in city and country. The Albany "Morning Times" of the 16th October, 1856 — an anti Maine Law paper — said: —

"The Penitentiary is filling up. The inmates amount to 270. Of this number, 180 are women. The number of prisoners is greater than it has been during the past eighteen months."*

159. On the 27th August, 1853, the Hon. Neal Dow published the following: —

"At the time of the enactment of the law, rum-selling was carried on openly, in all parts of the State. In Portland there were between three and four hundred rum-shops, and immediately after the enactment of the law *not one*. The wholesale trade in liquors was at once annihilated. In Portland, large numbers of men were reformed. Temptations to intemperance were in a great measure removed out of the path of the young and inexperienced.

"At the end of the municipal year, 1851-2, an official report to the City Council was ordered to be printed and distributed; its statements were not at the time, nor have they since been, denied.

* We record one contrary sample, taken from the "Albany Atlas," Aug. 1853: —

"Practical Operation of the Maine Law. The following is an extract from a letter received by a commercial house in this city, from a large distillery and rectifying establishment in New York, which deals largely with the Eastern States: 'The fact is, that since the passing of the Maine Law we find it difficult to supply our orders; and should our own Legislature pass a similar law at their next session *we shall take measures to enlarge our works immediately*.'"

Why, then, did these people want the law repealed?

---

What statement is made in relation to the Albany Penitentiary?

159. What was the testimony of Hon. Neal Dow, in relation to Portland?

"*Ten Months' Effects* (*June* 1*st to March* 20*th*): —

| COMMITTALS. | 1851. | 1852. | Decrease. |
|---|---|---|---|
| To Almshouse | 252 | 146 | 106 |
| To House of Correction for *Intemperance* | 46 | 10* | 36 |
| Inmates of Almshouse *on* March 24th | 112 | 90 | 22 |
| Out-door aid to Families | 135 | 90 | 45 |

"At the term of the District Court, in March, 1851, there were 17 indictments; at the term for 1852 there was but *one* (for petty larceny), the result of a mistake."

We were ourselves in Portland a few days after this letter was published. At several hotels we asked for strong drink, but could not get it. In the spring of 1855, the Hon. Horace Greeley visited Maine, and in the "New York Tribune" gave the following testimony: —

"The pretence that as much liquor is sold now in Maine as in former years is impudently false. We spent three days in travelling through the State, *without seeing a glass of it*, or an individual who appeared to be under its influence; and we were reliably assured, that at the Augusta House, where the governor and most of the Legislature board, not only was no liquor to be had, *but even the use of tobacco had almost entirely ceased.*"

During the mayoralty of Mr. Dow, the House of Cor-

* Notwithstanding much greater activity of the police under the new law.

---

State the decrease in committals to Almshouse? House of Correction? Give Horace Greeley's testimony. What other testimonials are given?

rection was for a time empty. In a pamphlet of 100 pages, published at Toronto, entitled "The Maine Law Illustrated," being the tour of investigation made in February, 1853, by Mr. A. Farewell and Mr. G. P. Ure, on behalf of the Canadian Prohibition League, we find a vast number of testimonies to the same effect, from persons of the highest character, including bishops, judges, governors, mayors, marshals, magistrates, ministers, professors, physicians, counsellors, representatives, etc. Their own conclusion is thus stated: —

"It is almost universally acknowledged to be as successful in its operations as any other penal law that ever was enacted."

At Calais, on the New Brunswick border, N. Smith Jun., of the Executive Council, says: —

"Where enforced, the results are good; the only places where it can be said to have failed are where they have had anti Maine Law justices, — *irresponsible* for seven years save by impeachment. Many of those *who sold* liquor have turned their attention to other businesses, *and are now better off than when selling liquor*. They have far fewer bad debts, and more reliable customers."

Mr. Sydney Perham, Speaker of the House of Representatives, says: —

"My knowledge of the workings of the law extends over a large section of the State. I can assure you the law *works well*."

---

What was the result at Calais? What testimony does Mr. Perham give?

Professor Pond, of Bangor, says: —

"I have not seen a drunken man in our streets for the last six months. The House of Correction has been, at times, *almost empty*. I know not but it is so now. The expense of paupers is greatly diminished."

Under date of September, 1854, the "Edinburgh News Commissioner" thus writes of Waterville: —

"Ten or eleven years ago, the cost of pauperism rose, in a manner unaccountable but for excessive drinking, from $700 to $1,800 a year. I am told that this year, with twice the population, the public payments for the poor will not exceed $1,000. *The amount of crime is also greatly lessened.* Those who still deserve the name of drunkards are mostly Irishmen and French Canadians, the latter people having settled extensively in the northern parts of Maine."

On the 8th of March, 1852, the Marshal of Gardiner reports: —

"At the commencement of the official term of office there *were* in the city 14 places where intoxicating liquor was sold; some of them the *habitual resort of drunken, riotous, and disorderly persons.* . . . *But one person has been convicted of drunkenness for the last four months;* but *two* sent to the watch-house for the last six months. The law has been rigidly and *quietly* enforced."

The Marshal of Augusta reports for 1852, as follows: —

---

Prof. Pond? "Edinburgh News Commissioner"? Marshal of Gardiner? Marshal of Augusta?

"Augusta had *four* wholesale stores, business worth $200,000 a year; retail-shops, 25. The city was (officially) *exempted* from the new law for 60 days; one dealer made a profit of $900. As soon as the 60 days were out, three of the wholesale dealers sent off their liquors to New York. The remaining firm persisted in selling, until about $1,000 worth of their liquors were seized. Liquor *may* be sold at the principal hotels, but stealthily. One of the keepers has been twice convicted. . . The police *used* to be called up 100 nights in a year. *Since the passage of the law they have not been summoned once.*"

A gentleman well known to the philanthropic world, who has several times visited the western hemisphere in the interests of the slave, writes us as follows: —

"NEAR CHELMSFORD,
"8th month, 11th, 1856.

"ESTEEMED FRIEND, DR. LEES: —

"In the early part of the year 1854, whilst travelling in the State of Maine, we came to Augusta, its capital. We were driven through the city in a sledge, by our friend, J. B. Lang, of Vassalboro', who, as we passed along, pointed out to us the city jail, *the windows of which were boarded up*. 'This,' he said to us, 'is owing to our Maine Law.' I think he remarked, 'It is empty now.'

"Thy assured friend,
"JOHN CANDLER."

The Mayor of Bangor, in his message to the Council, April 22d, 1852, says: —

"On the 1st July, when I gave notice that I should enforce the law, 108 persons were selling liquors here, openly; 20 of them have left the city. Of the remaining 88, not one sells openly."

He furnished the following statistics: —

| | | | Decrease. |
|---|---|---|---|
| 1850–51. | Inmates of Almshouse and House of Correction, | 12,206 | |
| 1851–52. | " " " | 9,192 | |
| | | | 3,104 |
| 1850–51. | Number of public prosecutions................. | 101 | |
| 1851–52. | " " ................. | 58 | |
| | | | 43 |

How far the people of Maine were prepared to honor and enforce the law is best shown by their election of municipal boards: 117 towns elected temperance men; 8 chose mixed boards; and but 34 elected opposition councils. The towns in favor represent a population of 254,891; those against, 55,565.

In 1855, the prohibitionists in Maine lost the election of governor. The temporary repeal of the law, and substitution of stringent license, with pecuniary penalties, was ALL FOR THE BEST; making the enemies of truth to illustrate it by the workings of error. Did the stringent license law succeed in *restraining* that drinking which the "State of Maine" newspaper affirmed the prohibitory law had *increased?* The "Portland Journal" reported a vast increase of drunkenness, rows, burglaries, and other crime. The "Bangor Mercury" said: —

"We are informed by a person in the express business, one who has good opportunities for seeing and knowing whereof he speaks, that the quantity of liquors brought to this city this season *is tenfold greater than it was last year.*"

---

What statistics does the Mayor of Bangor give? State the result of the elections in Maine. What occurred in 1855?

The "Calais Advertiser" said: —

*"We have seen more men reeling drunk through our street the last three months than we have seen before in the last three years."*

160. Southward, we pass to Massachusetts. The Hon. H. W. Bishop, judge of the Court of Common Pleas, says: —

"The violations of *the law itself* add to the criminal business. The operation of this new law has diminished *the other class* very much. Crimes of personal violence have *hitherto* constituted *two-thirds* of all our criminal business. Several years will pass before the courts are satisfied as to the bearing of this new law."

In January, 1856, it was announced that

"The law has evidently driven the open liquor trade out of three-fourths of the State. There has been a decrease of 50 criminals in the State Prison."

Mr. Counsellor Chapman said: —

"There is not the one-hundredth part of the drinking in Springfield that there was before the temperance movement commenced. Even those who, in their own families, use their wine, give their influence in favor of the Maine Law. Assaults were almost always committed under the influence of drink, and already that *class of crimes has nearly ceased.* Legal and moral agencies should be combined. They are like the soul and body, and cannot act well separately."

---

**160. What statement was made by Judge Bishop of Massachusetts? What by Counsellor Chapman?**

Mr. Morton, police justice, says: —

"The city is *much more quiet* than it used to be. The police books will give no correct information in regard to *drunkenness,* because persons now seen intoxicated are arrested, *which was not the case before,* and persons will now *sell* in violation of the law. In this way the criminal business *appears* to have increased, but as the other class of offences which formerly constituted the chief business of the Police Court *has almost entirely disappeared,* this new class will soon be worked out."

The Rev. Mr. Seeley says: —

"Its beneficial effects are remarkable. It evidently made a very great change in the moral state of the entire city. Its effects are very marked upon our young men. *Our Lyceum lectures were never half so well attended.*"

In Worcester, the number of commitments for drunkenness, from June to September, 1853, was 64 less than in the same months in 1852; 106 less than in 1850.

In 1857 the magistrates did *not* enforce the law. The consequence was that there were 60 per cent. more prisoners in the jail than in 1855.

In various parts of the State there were held musters, cattle-shows, public celebrations, at which the peace and order surprised all spectators, and opened a new era in the history of such assemblages. The diminution of arrests for drunkenness was 77 per cent. If there has

---

What by Police Justice Morton? Rev. Mr. Seeley? How did the commitments in Worcester, in 1853, compare with 1852? What diminution in drunkenness was reported in different parts of the State?

since been a relapse, it was from no defect in the law; *it was enforced long enough to show its power.*

In the city of Lowell, according to the Hon. Mr. Huntington, the mayor, for the two months ending September 22d, 1851, there were committed to the watch-house 110 in a state of drunkenness; reported as being *seen* drunk, not arrested, 390; total, 500. In the corresponding period of the next year, when the law came in force, there were committed to the watch-house for drunkenness, 70; reported as seen drunk, but not arrested, 110; total, 180; *diminution*, 320.

Mr. D. W. Alford, of Greenfield, said: —

"A year ago there were from 20 to 30 grog-shops; I don't think there is *one* now. *The law has been a blessing beyond anything we ever had.* I was afraid to send my own child, a boy of ten, into the streets unprotected, a year ago. Now females are perfectly safe."

Dr. J. W. Stone, one of the representatives for Boston, says: —

"From the best evidence I can gather, concerning the influence of unaided moral measures, the average effect of pledges is, that 50 per cent. adhere for a single year, 33 for five years, and 25 per cent. *permanently*. . . I looked upon the law, when first enacted in our sister State, with some suspicion. It is one of the peculiarities of this law, whatever theories drawing a different conclusion we might in advance apply to it, that *where it has been most efficiently executed, there the greatest results in the suppression of crime have been satisfactorily achieved;* and it has seized with such strong hold upon the hearts of the

---

What was said by Dr. Stone, of Boston?

people, that its popularity has in those places become invincible."

Speaking of a great political meeting, held in September, 1856, the "Boston Telegraph" says: —

"*We did not see a drunken man on the ground. This was owing to the fact that liquor was not sold.* Two or three men attempted to sell, but were soon *routed*, and took to their heels."

161. Proceed we next to Connecticut: First, of Hartford, Mr. H. Y. Phelps, says (February, 1855): —

"The fighting and rioting, so common, have entirely disappeared. Open drinking is stopped."

Rev. Dr. Clark says: —

"The general effects of the law are good, — *very* apparent in connection with our City Mission."

Chief Justice Williams says: —

"There *are* more prosecutions for drunkenness. Since the 1st of August, 1854, I have not seen more than one or two instances of intemperance in the streets."

Judge Bulkeley says: —

"There is *much less* drunkenness, much less liquor sold now. It is not sold openly at all, but is driven into secret places. The number of *misdemeanors* is far less."

---

161. Give the statement of Mr. Phelps of Connecticut. Of Dr. Clark. Of Chief Justice Williams. Of Judge Bulkeley.

Mr. B. Mann says: —

"I have been police justice here for 20 years, and *I know a very great difference* since the law went into effect."

Mr. L. S. Cowles says: —

"I have seen ten men drunk before this law passed, for *one* seen since. It was only when a drunken man was making some *assault*, that he was taken up formerly."

Mr. D. Hawley, city missionary, says: —

"I have a mission Sabbath school. Since the 1st of August it has *increased one-third.* I have seen in my rounds, wives, mothers, even young women, the worse for liquor, — *but all that has changed;* and in my conversations with the poor, many of them say that the law must have come from heaven, — it is too good to have been framed by man."

Of Hartford, containing 20,000 people, a resident said he had *not seen a single intoxicated person during the year!*

The "Hartford Courant," of December 21st, 1854, has this: —

| | | | | |
|---|---|---|---|---|
| "July, | 1853. | Committals *to* Workhouse | | 16 |
| July, | 1854. | " | " | 20 |
| August, | 1854. | " | " | 8 |
| *August to December*, 1854, discharged *from* the House | | | | 23 |

"On September 9th, there was *not a single male person* in

Of Mr. Mann. Of Mr. Cowles. Of Mr. Hawley. What statement is made of Hartford? Give the figures of the "Hartford Courant."

the workhouse, — which, except for two females, would have been *tenantless.* There has not been a parallel to this at any season, for eight years at least, — how much longer we do not know; but we presume there never was. Is there a sane person who doubts for an instant *what* has caused this result?"

In Middletown, police expense was reduced by $1,200. For year ending October, 1854, cost of paupers, $2,218 — for 1855, $1,644. Vagrancy lessened.

Mr. Freeman, of Haddam village, says: —

"Paupers reduced from 10 to 4. Quite an improvement in *the sale of necessary articles* of life."

Mr. Day, of East Haddam, says: —

"Drunkenness diminished decidedly. Persons in almshouse, previously, 24; now 16. No person sent to jail since the law enacted."

Dr. F. Farnsworth, of Norwich, January, 1856, says: —

"*The amount of disease in poor families, is not one-tenth what it was. Casualties* are largely diminished."

The "Norwich Examiner" has the following statistics: —

"COMMITTALS.

| (*August* 1, *to July* 31.) | 1853–54 | 1854–55 | Decrease. |
|---|---|---|---|
| To Norwich Almshouse | 61 | 40 | 21 |
| To New London County Jail | 220 | 127 | 93 |

---

What was the result in Middletown? East Haddam? Norwich?

"Of the 220 cases, 73 were for drunkenness, and 4 for selling; of the 127 cases, 35 were for drunkenness, 2 for getting liquor under false pretences, and 16 for selling; and these cases must obviously, under the continued operation of the law, cease.

"*Number in jail August* 1*st*, 1855, 16. Four times as many sellers have been committed the past year as during the previous year; *but only half as many drunkards.*"

The "Home Journal," of July 7th, 1855, says: —

"The Maine liquor law has ruined the jail business completely. The jail at Wyndham is *to be let for a boarding-house.*"

Mayor Brooks, of Bridgeport, gives emphatic testimony in favor of the law, in his report to the Common Council. He says that when mayor, three years ago, he was called up three nights out of five, throughout the entire year, to disperse brawling and noisy mobs.

"During the past year I have not been called upon in a single instance, by watch at night, to suppress or disperse any assemblage of riotous persons. All this change I attribute to the working of the new liquor law. It is a rare sight to see a person drunk."

"Chambers' Journal," January 20, 1855, cites as follows: —

"On the 1st of August, 1854, the new law came into opera-

---

What was the result in Bridgeport? What testimony in favor of the law is given in "Chambers' Journal"?

tion in Connecticut, and was carried out in a very stringent manner. A great change was visible immediately after, in New Haven, the capital. The noisy gangs of rowdies disappeared, and their midnight brawls ceased; our streets were quiet night and day; and the most violent opponents of the law said, 'If such are the effects of the law, we will oppose it no longer.' A few persons got intoxicated upon liquor from New York, and were promptly arrested, and fined 20 dollars and costs, which they paid, or went to jail. As to the prisons and almshouses in the various parts of the State, they are getting empty. A large number of our most desperate villains, who formerly kept grog-shops and gambling-houses, have emigrated, finding business so bad. Several who kept *gambling-saloons and disorderly houses*, in defiance of law, declared that *neither one nor the other can be supported without liquor*, and have moved to New York, where they can continue their infamous business advantageously."

The "Puritan Recorder," in the spring of 1856, contained a letter, from which we transcribe the following paragraph, showing how the law cherishes charitable feeling and forethought: —

"Another characteristic has marked the past winter. There was less complaint than usual on the part of the poor. *The attention was more awake on the subject;* more had been *contributed* and *done* to secure the relief needed. The poor more economically husbanded their own resources. The operation of the Maine Law had sensibly counteracted the *sources* of want. These beneficial effects have been perceived to be increasing ever since the law began to take effect. Another fact tells with emphasis. It is the *marked diminution of fires.* Since August 1st, 1854, the loss of property from this cause has been *fully one-half less.*"

---

What testimony in the "Puritan Recorder"?

The Rev. Leonard Bacon, D.D., of New Haven, says: —

"The operation of the law for one year is a matter of observation to the inhabitants. Its effect, in promoting peace, order, quiet, and general prosperity, no man can deny. *Never for twenty years has our city been so quiet and peaceful as under its action.* It is no longer simply a question of temperance, but a governmental question — one of legislative foresight and morality."

Governor Dutton said: —

"Criminal prosecutions are rapidly diminishing. The *home of the peaceful citizen was never before so secure.*"

162. Rhode Island comes next, — where, however, various obstacles have been placed in the way of the enactment. Mr. Barstow, the Mayor of Providence, said: —

"After the law had been in operation *three months*, I published statistics, showing that the law, in that short time, had made a reduction of nearly 60 per cent. in our monthly committals.

COMMITTALS.

| | | | Decrease. |
|---|---|---|---|
| 1851. | To Watch-House for drunkenness and assaults.. | 282 | |
| 1852. | " " " .. | 177 | |
| | | | 105 |
| 1851. | To County Jail.................................. | 161 | |
| 1852. | " .................................. | 99 | |
| | | | 62" |

163. In Vermont the law has been still more successful.

---

What testimony by Leonard Bacon?
162. What statistics are given by Mr. Barstow, of Rhode Island?

In July, 1853, Mr. L. Underwood, States' Attorney of Chittenden County, wrote from Burlington: —

"The law has put an end to drunkenness and crime *almost entirely.* Within this town, from December 1, 1852, until March 8, 1853, complaints were made to me, almost daily, for breaches of the peace; and, on investigation, I was satisfied that nine-tenlhs of the crimes were caused by drunkenness. *Since the 8th of March, two complaints only have been made for such offences*, and only one was caused by drunkenness."

Mr. M. L. Church said, February, 1855: —

"I am very much pleased with the law. You might stay here for a month, and you would not see a drunken man in the city."

The Grand Jury in their report said: —

"We feel highly gratified to find *the jail destitute of inmates*, — a circumstance attributable, in a very great measure we believe, to the suppression of the sale of intoxicating liquors."

Professor Pease, of Burlington University, says: —

"There is a very great diminution in the use of liquors by the students. We have not had, for a year past, any rowdyism."

At the fall elections of 1856, General Fletcher, the president of the State Temperance Society, was elected

---

163. What important testimony is given by the State Attorney of Vermont? What by Mr. Church? Give the Report of the Grand Jury. What was the result of the election of 1856? Give Gen. Fletcher's testimony.

governor of the State. On the 9th of October, in delivering his message, he used these words : —

"Coming from all portions of the Commonwealth, *you have personal knowledge of the practical operation of this law, and its adaptation to accomplish the purposes for which it was designed.*"

164. Last of the New England States, comes New Hampshire, which had been so long the "grog-shop" for the "thirsty souls" of the bordering States.

In March, 1856, the "Journal" announced that

"The law works admirably in all parts of the State. *Pauperism and crime are almost unknown.*"

The General Association of the Congregationalist churches, held on the 26th August, 1856, in their report say : —

"*We are called upon to give thanks* to God for the prohibitory law, which has been attended with such happy results."

The "Enquirer," published at Dover, says (September, 1856) : —

"The jail, which usually has a good supply of tenants, *has been entirely empty for several weeks past.*"

Another report from Strafford County announced that "for several weeks *the jail has been empty.*"

The "Tribune," Indiana, published the following, in

---

164. What was New Hampshire called? What was the happy result of the law? Give the testimony of the General Association. "Enquirer." What account is given in the "Tribune" in reference to prisoners?

April, 1856. Committed to penitentiary, 5 months preceding June, 1855, when the law went into effect, 83. Committed during 7 months after, 51, — a reduction of 50 per cent. Since the law was annulled by the Court, drinking and gambling have held carnival.

IOWA. — A letter from the State's Attorney says: —

> "*The prohibitory law in this State is doing considerable good. It works well.* If vigorously carried out, it will effect more than all the moral-reform lectures that can be mustered into the service."

A correspondent, under date of August 14th, 1856, says: —

> "There are many towns in Iowa where there is not a glass of liquor sold, and, if the reformation continues, all the citizens of that lovely prairie State will soon be free from the withering and blasting effects of the liquor traffic."

Under a knowledge of such facts as we have detailed, can we wonder at the expression of the Rev. John D. Lawyer, chaplain to New York State Prison, at Auburn? — "Give us the Maine Law, and in five years Auburn Prison is no more."

165. In Canada the agitation on behalf of the Maine Law has been carried on with varying success, but with substantial progress. After long effort, the temperance men succeeded in turning the attention of their Legislature to the traffic in strong drink, and, as a result, in 1855, a prohibitory law passed their legislative assem-

---

What account from Iowa? What was the expression of Rev. J. D. Lawyer, of Auburn? What was the progress in Canada?

bly by a vote of 51 to 29. The bill, however, was obstructed in every way, and at last thrown over, on a technical objection, referring to some omission in the forms of the House. This but increased the ardor of the friends of the bill, whose exertions were redoubled. Petitions poured in during the next session. The petitions in favor were signed by 108,417, in proportion to every 4,388 against it. Amongst others, the Roman Catholic Bishop of Montreal, with 20,000 of his parishioners, signed a petition, praying the Canadian Parliament to outlaw the liquor traffic. The petitions against the measure emanated from the large cities, and from those localities in which the influence of the traffic was most powerful. Though the faith of some who had undertaken to pilot the bill through the storms of the opposition was shaken by the temporary disaster in Maine, and they deserted the helm at the most critical moment, — the measure being again stranded in consequence, — it was yet felt that indifference to the claims of popular feeling could be no longer assumed. Special committees of inquiry were appointed by the House of Assembly and the Legislative Council. Both committees reported the results of their investigation. That of the Council recommended the license law which replaced prohibition in Maine, — a law which, defective in itself, would yet be an immense step in advance of any then existing in Canada. But the Assembly committee repudiated all such jejune and unsatisfactory con-

---

How many petitioned for the passage of the law? How many against? What stand was taken by the Roman Catholic Bishop of Montreal? What was the position of the Assembly and Council? What partial laws were adopted?

clusions, and reported in favor of downright prohibition, declaring that "no legislative reform had been demanded with such unanimity."

Though a Maine Law has not yet been adopted, many landmarks have been erected to mark progress. In 1853 the principles of the law were applied to localities in which public works were in progress; it being forbidden "to sell, barter, or dispose of any kind of intoxicating liquor within a distance of three miles of any public works declared to be in progress." In 1855, a new "Municipal Act" enabled County Councils to free their districts from the traffic by their own ordinance.

Already this power has been put into force; for, notwithstanding that Upper Canada has shown more favor to prohibition, Lower Canada has, in nine County Councils, determined "to prevent, so far as in their power, the traffic in intoxicating liquors within their limits."

In Nova Scotia a prohibitory liquor law is steadily demanded. In 1855 a bill was introduced and carried through the House of Assembly, which passed on the second reading by a vote of 29 to 19, and, on the third, without a division. In several counties, however, the traffic is suppressed with great benefit.

In the Province of New Brunswick, prohibition has still further developed itself. In consequence of the vigorous agitation kept up by the temperance men, a law was adopted in 1853, which prohibited the sale of *spirits*, but allowed the license for other intoxicants. As might be expected, a measure so partial failed in obtain-

---

What progress was made in Nova Scotia? What was the result of the agitation in New Brunswick?

ing a satisfactory result, and it was repealed in 1854. From the first this measure has been regarded by the friends of prohibition as an insidious triumph of the liquor interest, which sought, through its failure, to retard the coming struggle. The failure of the law of 1853, however, did NOT disgust the people with legislation, but only made them resolve that their future legislation should be sounder. At the next election a strong temperance House was returned, the most earnest of that party entering the government. Nothing could be more emphatic than the decision of public opinion. Accordingly, in 1855, a law was passed "totally prohibiting the manufacture, sale, and importation of all intoxicating drinks," to take effect from January 1st, 1856. The bill was sent to the mother country for ratification by the home government, accompanied by a despatch, containing thirty elaborate paragraphs intended to dissuade the government in England from recommending the queen to sanction the measure. The bill was referred to a committee of the Privy Council, and, on their report, ordered to go into operation as fixed and declared. Every effort was directed to defeat the operation of the law; mobs were organized, disturbances initiated; but these attempts of the trade only stimulated the enthusiasm of the upholders of the bill. Mass meetings, in favor of prohibition, were held, and energetic steps adopted for enforcing the law. *During the first twenty days of January*, 1856, *notwithstanding all difficulties, the intemperance of the city of St. John was reduced* 80 *per cent.*

---

What result was produced in St. John?

In the Legislature a motion was made to dissolve the House, and appeal to the people while laboring under the excitement of the struggle and of baffled appetite. This ruse was negatived by an emphatic vote of 29 to 11, and the law sustained. At last a willing hand was found to deal a blow at the law. The lieutenant-governor, *on his own responsibility, dissolved the Assembly*, the ministry resigned, and then, with a new ministry, the lieutenant-governor precipitated an election. The stratagem was successful, and the law fell, under the pressure of prerogative never before exercised in the colonies since the recognition of their independent constitution, and which has not been asserted in the mother country since the bad days of the Stuarts.

166. In the meanwhile, the temperance movement achieved its partial triumphs in other countries. In Norway it had a saving effect, and arrested the downward progress of its people, but in other parts of the continent of Europe, after a few spasmodic efforts in Poland, in the Netherlands, and in Germany, — where Pastor Böscher, of Kirchrode, Hanover, attempted much with indifferent success, — the cause has all but died out. The beer-drinking and wine-soaking of the continent seems to have killed the soul of Christian self-denial, and to have made "pleasure" the great end and aim of life. In Britain the cause has fared better, especially in Scotland, the north of England, and Wales. The Free Kirk and the Evangelical Union of Scotland have generally

---

What action was taken in the Legislature?

166. What has been the progress of the cause abroad? In Norway, Germany, etc.?

patronized the movement, and the Scottish Temperance League, and Scottish Permissive Bill Association, are now two powerful organizations, — the former having a large and successful publishing establishment. Both societies have organs of their own, — the first-named a weekly journal, the second a monthly issue, "The Social Reformer." In Ireland, too, especially in Dublin and the north, there is considerable activity, but no *national* life. A large number of the Presbyterian divines of Ulster are abstainers; but their fervor is lessened, and their usefulness limited, by dogmatic prejudices in favor of wine, based upon the popular misinterpretations of Scripture. In England there are thousands of temperance societies, and four or five general leagues, working in several districts or counties, as East, West, and North. The Episcopal Church (Church of England) has a society of its own, upwards of 600 of its ministers having joined it. They publish a monthly magazine. The Wesleyans also have their societies. Three associations, however, are specially noticeable for their peculiarities and their influence. First and oldest, the *British Temperance League*, founded in 1835, which employs a staff of agents, and publishes a monthly organ. Its head-quarters are at Bolton, Lancashire. Its principles are thorough on all points. Second, the *National Temperance League*, the operation of which is chiefly confined to London and the South. It aims to operate especially, by special and semi-private action, on the respectable classes, so called, and its tone is

---

What in Scotland? In Ireland? In England? What are the three great English societies?

modified and moderated to suit its clients. It has in past years had an unfriendly, even hostile attitude, to *thorough* teetotalism and *legal* action, but has improved as the cause of prohibition and truth became more established in the national mind. It publishes a "Weekly Record" of its doings. Third and last, not least, is the *Grand Alliance* (as Lord Brougham called it, one of its vice-presidents), formed June 1st, 1853, "for procuring the total and immediate suppression of the liquor traffic." Its president is Sir Walter C. Trevelyan, Bart., supported by a host of distinguished vice-chairmen, including Mr. B. Whitworth, M. P., Sir Wilford Lawson, Bart., M. P., who, on the 10th of March, 1864, introduced the *Permissive Bill* into the House of Commons, and obtained forty supporters on its first discussion; and again, on the 12th of May, 1869, when he obtained ninety-three supporters, and greatly reduced the votes against him. The object of that bill is simply to permit, *by empowering*, the *Rate-payers* of a district (parish, town, or township), to VETO applications for licenses to sell inebriating liquors, a power *now* permitted to magistrates or justices of the peace, and which they generally exercise for the protection and purity of their *own* immediate neighborhoods. An executive committee of teetotalers, at Manchester, conducts the association, — which is called the "United Kingdom Alliance;" the working secretary is Mr. T. H. Barker; the honorary secretary Mr. Samuel Pope, an able barrister-at-law, and Recorder of Bolton. The annual income now amounts to about $60,000, which is effectively expended in the advocacy of temperance and prohibition. It

---

**Describe their specialities. What is the aim and agency of the Grand Alliance?**

publishes a one shilling quarterly called "Meliora" (Journal of Social Science), and a weekly newspaper, "The Alliance News," circulating upwards of 20,000 copies. Its peculiar province is political action, with the view of first limiting, and finally suppressing, the liquor traffic.

---

# IX.

## The Philosophy of the Temperance Enterprise.

167. It was said of old, that "History is philosophy teaching by example." If so, the glance we have taken at the history and results of intemperance in ancient and modern times should be full of instructive philosophy, seeing that the lesson is at once so continuous and so uniform. Like effects point to like causes, and the question of *cause* is that which, in regard to this subject, is at once most fundamental and most practical. No matter as to what period, or place,or people we go, for learning the effects of intoxicants, the same class of terrible FACTS are summoned up, and the fugitive past is but the photograph of the living present. *Drunkenness*, in its folly, its revel, its obscenity, its beastliness, staggers across the vision, — *Poverty*, clothed with the rags of innocence or the filth of vice, files past,—*Ignorance*, with her sightless orbs, attended by her sad and hopeless brood, gropes on to the darkness beyond, — *Prostitution*,

---

167. What is history? What lesson does it teach? What train follows drunkenness?

in flaunting robes of guilt, with heart-on-fire of hell, hurries, shrieking and mocking, onwards to the flowing stream beneath "the Bridge of Sighs," — *Disease* withdraws its curtain, that we may see its lazar victims stretched on their "bed abhorred," — *Idiocy*, with incoherent gibberings and lack-lustre eyes, shows itself, — *Insanity*, with her multiplied children, here "moping melancholy," there raving madness, comes up and vanishes from sight, — *Brutal Lust*, fiercely glaring upon outraged chastity, stalks by, — and the fearful panorama closes with *Crime*, apparelled in garments purple with the blood of victims!

Can any question be more important than that which refers to the *cause* and the *cure* of such a condition of mankind? Ten years ago, the London "Times" offered to the temperance societies, the following tribute: "They have in their day, and at intervals, done a good deal; they are not doing so much now. *There is a fashion in these things.* This machinery for acting on the human imagination is not always to be got up at the exact moment you want it. It depends on the turn of enthusiasm, on individual impulses, on the *unknown* succession of ideas in human society, which we can no more predict, with any certainty, than we can the temperature of the next winter and spring." The writer ought to have said the *known* succession of ideas, since it is the very business of the reformer — the mission for which he was called forth out of the needs of his epoch, — to *perceive*, inaugurate, systematize, and *promulgate*

---

Give the statement of the "Times," and explain its error. What is the mission of the reformer?

those ideas, whose function it is to work out a certain and determinate issue. It is the presence of this perception, the possession of this knowledge, which makes all the difference between the *real* and the *sham* reformer; as it is the possession of the art and skill of working, which makes the difference between the real and the pretended craftsman. While the mere empirics, the men of crotchets and experiments, attach themselves to a movement, like barnacles to the keel and sides of a stately ship, true genius steadily and persistently presses forward to the mark which inspires him by its greatness. It is the prerogative of such men to perceive the great *tides* of thought, — to feel and comprehend the *tendency* and *want* of an age, — to know, and so to prophesy, the coming event, and to seek its embodiment in appropriate form; and all this because they are *part* of that tide, — the deepest or the topmost wave of it, — and therefore its fitting, chosen, and successful exponents. In moral and social matters the reformer may exaggerate his idea, or give to it a one-sidedness; but that is not always a disadvantage; for it may tend to outweigh the indifference or the stolidity of the masses. If *all* minds were of the calm, unbiased kind, enthusiasm would be out of place in this world. As Providence prepares the thought in the reformer, so it prepares it less consciously in kindred souls; and thus it happens that when the master speaks, the disciple answers, as thought responds to thought, and heart to heart. In a country, therefore, where the press and platform are free, a great movement based upon truth, and born of social necessity, needs not to "depend on *turns* of enthusiasm," or "individual impulses." On the contrary, it *may* and it *ought* to proceed according to a known succession of ideas, which it is the business of intelligent and true leaders to found upon clear and certain grounds of fact and philosophy.

168. The "Times," indeed, as a true representative of commonplace ignorance, thinks that the fancied fact of there being "*so little to be said* about drunkenness and its cure" may account for the topic being ignored by fashionable social reformers, but concedes that "it is not a *very agreeable* subject," since the cure proposed demands *self-denial* as well as the reading of papers. After all, can that monster vice and opprobrium of civilization, especially of the Saxon race, — a vice that has so stubbornly defied so many remedies, social, legislative, and religious, — which has set at naught for centuries the hortations of the moralist, the anathemas of the church, and the penalties of the state, — can such a vice, in its origin and its growth, be really a subject on which *so little* can be thought and uttered? Or is not the fact really this, that everything but the right thing has been said? At any rate there must be a philosophy of its cause, even if there be no hope of its cure. Nay, if it be at once inveterate and invulnerable, — if, in relation to this disorder of the body-politic, we adopt a dreary, hopeless fatalism, — still it must, for that very reason, all the more have a philosophy fixed in the *necessity* of things, — something singular and unique to be discovered and discussed concerning it! This is an age of science, and we ought to have the science of this

---

**168. What *is* the philosophy of intemperance? On what condition shall the vice be extirpated?**

question, feeling assured, indeed, that whether the triumph of temperance is deferred, or hastened, depends very much on the activity with which we propagate just and potent *ideas* and *plans* among the people, and that again upon the clearness and vigor with which we grasp them ourselves.

169. Sometimes we hear, alike from friends as foes, now that "moral suasion has failed," and now that "legal suasion has failed." Neither have failed in fact, because men are disappointed in absurd expectations. Our blunders of method, our partial plans, are no ground for despair. The police is not a failure, because they do not make rogues honest, but only limit their roguery; and, on the other hand, the preacher is not a failure, because he does not convert the fool, the sot, or the burglar. "The *knowledge* of a disease is the first half of the *cure*." Until the nature and causes of our evil conditions are known, a full and adequate *remedy* is simply impossible; and so, until we are fully equipped, we have neither ground for expectation nor discouragement. When enthusiasm is embarked, without chart, in a ship not seaworthy, which can never reach the hoped-for port, a collapse of effort follows, and it is long before the undertaking can be renewed in the old spirit, even with wiser pilotage and in a fitter vessel. It is never the *delay* of reform that destroys the eager spirit demanding it, but the acceptance of an unsatisfactory and partial reform, proved to be a mockery by the vanity of the result. Opposition but rouses to an increased ex-

---

**169. Does either "suasion" or "law" fail? What are the results of *false* expectations?**

hibition of power, equal to the emergency; it is the *delusive concession* which paralyzes the reformer and postpones his triumph indefinitely. The only lasting revolutions of history have been the complete and radical ones, for those that were partial have had the elements of reaction within them. The English Beer Act is a memorable example of the perniciousness of a false reform, which tampers with effects instead of touching the *causes* of an evil. The church, the press, and the parliament, thirty-five years ago, were united in agreeing that the monstrous nuisance of the 60,000 PUBLIC-HOUSES of Britain must be abated. The remedy prescribed was the addition of 40,000 BEER-HOUSES, — in other words, freer trade in beer, and a cheaper article. After the trial and failure of this quack remedy, what *advance* has been made by the ruling classes? They have *retrograded* as a necessary consequence. The INSTITUTION has strengthened itself in the conservatism of society; and the magistracy, home government, and bishops can now, after all this additional evil, only propose to make the beer-shops subject to the same control as the original evil they were designed to destroy. With a worse disorder than of old, entrenched in vested interests, we are to have the old, unsuccessful medicine applied to a third more cases of disease, licensed by the law itself.

Agricultural science, if not of slow growth, had progressive steps, each development preceded by partial failure, and by much doubt and disappointment. At

---

**Give an example from English history of the folly of partial and erroneous methods of cure. Give an illustration from agriculture.**

first, farmers thought they had little else to do in order to realize good crops than to sow *good seed;* their ploughing was superficial, their dressing imperfect, their dunging defective. At last, they began to see the value of *appropriate* and *plentiful manure* as the needful food for the growing crop. Things then improved; yet often there was disappointment, especially in a rainy season. Then came the discovery and appreciation of the third great condition of profitable farming, — the draining, subsoil ploughing, etc.; in short, the *preparation of the land*, so that the good seed might not be killed, and the costly manure wasted, by the cold and wet of undrained fields. The failure was, in strictness, only as to the realization of the false and foolish *expectation;* for the objective fact illustrates the success of a partial agency, operating without those correlative conditions which make up the complement of the science of agriculture.

The application of this history to the temperance question will be evident; for it, too, has its stages of development, and its *complementary* conditions, jointly needful to complete and eventual success. We shall deduce these conditions from an analysis of the causes of intemperance, but now simply indicate them as, — "SPECIAL EDUCATION, ASSOCIATED EXAMPLE, and LEGAL PROHIBITION."

170. A preliminary objection must be met. Some writers have supposed that the extensive use of strong-drinks proves that mankind have a *natural instinct* for them; and in that case it is hopeless to attempt to ex-

---

What application is made to temperance?

170. What *objection* is urged, which, if true, would render the temperance enterprise hopeless?

tirpate their use. We cannot fight successfully against nature. There is, however, no just ground for the idea. As Dr. Rees long ago observed,* "The propensity for strong drinks seems explicable upon the general principle that all animals feel a pleasure in *living faster*, or, as it were, crowding a greater portion of existence into a shorter space than natural; an effect, in some degree, produced by the exciting qualities of such liquors." Nature has given no intoxicating drink, and can, therefore, hardly be supposed to have provided a specific instinct for it; for where the infant has the instinct for aliment, it at once detects and seizes the supply provided at the maternal fountain. Not only would the argument prove with equal logic that sin was *natural* because it is universal, but it would prove the naturalness of the most morbid tastes and abominable customs. Some years ago the "New York Herald" published an account of certain snuff-circles established amongst the fashionable ladies of New York; but it would be as rank folly to infer that, therefore, they were specially born with an instinct for eating snuff, as that the Chinese consume opium by virtue of a natural impulse. The truth is, that such an appetite is never manifested in temperance families, but a very sensible disgust to the artificial drinks *is* experienced. Observant men have always noted this. "I fear," said Geddes, in Scott's "Redgauntlet," "it were no such easy matter to relieve thy acquired and artificial drought" (ch. xii.); and in "The Strange Story," Sir Bulwer Lytton remarks, "No

* "Cyclopædia," London, 1819.

---

**Show the folly of the objection. What is the *true* origin of the love of drink?**

healthful child likes alcohols; no animal, except man, prefers wine to water." The missionary, J. L. Wilson, in his work on Western Africa (1854), says: —

"The Banaka people, on the Gabun coast, are sufferers from European intercourse. Foreign vessels had no trade with them until within the last fifteen years. Previous to that time they had no relish for spirits, and *it was with difficulty any of them could be induced to taste of it in the first instance.* But those days of happy ignorance are gone; *the taste has been acquired,* and nowhere is rum now in greater demand."

On this we need only observe, that there is no difficulty in inducing a small child to drain its mother's milk; instinct manifests its tendencies and tastes at once, whereas abnormal appetites grow only with gratification and what they feed on. Our conclusion is, that the appetite for opium, alcohol, and tobacco, is a pure perversion of nature, for which man, the sinner, is accountable, and not God, the wise creator.

171. In the year 1834, the intelligent and patriotic member for Sheffield, Mr. James Silk Buckingham, moved in the British House of Commons, for a committee of inquiry into the causes, extent, and consequences of drunkenness. Half in joke, and half in ignorance, the motion "was opposed on the ground of the cost and trouble being needless, seeing that the *cause* of drunkenness was so plain and palpable, — namely, *drinking!*" The committee, however, was granted, and ultimately published a valuable body of evidence, and a report recommending a series of excel-

---

171. What famous inquiry was moved for in 1834? What is the *real* question as to drinking?

lent measures, which remain to be applied by a wiser parliament than Britain has yet seen. That "drinking intoxicants is the cause of drunkenness," whether we mean the temporary state or the abiding appetite, is little more than a truism, and, therefore, of no practical value for our present purpose. If a congress of men were met to consider how the crime of arson, or rick-burning, prevailing in a country, was to be stopped, he would be regarded as anything but a statesman who should announce that "the property of matches to ignite, and that of wood and straw to burn, was the cause of arson!" He would be immediately asked *why* men used these properties to effect the end, — in other words, what induced this criminal condition of mind which issued in such criminal actions?

The reformer who is bent on the removal of a great evil must not only know the *proximate*, or immediate cause of its existence, but THE CAUSE OF THAT CAUSE, — the ultimate foundation on which the evil rests.

172. It is obvious enough, that, *if* nobody *drank* liquors that intoxicate, nobody could get *drunk* with them; but it is equally clear, that to prevent persons from drinking, you must go back to the *reasons* and *motives* which induce them to drink. A philosophical inquiry into this subject must, therefore, go behind and beneath the superficial truism, — must begin with the *moving cause* of action in the subjective nature, and the essential relations of the human soul. The first inquiry really is, — the inquiry which alone touches the primal

---

**172. Why do men drink? To what *two* sources must all action be referred?**

cause of those steps and consequences which terminate in drunkenness, — *Why do men drink?*

People generally, were they honest and perfectly sincere, would have to reply, "We drink because drinking is pleasant;" or, "Because it is the fashion to drink;" and, perhaps, the next best thing to not drinking at all is not to drink on false pretences. Still this explanation does not fathom the causation of the phenomenon, since, very clearly, the custom rests upon some antecedent motive which *first* established it, while the "liking" now generated must be regarded as a consequence, rather than the original cause of drinking. The inquiry does not so much concern the present motive for drinking *now*, as the original reason for *beginning* to drink. What, then, is the great cause why individual men BEGIN to use intoxicating drink? The explanation must be referred to one of the two parts of our double nature, — the *head* or *heart;* or to forsake the figure for the literal fact, either to a "reason" or belief in our INTELLIGENCE, or to an emotion or FEELING in our sentient and psychological nature.

173. A love of "pleasure," and a dislike to "pain," are instinctive conditions of human nature. Whatever promises the one, or offers relief from the other, is eagerly seized, and becomes a SOLICITING, often a seducing, motive of action. Against mere impulses of this kind, we have an interior set-off of higher principles, — a desire for *good*, as good, — and aspirations after the true, the right, the beautiful, the pure. These are in-

---

173. What are the two instinctive conditions of human action? What *duties* of society follow from those conditions?

nate elements of our proper being; designed to instruct and influence our will, and to curb and control the action of the inferior impulses. The question as to what physical conditions and agencies promote or retard the *harmony* of these varying, and possibly conflicting, powers, — exciting the one or repressing the other, — becomes, therefore, a point of high ethical importance. Man, like any other vital organism, can only grow according to the *conditions* by which he is surrounded. Take, for example, a person who lives and works amidst depressing and unwholesome agencies. The instinct for "pleasure," combined with the feeling of "depression," becomes *relatively stronger* to him than if he were more happily placed; and the grog-shop and beer-saloon, consequently, present a temptation which operates with greater intensity on him than if he had no "relief" from a morbid monotony of life to seek, or had the perception of higher duties, and the capacity and opportunity for purer enjoyments. It is, therefore, the prime and principal business of man in society, first, to *prohibit* all avoidable evil, and second, to *create* those normal conditions upon which human nature is dependent for its true development, — in short, the office of government is to make it *easy to do right, and hard to do wrong.* How do these principles of human action stand related to the drinking system? In the first place, drink promises *good* — benefits of several kinds — to all those who think it good. In the second, it is a known means of *pleasure*, and pleasure is not only inviting, but, in proper degree and circumstance, legitimate. In the third place, strong drink, like other narcotics, presents a ready means of *relief* to any feeling of depression, discomfort, or care, — whether connected with mind or body. So far, therefore, as these relations are concerned as original causes of drinking, the temperance reformer has a corresponding duty to discharge: —

1st. To dissipate the delusion as to the *excellence* of the drink itself.

2d. To point out the *danger* of the drink, and to show that the drinker "pays too dear for his whistle."

3d. To promote the institution of those physical, educational, sanitary, and social conditions which are the *conservators of temperance*, and the absence of which tends to the degradation of humanity.

174. An advocacy of temperance on mere "expediency," it is plain, can never touch the first great cause of drinking in the world at large, or operate for any length of time; all fallacies and shams are sooner or later found out; for the intellect of man is, in the long run, sternly logical. If drinking be the cause of drunkenness, then the curse can be destroyed ONLY by the abandonment of drinking. But WILL the world give up drink, so long as it is persuaded that it is "good"? As Selden sagaciously observed long ago (1620): "It seems the greatest accusation upon the Maker of all good things. If they be not to be used, *why did God make them?*" The expediency man has no sufficient answer.

The *first* duty of temperance societies is, therefore, to explode this error, — to teach, by press and platform, by example and organization, that alcohol is not food

---

Name three corresponding duties of temperance men.
172. Why must "expediency" fail? Give Selden's remark.

but poison, not good but evil. It is especially important to teach this to our young, — our "Bands of Hope." The Rev. W. Jones, in his celebrated letters (1760), has well put the case: —

"It will be too late to persuade, when the judgment is depraved and weakened by ill habits. Gulosus was a country gentleman of good parts, friendly disposition, and agreeable conversation. He was naturally of a *strong constitution* and might have lasted to a good old age, but he is *gone before his time*, THROUGH AN ERROR IN OPINION, which has destroyed more than the sword. He asked a friend, a valetudinarian, how much port a man might drink without *hurting* himself; who gave it, as his private opinion, that a *pint* in a day was *more* than would do any man good. 'There,' says he, 'you and I differ; for I am convinced that *one bottle* after dinner will never hurt any man — *that uses exercise*.' Under this persuasion, in eating and drinking as much as he could, his life was a continual struggle between fulness and physic, till nature was wearied out, and he sank all at once at the age of forty, under the stroke of apoplexy. The time hath come upon many great nations, when ill-principles and self-indulgence, and that *infatuation* which is the natural consequence of both, have brought them to ruin."

In Britain, at least, all the highest authorities in medical science are now upholding the temperance platform, — such is the resistless might of truth. Dr. W. B. Richardson, F.R.S., in lecturing on December 15, 1868, before the Philosophical Society of Hull, asked: —

"What is alcohol? *Is it food or poison?* or is it something like chloroform, or ether, — simply a sleep-producing agent?

---

Give Jones' illustration. Give the testimony of Dr. Richardson.

There were many theories as to the causes of the physiological action of the spirit. First, increased combustion; next, arrest of combustion; and next, increased tension. This was a solemn subject. The primary effects might go through their series of stages in a youthful subject, who had rashly become intoxicated for the first time, and leave him comparatively uninjured, but *the continued use of alcohol was merciless, in that it left no important part of the body uninjured.* The brain underwent changes even in its structure, and symptoms of imbecility, of melancholia, of mania, and of paralysis, were often the result of its action. The vast majority of patients in the asylums who suffered from acute or intermittent mania, with a measure of paralysis, were cases of alcoholic production. *There was also a peculiar condition of the lung produced by alcohol.* It occurred to him to first point this out, and the disease was well known as *drunkard's consumption.* Then there were peculiar changes occurring in the glandular organs; in the liver, for instance, changes of induration. These came on mainly by drinking spirits, especially when consumed neat.

"Alcohol, in the shape of malt liquors, produced *a strange change of structure in the muscles, by which they became weak.* The *heart* especially was affected, and dropsy and early death was the result. On these accounts the prisoner at the bar could not possibly receive any mercy. He had been asked his opinion with regard to the value of alcohol in disease. He regretted to say that he knew of no distinct series of observations made with what was *known* to be ethylic alcohol. They would have heard of alcohol being recommended in fevers in the form of wine, brandy, and sometimes other spirits; but, in truth, there was no evidence as to the *quality* of these agents.* But as to the general use of alcohol in disease, he was quite open to say, that *every form of disease would be better treated without alcohol than with it.* It was not more essential to the existence of animal life than to the existence of anything else which was put in motion by some other force. The use of alcohol was simply the result of our own free will: we took it as a *luxury.* He should not expect the use of alcohol to be

* See § 86.

abandoned until the *reason* which was given to us had become more highly developed; then those things which were hurtful and injurious we should gradually *eliminate* from our lives."

Dr. King, the president of the society, "thought the smaller the dose the better, and it ought to be disused as soon as the physiological changes were produced." Dr. Munroe quoted the crucial fact, "that in hospitals where the largest amount of alcohol was used, *there* was the greatest percentage of deaths."

175. *Secondly*, we must teach the seductiveness and danger of drinking; the folly of exposing one's self to grave risks for the sake of transient pleasures which leave a sting behind. The *fact* can hardly be denied, for even the "Westminster Review" has admitted that "alcohol is a *dangerous* and *tricksy* spirit," and that "Moderation oils the hinges of excess,"—a figurative style of expressing a deep physiological truth. Nay, Thackeray himself, in his "Virginians," is compelled to declare the truth "in the face of all the pumps!"

"There is *a moment* in a bout of good wine, at which, if a man *could* but remain, wit, wisdom, courage, generosity, eloquence, happiness, were his; but the moment passes, and *that other glass somehow spoils the state of beatitude*." Truly, "wine *is* a mocker."

176. *Thirdly*, temperance reformers must be something more than sectarians. They must be general edu-

---

Give the testimony of Dr. King. Of Dr. Munroe.

175. What is the second subject that must be taught concerning Alcohol? Give the description of its *deceptiveness*, from the "Westminster Review," and a celebrated satirist, himself a victim.

cators, physiologists, sanitary teachers, politicians, patriots, — and they must supplement their moral suasion and example by appropriate *social action*. If abstainers could but take comprehensive views of their mission and their work, and band themselves together on a broad and deep principle of ORGANIZATION, their influence on the world of thought, of fashion, and of politics, would be irresistible.

But temperance organization is as impossible without a principle, a pledge, a banner, or a bond, as a political party without a "platform," an army without a captain, or a church without a discipline and a faith. Hence the absurdity of objections to pledges. All life is a pledge, or manifestation, — the revealing of the *inner* quality by the *outer* form. Dean South, commenting on the apostolic injunction, "*Show* me thy faith by thy works" (James ii. 18), very wisely and wittily observes: "Every action being the most lively *portraiture* and impartial *expression* of its efficient principle, as the complexion is the best comment upon the constitution. When a man's piety shrinks only to his *intention*, — when he tells me his *heart* is right with God while his *hand* is in my pocket, — he upbraids my reason, and outfaces the common principles of *natural discourse* with an impudence equal to the absurdity. He who places his Christianity *only* in his heart, and his religion in his meaning, has fairly secured himself against a discovery in case he should have none. Those, in a very ill and untoward sense, verify that philosophical maxim, that

---

176. What is the third step? On what can *organization* be founded? Give Dean South's answer to the objection against *expressing* what is in us.

what they so much pretend to be chief and first in their *intention* is always last, if at all, in the execution."*

A temperance pledge has manifold virtues and meanings, and has been amply justified by its fruits. It is, (1) the *expression* of a *conviction* or truth; (2) the declaration of a *purpose;* (3) the utterance of a *protest;* and, therefore (4), a bond of *sympathetic union* or co-operation.

177. The perception of the fact that an opinion of the excellency of the drink was the first cause of drinking, as drinking was the proximate cause of drunkenness, led many of the early temperance men to place too much reliance upon the proclamation of *personal* abstinence. The leaders of the reformation, however, never fell into this fallacy of a partial remedy; it was confined entirely to the secondary, compromising men, and to certain earnest but somewhat narrow-minded disciples, with whom the personal pledge of abstinence was everything. Thus one party ignorantly held that abstinence was all that was *needed*, and the other tenaciously maintained that it was all that could *prudently* be adopted. Hence in Britain arose the battle of the pledges, — finally decided in Exeter Hall against the short pledge, in favor of the long pledge, discountenancing *all* the *causes* of intemperance. Short-sighted people imagined those discussions, like many others, were not only unnecessary, but injurious; but we who survey the past from the impartial future can now clearly see that the contest was

* "Sermons." Oxford, 1698.

---

What are the *four* attributes or elements of the temperance pledge?

a *necessity* in the development of the permanent philosophy of the enterprise. The attack on *custom* was the second great practical step,— the application of the second great remedial agency for extirpating the vice of the civilized world. The "Times," in an article on the temperance question, justly pointed out the cardinal importance of "abstinence," and "sympathy."* The first, so far as it can be carried out, at once excludes temptation to drink, and keeps in abeyance that appetite which, once roused, is uncontrollable, even in men of strong wills and robust natures. The great Dr. Samuel Johnson, who declared that "abstinence was easy, moderation impossible," is the type of a large class of our fellow-creatures. The *pledge*, therefore, is to such a moral *punctum*, — a pivot upon which their will easily and safely turns. As the "Times" declares, "in some cases" — it might say, ten thousands of cases — "it had complete success; the devil was fairly cheated; the victim was enabled, by means of the aid given to his will in the abstinence he promised, *to rise to a higher moral level*, upon which he then advanced to permanent (or habitual) abstinence." Associated pledging also increased sympathy, and communicated power to the infirm. Never-

* This "sympathy" may be more distinctly analyzed. The power of fashion rests on three principles of human nature. First, instinct of *imitation.* second, *love of approbation.* Third, *fear of reprobation.* Which last is the result, partly, of the second principle being too strong, and of self-esteem being too weak. It is the business of reason and conscience to subordinate those feelings to the rule of right.

---

177. What was the second great practical step in the movement? What does "sympathy" include? What was the working of a *rule* (or pledge) in the case of Dr. Johnson?

theless, it was a partial and imperfect application. It virtually ignored an antagonist sympathy counteracting itself. Why, for instance, should we together pledge to abstain from drinking ourselves, and not together pledge ourselves to discountenance drinking in others? If we influence *each other*, it is equally clear that *others* must influence us; and consequently, if a pledge of abstinence breaks the power for evil in one direction, it must be equally necessary and effectual in another.

178. The short pledge very obviously meets but one cause of drinking; wields but one arm of social sympathy. Hence the importance of a correct, complete, and consistent pledge. The action which we take against the enemy must be *as broad* as the basis of his own operations. We must outflank the forces of intemperance before we can rationally expect to conquer. This truth was early perceived by Mr. Dunlop, and ably expounded in his work on "The Drinking Usages." He pointed out the adverse influence of some hundreds of *usages*, penetrating and permeating every vocation of life, and entrenched in almost every place, from church and mansion to the meanest cottage and the humblest workshop. He insisted upon the fact, that customs were amongst the most potent and practical of all teachings, since they address themselves to the *instinctive*, the *imitative*, and the *active* powers of man. He finally declared, with just emphasis, that UNLESS TEETOTALISM ABOLISHED THE DRINKING USAGES, THE DRINKING USAGES WOULD IN THE END ABOLISH TEETOTALISM. It was those

---

178. What is the defect of the short pledge? What is the true plan of battle? What did Mr. John Dunlop teach as to usage?

considerations which finally compelled to the general adoption of the *long pledge*, which involves, not only a declaration to abstain from the use of intoxicating *beverages*, but a promise not to give, offer, or provide them; and to discountenance, in *every proper way*, all the direct *causes* of intemperance. No doubt *much* has been achieved by this social protest, imperfect as it has been. It has destroyed the despotism, if it has not abolished the tyranny, of drinking customs. Even at royal and lordly tables, men endowed with moderate wills may now practise abstinence with comparative ease; and history will yet rank this work of liberation from the depotism of social custom amongst the most signal revolutions of the nineteenth century.

179. The enormous power of custom and fashion has perhaps never yet been duly estimated by the bulk of temperance reformers. It is not only that which induces many to begin to drink, and to continue drinking, — many who have no faith in the virtue, and many who even strongly suspect the evil, of the drink, — it is that which surely antagonizes, by silently *undermining*, the reformation. Dr Beddoes * puts the case strongly, but truly, when he says that "*crimes* of moderate magnitude do not excite so much repugnance as an oversight in any of the *minutiæ of fashion*." Who, indeed, can bear to be stigmatized as "ungenteel" or "vulgar"? To bear *that* for conscience' sake — resolutely to ignore what Mrs. Grundy may say — is the very height of heroism, though

* "Hygeia," 1802.

---

179. What are the two great *social* antagonists of temperance? Give Dr. Beddoes' words, and explain the nature of the tyranny.

it may not wear the "crown." Fashion is a kind of slavery, wherein there *is* no slave-master; but all the men and women are the mutual slaves of their adopted notions. A dandy or dandizette, an idiot *beau* or *belle*, may set the fashion, which king, lords, and commons will servilely follow, till some new idol or fresh whim displaces the old one. Fortunately, one can see that fashion and custom are powers which can be turned against themselves. When bad customs conspire to tyrannize over men's better knowledge and purer aspirations, it is the duty of good men to combine and establish COUNTER-CUSTOMS, and to make them honored and respected by their own virtue. This custom, as Bacon says, must be "*copulate* and *collegiate*," for "the great multiplication of virtues upon human nature RESTETH UPON SOCIETIES WELL ORDAINED."

180. By this, however, is meant something more complex and compact than the pomp and show, on which the "Times" insists in the following significant passage: —

"It is a known fact that men can do together and in company what they cannot do by themselves. We may call this the effect of imagination, but, if it is, then all we can say is, that imagination is a great thing in morals, and we should advise you to make friends with it as much as you can. Imagination, indeed, does wonders in this way. Who could possibly stand for one hour to be shot at by himself? The trial would be too great for human courage, and long before half the time was out, it would occur, and we must think very naturally and

---

How must *custom* be met?

180. Give the gist of the "Times'" doctrine as to *sympathy* and *organization*.

justly, to our isolated target, that this was not the sort of trial that human nature was intended to submit to; that we are intended to rough it in many ways, and take our chance, but that this sort of discipline was *extra-providential*, and formed no part of our allotted probation. . . But put fifty men in a row, with fifty men behind them, and another fifty men behind these, and they will stand to be shot at a whole day. The soldier depends entirely on sympathy, on the sensation that he is in company, on the fellow-feeling created by the consciousness of the same danger, for his power to go through the awful scenes in which he is placed. But this principle does not apply to courage only. *Anything that is difficult to do, any exertion of resolution, any kind of self-denial, is made easier by the aid of sympathy, by knowing that other persons are doing the same thing that you are.* The temperance movement, accordingly, made large use of this principle. There was much tact, and knowledge of human nature, in its policy. *It made a great parade of the work of reformation, a grand show or pomp of it. There were meetings, inaugurations, ceremonials, with banners, trumpets, and drums, colors flying, shouts rending the air, speeches, and processions.* All this was in order to bring the task of reformation out of its damp, dark, and dreadful cavern in the solitary human heart, where the torturing demon sits amid coiled snakes and scorpions, hissing hydras, gorgons, and chimeras dire, into the open air and open light of day, to set men to work upon it *together and in crowds*, and give them the sensation of only doing what numbers were doing all around them. That was a great step gained. The old proverb of *omne ignotum pro terribili* * applies especially to a new piece of self-denial; it is dreaded not only as being something disagreeable, but because the kind of disagreeable which it is is unknown. A drunkard has known what it is to go without drink when he was in his *natural state*, but he does not know what it is to go without it when he has got used to it. He dreads this unknown pain as a child is afraid of being in the dark. Then bring him and others in the same case together; *make reformation a social,*

* That is frightful which is unknown.

*open, large, multitudinous thing, and you deprive it of half its difficulty.* It is then no longer a number of scattered wretches, each in his own hole and corner, trembling at the bare idea of a *single* encounter with duty; but it is a crowd of men who are working together, and dividing, as it were, the pain and burden among them. These are *the only two * great aids* that have been as yet discovered for easing the return of the drunkard to sobriety. They have in their day, and at intervals, done a good deal."

181. We would particularly guard against mistaking the pomp of badges, banners, and regalia for the true power which they ought to symbolize. BADGES — if simple, chaste, and unobtrusive — are very well and appropriate; but the real question concerns their *distribution* and their *significance*, — the duties they indicate, the trained faculty they mark, and the privileges they confer. It is an organization of spirit, not merely a spirit of organization, which is needed; and we see no prospect of achieving *great* conquests over fashion in any other way. Temperance societies, as hitherto organized, have realized no fixed social and political influence at all adequate to the just and intrinsic claims of the reformation. In fine, it appears to us that we need a broad and firm *organization of virtue into fashion*, — an organization and machinery of brotherhood and philanthropy, — which, by reason of its utility and labors, its nobleness, its lofty aims, *and even its exclusiveness*, shall

* There is a *third* great complementary aid which we shall unfold in another section. It is necessary to pledge ourselves to do good, but equally necessary to remove stumbling-blocks out of the path.

---

181. What are badges?

irresistibly attract the respect, and compel the homage, of the world. The true "sons and daughters of temperance," who are awake to the dignity of their cause, to the holiness of their mission, and to the vastness of their work, should constitute themselves into an ORDER OF MERIT, — a legion of honor, — a sodality "well-ordained" within the loose, atomic aggregate of general society, — which would speedly emancipate mankind from the vulgar fashions of the drinking system, and inaugurate a more beautiful and happier mode of social intercourse. The young and generous, the aspiring and broad-hearted, the earnest workers and deep-cultured intellects, now associated in the movement, wait to be organized into a PHALANX OF PHILANTHROPY which shall rise above all sects and parties, and, inspired with an *esprit du corps* like that which animated the legionaries of old Rome, shall go forth to the conquest and colonization of a new social world, governed by "simpler manners" and "purer laws." *

* In Britain, so far back as 1837, a Benefit Society, calling itself the INDEPENDENT ORDER OF RECHABITES was formed, which at one time rose to considerable influence, but, owing to erroneous tables and indiscreet management, received a serious check some years ago. A similar order, in 1842, was introduced into the States, the chief office being now at Utica, New York.

In England, at present, the order of the SONS OF TEMPERANCE seems to take the lead in popularity. This organization was established in 1840, by Messrs. Oliver, the printers, of New York, to supplement and uphold the WASHINGTONIAN movement (§ 138). It has 37 Grand, and nearly 2,000 Subordinate Divisions, extending into twenty-five States and territories, besides the British Dominions. During the past twenty-seven years, it has

---

What kind of Brotherhoods are needed? *Note.*—On the "Sons of Temperance" and other secret orders and benefit societies. State the peculiarities of the "Templars," etc.

182. The influence of custom, fashion, or flunkeyism is, indeed, the standing hindrance to human improve-

numbered over 2,000,000 of persons, and is steadily advancing, with increasing force and swelling ranks. Its entire freedom from the machinery of signs, grips, or degrees, leaves it free for effective *missionary* work, and it embraces some of the ablest and most moral and religious elements in the land. The order now numbers about 200,000, exclusive of Great Britain.

In 1845, was organized the TEMPLARS OF HONOR AND TEMPERANCE. It embraces Grand Temples, with subordinates, in twenty-one States of the Union. It is intended as a higher temperance and fraternal organization, *with advancement by degrees as its members are proved worthy.* It has six degrees, in addition to the initiatory, besides the Social Temple, with three degrees, where *ladies* are received into full membership. Its beautiful ritual and fraternal maxims unite its members in a bond of union and friendship not easily broken.

In 1846, the CADETS OF TEMPERANCE, for boys, were organized. It has a ritual, passwords, and regalia. About 25 sections exist in New York State, and many in other States.

In 1847, the GOOD SAMARITANS were also organized in New York city,—a benefit society, and the first of the order to admit colored citizens to their lodges. The society extends to all the States of the Union, and includes about 22,000 members.

The FRIENDS OF TEMPERANCE is an organization formed in the Southern States, composed of whites, numbering over 100 Subordinate Councils, located mostly in Virginia and North Carolina. It was organized by former "Sons of Temperance," who preferred a Southern organization. Women, old men, and children are admitted as associates.

In 1856, the order of the COUNCIL OF FRIENDS arose in the West (Indianapolis), and now numbers over 300 Subordinate Councils, and 15,000 members. It is designed for the tried and true, and admits only those who have been a member *for one year previous, of the Sons of Temperance, Good Templars,* or some other known temperance society. The initiation fee is not less than five dollars, and one black ball rejects a candidate. It is, therefore, an *aristocratic* order, in the original and best sense of that word.

The KNIGHTS TEMPLARS OF TEMPERANCE is an order started in 1860, as a side degree of the "Good Templars," but is now an entirely independent organization. *Its platform is prohibition, and it proposes to operate through the ballot-box.* Its pledge is for life. Ladies are admitted, and its membership is estimated at from 10,000 to 20,000.

Last, but not least, comes the order of the GOOD TEMPLARS themselves. This organization was instituted in 1851, and now contains 32 Grand, with 4,000 Subordinate Lodges, scattered over 29 States, and in Canada, Nova Scotia, and Prince Edward Island. It has a liberal financial basis, is everywhere scattering a temperance literature, supporting lecturers in the field, holding county and district conventions, and is rapidly increasing its numbers

ment, and ought to be rebuked, ridiculed, and denounced by every earnest man. Mr. J. S. Mill, in his work "On Liberty," says: —

"In our times, from the highest class of society down to the lowest, every one lives as under the eye of a dreaded *censorship*. It does not occur to them to have any inclination except for what is *customary*. Thus the mind itself is bowed to the yoke; even in what people do for pleasure, *conformity* is the first thing thought of; they like in crowds. Now, is this, or is it not, a desirable condition of human nature?"

But whence is the hope of freedom to come, save from *combination* on behalf of freedom? For we must recollect, in the language of Mr. Buckle, the historian of civilization, that "whatever may be the case with individuals, it is certain that the *majority* of men find *an extreme difficulty in long resisting constant temptation.*" Hence the necessity of those "organizations" just sketched.

183. There now starts up another question: Whence the *peculiar consequences* of drinking intoxicants? It is a fallacy to refer everything to the law of habit; for this

in almost every State and territory. It has *degrees*, and *methods* of recognition. Its membership is estimated at nearly half a million. Its three degrees correspond to the three conditions of *Self Respect*, *Brotherly Love*, and *Loyalty to God*. To build up such a "Living Temple" is a noble aim.

Finally, the British-American Order of Good Templars was started in 1858, at London, Ontario, Canada, and now numbers 200 Primary Lodges, with 5,000 members. It acknowledges no supreme head beyond its own Grand Lodge officers. The order is doing much toward circulating temperance literature, rightly believing that to be one of the most effectual ways of reaching the masses of the people.

---

183. What are the *peculiar* consequences of drinking alcoholic liquor?

is really ignoring, not explaining, the peculiar facts. The habit of smoking paper does not engender a *passion* for smoking, and lead to the continued and general increase of the quantity smoked. The habit of taking bread-pills is not attended by the same kind of consequences as taking opium-pills. Tobacco, opium, spirits, compared with food, have all marked peculiarities. Disgusting at first, they create by use an intense and irresistible craving for themselves, which "grows by what it feeds on."

Tobacco at first excites disgust and vertigo, — even insensibility in some. After a period of probation this effect disappears, and the smoker finds a peculiar fascination in the noxious weed. He has passed through the purgatory of disgust to the paradise of fools, is the bond-slave to his pipe!

So with opium. It is not the *habit* of using it, but the *property* of the drug, that enslaves the man to the habit. As Awsiter says, in his "Essay" (1763), "There are many *properties* in it, if universally known, *that would habituate the use*, and make it more in request with us than the Turks themselves, the result of which knowledge must prove a general misfortune." Nor is the law of this far to seek. The "Cyclopædia of Practical Medicine" observes (1834), "Narcotics lose their influence when they have been taken daily for a considerable time." But the pleasure they excite is desired again, and, as the same quantum will not suffice, a *larger* is taken; and then follows the collapse of the system,

---

**Explain the law as to opium. What is the fallacy as to "habit"? Show what it means.**

attended by uneasiness and craving, which furnish a second and stronger motive for repeating the increased dose or draught. Thus, says the "Medico-Chirurgical Review," writing of opium, hashish, etc., "It is the effect [rather tendency] of all these narcotic poisons, in common with alcohol, *to cause an ever-increasing desire for them.* There can be no doubt whatever, that everything that exhausts the sensorial or motor power, *conduces* to excite this irrepressible desire for stimulants." *

De Quincey truly remarks, that "Wine *disorders* the mental faculties, unsettles the judgment, constantly leads a man to the brink of absurdity." All this, by lessening the internal controlling power, increases the intensity of the general narcotic law.

Now, as no man is born with an *appetite* for such things; as children and savages at first reject them with abhorrence or disgust; as the *taste* for them is slowly raised upon the ruins of pure and aboriginal instinct, — we can be at no loss to discover the secret of

* Hence the folly of ascribing to teetotalism the spread of opium-eating; as if conscientious abstinence from one narcotic did not tend to abstinence from every other! Mr. De Quincey, in his "Confessions of an Opium Eater," so far back as 1823, spoke of "an incredible number" of opium-eaters, and showed that the *use* of ale and spirits had first generated the *necessity* or craving. He says :— "I take it for granted

"'That those eat now who never ate before,
And those who always ate, *now eat the more.*'"

So, too, with alcoholic drinks, which are even more mocking and dangerous than opium, because, as the same witness remarks: —

"The pleasure given by wine is always rapidly mounting and tending to a *crisis*, after which as rapidly it declines; that from opium, when once generated, is *stationary* for eight or ten hours."

---

Give the observations of De Quincey.

intemperance. Here is its proximate cause, — its true *etiology.* It does not spring up native from the human heart; it has no relation to any faculty or function of human nature; it is a physical and moral effect of a physical agent, and of that alone. The late Mr. Conybeare, in the "Edinburgh Review," has well put the facts: —

"The passion for fermented drinks *is not instinctive.* A rare accident taught some sleepless Arabian chemist — torturing substance after substance in his crucibles and alembics — how to extract the FIERCE SPIRIT from these agreeable drinks, and brought up, as it were, from the bottom of Pandora's box, that *alcohol* which has since inflicted so many evils upon the world. . . They exhilarate, they enliven, they stimulate, and exalt the mental powers. Some [men] they stupefy, *some they convert into irritable savages,* some into drivelling idiots, and some into mere pugnacious animals. All, if long and largely used, they brutalize, prostrate, and, in the end, carry to an untimely grave. . . . . But more wonderful than these *poisonous* and destructive effects, is the *passion for indulging in them which these liquors awaken* [originate] *in a large proportion of our fellow-men,* — the irresistible love with which these unfortunates are smitten by them, — the *fascinating influence* by which they are charmed. The will becomes absolutely spellbound *through the action of alcohol on the bodies of some,* and reason is dethroned, even where it formerly exercised clear and undisputed sway. . . . . IT IS FROM THIS FASCINATING POWER THAT THE DANGER OF USING THEM PRINCIPALLY ARISES."

184. But still more clearly was the principle stated long ago, by Dr. Thomas Reid, the Scottish philosopher: —

---

**Give the observations in the "Edinburgh Review;" of the philosopher Reid.**

"Besides the appetites which nature has given us, for useful and necessary purposes, we may *create* appetites nature never gave. The frequent use of things which stimulate the nervous system *produces a languor when their effect is gone off*, and a (consequent) *desire to repeat them*. By this means, a *desire* of a certain object is created, accompanied by an *uneasy sensation*. Both are removed for a time by the object desired; but they return after a certain interval.* . . . Such are the appetites which some men acquire for the use of tobacco, for opiates, and for intoxicating liquors."

185. Looking back at the preceding sections (167, 182), we are brought to the old conclusion, — not that moral-suasion and temperance societies are FAILURES (for they have done *much* they were adapted to do, indeed quite *as much* as we had a right to expect them to accomplish under the circumstances of imperfection in which they originated), but that they are INADEQUATE to meet the *whole* causality of the evil. Until the remedies of an evil are as broad and deep as the circle and fountain of the cause, the effect *must* continue, by necessity of divine law. Whatsoever we sow, *that* we

* "Works of Dr. T. Reid," Sir W. Hamilton's ed., p. 553. He adds: "This differs from natural appetite *only* in being acquired by *custom*." But he is wrong. The true difference is, that while a pint of milk, or a pound of bread will always fulfil the same ends, the *same effect* cannot be produced by the *same dose* of a narcotic *continuously*. Hence, from the desire for pleasure, and the dislike of pain, — the two essential instincts of life, — in relation to this physical law, arises the *tendency* of the little use to beget the ever-growing use (called abuse), which satisfieth not, as *food* does. If a man is a glutton, it is *in spite* of the food, which tends to satisfy. But if a drunkard, he is so *because* of the tendency of drink to create an ever-increasing appetite.

---

What is the difference between the law of food and the law of narcotics?
185. What is the sum of the preceding argument?

must also reap. No mere deprecations or lamentations, no hopes, no aspirations, no prayers, will in the least avail, if at the same time we do not touch the *actual causes* of the evil effect deplored. Faith is emphatically dead and barren without works, in this case; for the same reason that no amount of trust will cause wet powder to explode. Multifarious and majestic as the labors of the temperance societies have been, there are causes which they cannot successfully cope with and conquer; causes which win back from them some of their proudest trophies and most promising conquests, and occasion many of their valiant soldiers to relapse into fatalism or despair. Fields that were once white unto the harvest have been covered with blight and blackness; fruitful orchards once ruddy with health, and advancing to a ripe and rich maturity, have been withered by some baleful blast; thousands who, under the aspirations of enthusiasm, signed pledges of abstinence, have gradually declined and narrowed into units. Such is the history of temperance societies everywhere! They have, by immense and herculean efforts, raised embankments to shut out the swelling tide of intemperance, and *for a time* succeeded; but, ere long, some current has set in, or the incessant return of the tide has gradually destroyed the works in some part or other, and the waves have come in again with destructive power. The reason is plain. Philanthropy can work only by *fits* and *starts;* it tires and relaxes, and is carried on of necessity by a system of *relays;* whereas misanthropy and mammon have a ma-

---

Why must *mere* philanthropy fail to accomplish the reformation? What do *vested* interests involve?

chinery and motive-force which are compact, incessant, and untiring. They know no repose and need no rest; their lever and fulcrum are unfortunately pivoted upon the very LAWS, upon vested INTERESTS and licensed INSTITUTIONS; and they are worked by the remorseless instincts of selfishness, greed, and fear.

186. While such a social anomaly exists as institutions for the *theoretical* teaching of temperance and morality, side by side with a hundred thousand seminaries devoted to the *practical* training of drunkards, paupers, and criminals, it is sheer madness to expect anything like general sobriety and virtue. Moral palaver passes by with little influence, when uttered amidst the pressing and hourly *temptations* of life. The virtuous theory held up before the intellect is weaker than the vicious temptation which appeals to the active powers; the corruption within is far stronger as a motive-force than simple intelligence. *Video meliora*, etc., — "we know the right, but do the wrong." That which appeals to the evil habit cannot tend to strengthen the moral nature. Of all the strange paradoxes of our time, therefore, the strangest seems to be that of a moral suasionist *opposed* to prohibition, — a teetotaler who is an anti Maine Law man! For what have we here?

A person who, *as a temperance member*, teaches that intoxicating liquor is physically evil and morally and socially seductive and corrupting; who warns the public against the tavern, as a trap and a temptation to ruin; yet —

---

186. What is the great practical *temptation*? Why is a moral suasionist inconsistent? Explain the force of *circumstances*.

A person who, *in his relation of citizen*, takes part in the election of men who make the laws which *open* the public house, and *sanction* and *license* the sale of the drink which, as teetotaler, he decries and denounces! It is worse than folly, however, — it is inconsistency, contradiction, and perversity. It is profession flouted by practice; it is moral suasion counteracted by legal temptation; it is the blasphemy of converting LAW, that most sacred of attributes, into the cloak and apology for a system which is the perpetual fountain of social misrule and mischief.

187. Let us review the argument. The *first* cause why many *begin* to drink must be one of two, springing out of a mental state, — either a desire to realize pleasure or relieve pain, arising from a knowledge of the anæsthetic properties of alcoholic drinks, or a belief in their dietetic advantages. This source of drinking requires to be combated by *special education* as to the true nature of alcohol, and by pointing out its danger or seductiveness. The *second* cause why men begin to drink, is the influence of fashion and custom, — one of the standing hindrances to human progress. This can be resisted only by combination,—that is, *associated example*, — and the particular fashions connected with drinking require a confederation more complicated, perfect, and august than any we have yet seen in operation; we invoke support, therefore, to the higher organizations,— the new *orders of merit* founded upon work, on intrinsic and tried worthiness, — organizations which combine the vir-

---

**187. What is the lesson of the whole, in relation to the three evils and *the three remedies*?**

tues of Free Masonry, the benefits of Mutual Assurance, and the dignities of Intelligence and Virtue. But, drinking from any influence, to begin with, generates by physical law the *liking* for strong drink, which is, in fact, the initial degree and universal inauguration of the world's drunkenness. The sole *proximate cause* of the drunkard's appetite is the physical operation of the drink, inducing the gradual disorganization of the normal nature of man, first of his nervous system, and second of his mental associations. This is the secret of intemperance, which is the condition we desire to remove, and which, of course, *can* only be removed by the destruction of its cause. It is this acquired *liking* — this subjective susceptibility within men — that gives such tremendous power to the ramified temptations of the traffic. The *enemy*, as it were, has friends already within the citadel, willing to open the gates. So when the drink is impeached and placed at the bar, the jury are bribed and prejudiced in its favor. The traffic surrounds the people with ready drinking facilities, and presses upon them perpetual suggestions, at once in *harmony* with ignorance, with custom, and with appetite. Hence its potency and the tenacity of its grasp. Law has entrenched and emblazoned it, and law to the multitude is a powerful teacher; and what the law has raised into power, the *law* can alone destroy. It has, in fact, raised a monster; has constructed and vivified a social Frankenstein, whose "daily bread" is confusion and crime; and no lesser agency can now annihilate it. It is too strong for mere suasion; it demands *legal prohibition*, called forth by the voice of the people, and armed with executive power, — prohibition as expressive of the wisdom and virtue of the community, and solemnly realizing in their social constitution, for the benefit of the great masses of the people, that *protection* for which the Christian petitions God on his own behalf, — "Lead us not into temptation, but deliver us from evil."

When our remedies are thus coextensive with the causes of the disorder, we may expect the temperance enterprise to go on to an assured and complete victory. Prohibition, by removing the hindrance, will give fair play to moral suasion; or, to change the figure, prohibition, by *draining away* the poisoned waters that kill the seed of much truth, will allow the germs of knowledge and virtue to fructify in an appropriate soil, and to grow up to a fair and fruitful harvest of social happiness.

188. It has been shown that the moderate use of drink is the *only* proper and proximate *cause* of drunkenness, and that all attempts to get rid of this vice, without abstinence, will necessarily fail. The *surroundings* of men, playing upon their feelings and perverting their unformed judgments, is a more powerful teacher than any mere words. This truth, Byron saw when he apostrophized

> "Circumstance, thou *un*spiritual God and miscreator,
> Whose touch turns hope to dust,
> The dust we all have trod."

Still, it is quite true that temperance requires its bulwarks, — certain exterior and *supplementary* work, which the enlightened temperance man should partly inaugu-

---

188. What is meant by the "Bulwarks of Temperance"?

rate, and partly stimulate others, less advanced, to perform. These "conservators of temperance," as we may call them, are, as the auctioneer's catalogue phrases it, "too numerous to mention" in detail; but the class may be known by a few samples.

189. Education is the first of these, — using the word in its proper and original sense as an *educing*, or bringing out, the latent and higher powers of the mind. For though mere cramming, learning, and instruction — or *knowing*, as dissevered from feeling and habitual *being* — is no safeguard against the encroachments of sensuality so long as the physical *causes* of appetite are fostered, it is yet very important to recollect, that a thirst for knowledge, a taste for reading, a perception of the beautiful in nature and art, — in brief, the pursuit of intellectual and refined pleasures, — must positively and powerfully tend to conserve wise and pure habits of temperance, and negatively, as regards time and opportunity, tend to narrow the dangerous platform of temptation. He who has pure tastes and good habits will be least susceptible to the evil influences of bad customs, least attracted by the gross seductions of the impure social circle. As the ale-house is the *antagonist* of the school, so are the school, the mechanics' institute, the gallery of art, the oratorio, the free library, and the lecture-room the *rivals* of the drinking saloon.

190. We remember once hearing an advocate of tem-

---

189. What is the function of Education, and how does it bear upon the cure of intemperance?

190. How does sanitary reform stand related to the Temperance Reformation?

perance weakly decrying sanitary reform as *needless*, where we had teetotalism! Nothing can be more absurd, nothing more calculated to bring contempt and derision upon the cause he was so foolishly pleading. Not to insist on the truth, that the very thing repudiated should be one of the *uses* of temperance, — one of those *ends* that give value to the *means*, — the advocate had clean forgotten that bad sanitary arrangements, by inducing a low tone of health, and fostering a morbid condition of the mind, at once increase the susceptibility to temptation and lessen the power of resistance. The felt *want* of the physical system may be said almost to *drive* the victim of dirt, malaria, and deficient ventilation to the use of such narcotics and stimulants as will afford undoubted temporary relief. The truly enlightened advocate, therefore, must also be the friend of every kind of real sanitary and dietetic reform, the supporter of sanitary law, and of baths and wash-houses for the people. Ventilation, and the absence of dirt and decomposition from the homestead and the street, is but another name for *bathing the blood* in pure air; while the bath and the wash-house are the instruments for securing the purity, or *ventilation*, *of the pores* of the skin, thus completing the purification of the circulating vital fluids. If "cleanliness be next to godliness," — by tending to put the soul in a better attitude of attention, — it may be said with still greater emphasis, that "cleanliness is part of temperance."

If "bulwarks" and "preventatives" are needful to the normal and unvitiated members of society; if, to sustain them in virtue, even *their* circumstances must be in harmony with the theory of well doing, it is evident that special teaching and discipline, through fitting institutions, should exist for the developed victims of strong drink. At last, physiologists and statesmen have begun to acknowledge that the drinker's appetite is a true mania, and must be treated as such. Hence the establishment of "Inebriate Asylums" in various parts of the States, where, as regards the male sex, it has been found that nearly 80 per cent. of those under treatment, which is both physical and moral, hold steadfast to the principle of abstinence.*

In the case of persons having latent cravings for drink, we know few things more efficacious than a short course of that peculiar method of cleansing, which, borrowed from the Orientals, has been recently introduced into many cities, — we mean, the *Turkish bath*. Who, suffering from morbid accumulations incident to town life, that has ever tried these processes has not felt a wonder-

* The following are the places where such establishments exist at present date (1868): —

BINGHAMPTON, N. Y. Dr. Willard Parker, President; Albert Day, M. D., Superintendent.

BROOKLYN. *Kings County Inebriate Asylum.* Hon. J. S. T. Stranaham, President; Rev. John Willetts, Superintendent.

*Ward's Island Asylum for Inebriates*, near New York city. Under charge of the Commissioners of Charities and Correction. Dr. W. R. Fisher, Resident Physician.

BOSTON, MASS. *Washingtonian Home*, 1009 *Washington Street.* Otis Clapp, President; Wm. C. Lawrence, Superintendent.

CHICAGO, ILL. *Washingtonian Home*, 570 *West-Madison Street.* C. J. Hull, President; Dr. J. A. Ballard, Superintendent.

MEDIA, PA. *Inebriate Asylum.* Dr. Joseph Parrish, M. D., Superintendent.

---

What is the nature of Inebriate Asylums? What special bath is useful in the case of drink-curing? and also as a preventive?

ful increase in the vital *elasticity* of his frame? It is as though a heavy weight had been lifted from the bent spring of life, permitting fuller and freer play to the vital machinery, and creating a feeling of sympathetic purity in the soul.

191. On the same principle of the acknowledged connection between body and mind, — of a right condition of the physical with a normal condition of the spiritual, or the sensuous, — we should be the friends of all innocent recreation; for, be assured, such *has* a *re-creating* effect, — a highly ameliorating tendency upon the temper and spirit, both of boys and men. Our very proverbs teach this. "All work and no play makes Jack a dull boy." Why? Because it puts his body and brain in a false and unnatural state. Again: "The devil tempts the idle." Why? Because dammed-up physical energies are apt to get into wrong channels, and thus produce devastation. Lust, in a multitude of cases, for example, is dependent for its development more on rich *diet* and *idleness* than anything else, and the best antidote is intellectual occupation, simple diet, moderate exercise, and innocent recreation. Morbid physical conditions tend to moral evil; and so, contrariwise, recreation, in proper time and method, is a condition of healthy life which tends to purity and temperance; which, at least, prevents the addition of evil to the original defect and depravity of man. When will people learn the duty of giving our original and better nature "fair play"?

192. The establishment of TEMPERANCE HOTELS is

---

191. Show the value of innocent recreation, and its bearing upon this question.

another *desideratum*, — not hotels set up by untrained and incompetent persons, or mere speculators: hotels where one is ashamed to take our friends, or be seen ourselves; houses which are nasty and *not* cheap, — but hotels which shall be patterns of liberal economy, neatness, and comfort. The conversion of respectable publicans would be the *best* thing; but, failing that, why should not our organizations see to this? What else are they for, save to accomplish work beyond the power of *individual* effort? When a sufficiency of respectable houses of this character shall be provided, not only will a great excuse and apology for drinking be removed, but the *institution* of such houses — houses of which we shall be rather proud than ashamed — will be a powerful teaching in itself.

Once more, and in conclusion, we suggest a more powerful organization of our friends and forces, upon the broadest basis and in the highest spirit, for the removal of the great positive causes of intemperance, and the inauguration of those social conditions which shall permanently conserve the fruits of the temperance reformation.

193. Laws and institutions which promote a low state of intelligence and industry will, *other things being the same*, tend to intemperance; on the principle explained, that the temptation to happiness must be of the sensual kind, rather than of the moral or social. A degraded peasantry, like a tribe of savages or Indians, or the pariahs of our towns, will be *sure* to fall before the

---

192. What is needed as a substitute for drinking saloons, bar, and grog-shops?

temptation of the drink, if presented. On the other hand, *mere* ignorance will not necessarily have this tendency. This is seen in the state of the peasantry of Ireland, of Italy, and especially of France, where, with profound ignorance there is great comparative sobriety. Besides the limited number of drinking-shops, we have there the strong antagonist passion *for saving*, which, combined with higher education and better social arrangements, is capable of being turned to good account in the cause of temperance and progress. Nassau, and other agricultural districts of Germany, when the feudal system was broken-up and the land distributed among the people, became at once more educated, wealthy, and sober. The peasantry had an *interest* in social life and its ambitions, and when permitted to thrive, became economical instead of careless, dissipated, and drunken. The same tendency would be developed in our large towns, amongst the high-paid artisans, — now the greatest drinkers, — *if only the temptations were removed*, and a systematic attempt were made to show them that a better life was possible. But "circumstances" doom them to evil ways, and the high wages which, through temperance, economy, and co-operation, might enable them to redeem their class, become an instrument of their degradation. It is their *feeling* of this in Great Britain which makes them such ardent supporters of the Permissive Bill for the suppression of the traffic.*

* The large Whitwood Colliery, near Leeds, which formerly was notorious for its riot and drinking, is now a model village, owing to the happy introduction of co-operation between masters and men. The men have a *share* of the profits, and a voice in the management. Mr. Briggs, the chief proprietor, thus describes the results (Dec., 1868): —

"They had worked out there a true remedy for the evils described; *not a*

These principles are of universal application, and show in how various ways, when once the traffic is down and the social usages are shattered, we may conserve true temperance.

---

# X.

## Summary of the Argument.

1. **Temperance** is the *proper use* of things. It primarily, therefore, refers to quality, not quantity. Like sin in general, the special vice of intemperance is not the

*cure merely, but a prevention, and a remedy which had transformed the village from a hot-bed of strife and ill feeling between employer and employed, into a model of peace and good will.*

"While great improvement was being effected in the *financial* results of the business, a *corresponding change was taking place in the social and moral condition of the village.* Many had expressed a *fear* that the distribution of an unwonted amount of money, as *bonus* among the men, *would result in increased drinking, gambling, and other evils;* but they had not found this fear realized. Of course, among the large number of recipients there would be some who would make a bad use of their unaccustomed riches; but such cases were extremely rare. While many paid in their *bonus as a deposit towards a share in the company, or paid off some old debt to the neighboring shopkeeper*, a still larger proportion spent their *bonus* in some long-wanted article of furniture, or in new clothes; while instances were not rare of a pig being added to the live stock of the family, to be fattened for Christmas."

Mr. Pyrah also said: "*They had no 'Collier Monday' now, and had not made a play-day for nine months. The scheme had produced a wonderful good feeling between the workmen;* and as he was determined to do all in his power to reduce the misery which had existed, he should give the scheme his utmost support."

---

1. What is Temperance? What is the special vice of Intemperance?

use of a little, or of a large amount of food or drink, but the conscious free choice of the worse in presence of an attainable better. It is, consequently, always a question of *fitness*. What Reason cannot justify, Morality must condemn.

2. That Alcohol, the intoxicating constituent of inebriating liquors, is the product of the artificial fermentation of *natural* elements of food, *sugars* of various kinds, which exist ready formed in fruits, or produced by the malting of grain. *Alcoholic liquors* are no more found in creation, than pistols and powder, bullets and bowie-knives. That all power wielded by man is *derived* through natural law, but man is responsible for the *mode* of its use, and its *effects*. God creates iron, but man makes guns; grain grows, but the brewer malts and ferments it into drink. Alcohol is a special combination of atoms, not pre-existing in sugar, but induced by art. The only known creature, save man, that has a claim to the production of alcohol, is a very low species of plant, — a child of darkness, like the cryptogams, — called *Torula*, the cells of which are said to secrete an infinitesimal amount of Alcohol, — a fact parallel to the secretion of *formic-acid* by the red ants; but the one fact no more points to the consumption of alcoholic liquors, than the other to *chloroformic*, which results from combining *formyle* with *chlorine*.

3. That Alcohol, judged by experience and known by its fruits, must be condemned *as food*. In all climates,

---

**2. What is Alcohol? From what is all power derived? How should it be used?**

**3. What is Alcohol, judged by experience? Of what is it productive?**

temperate, torrid, or arctic, — in all departments of labor, civil, naval, or military, in mine, field, workshop, or study, — it has been found productive of weakness, and of increased sickness and excessive mortality. That Alcohol cannot "*nourish*," because it does not contain the matter of the body to assimilate to it; that it cannot "*warm*," but, on the contrary, narcotizes and chills; and that it *antagonizes* the known ends and qualities of *drink*. That the vulgar estimates of the value of wines and beers as diet are extravagant and untrue. That Alcohol does not *aid* "digestion."

4. That Alcohol is an agent properly termed "poisonous," because it *disturbs* the natural condition of the living organs, and thereby *wastes* the vital forces. That, in this respect, it is specially distinguished from all true foods, which warm without first burning, and build up without first pulling down. That Alcohol, like chloroform, is an *irritant narcotic*, a true depressor of vital power. That it inflames and indurates many organs, promotes muscular degeneration of heart and other tissues, and perverts the nutrition and functions of the brain, both through its molecular poisoning of the blood and its direct action upon nervous matter.

5. That Alcohol is not a *curative*, or truly medicinal agent, but at best, a mere "adjunct" to treatment. That in the great majority of cases where it is prescribed, it does nothing but harm, and increases frightfully the mortality of patients. That the *conditions* for its scientific prescription are generally unknown, and

---

4. What is said of Alcohol as an agent? What results from its use?
5. What is said of Alcohol as a medical agent?

its most plausible use is reduced to the solitary fact of its being an *anœsthetic*, or nerve-quieter.

6. That Revelation and Science accord in a remarkable manner upon the moral and physical question of the use of *intoxicating* wines, the Bible having plainly pointed out their poisonous, seductive, narcotic, and heart-deceiving properties, and nowhere given them its direct sanction. That Teetotalism, in all its parts, physical, social, and moral, is distinctly approved.

7. That history shows beyond denial, that Intemperance is no question of race or climate, but has prevailed in *all ages* and amongst *all people*, whether refined or barbarous, whether educated or ignorant, whether pagan, Jew, or Christian, *in proportion to the facilities for the use of intoxicants.*

8. That, in the language of Thomas de Quincey, "The most remarkable instance of a combined movement in society, which history perhaps will be summoned to notice, is that which, in our own days, has applied itself to the abatement of Intemperance. Two vast movements are hurrying into action, by velocities continually accelerated, — the great revolutionary movement from *political* causes, concurring with the great *physical* movement in locomotion and social intercourse from the gigantic power of steam. At the opening of such a crisis, *had no third movement arisen of resistance to intemperate habits*, there would have been ground for

---

6. What is the testimony of the Bible? Does the Bible sanction intoxicating wine?

7. What does history show?

8. What statement is made by Thomas de Quincey? What is the only remedy?

despondency as to the melioration of the human race." That the only remedy possible is a systematic *organization* of moral and political force, as against an insidious and cruel foe, which shall meet the various conditions which give support to Intemperance. That the history of the Temperance movement in America, and incidentally in Britain, is a providential development of the *remedies* required to meet those conditions. That prohibition, wherever fairly tried, *and so far as tried*, has succeeded.

9. That the philosophy of the Temperance enterprise is a question of *causation*, or of those factors on which the effect depends. That these three — (1) false notions and estimates of the drink; (2) social fashions and usages; (3) public facilities for the sale of drink — must be met by their corresponding cures, — suasion for the head; the fashion of a better *associated example* for the conventional usage; and *prohibition of the traffic* as the crown and complement of the Temperance movement.

---

**9. What three causes are given for the prevalence of Intemperance? What are the three cures?**

www.ingramcontent.com/pod-product-compliance
Lightning Source LLC
LaVergne TN
LVHW020235110826
845151LV00003B/931

* 9 7 8 1 4 2 5 5 2 9 9 3 2 *